Passing the Plate

CHRISTIAN SMITH

and

MICHAEL O.
EMERSON

with

Patricia Snell

Passing the Plate

Why American Christians

Don't Give Away More Money

OXFORD
UNIVERSITY PRESS

2008

OXFORD

UNIVERSITY PRESS

Oxford University Press, Inc., publishes works that further
Oxford University's objective of excellence
in research, scholarship, and education.

Oxford New York
Auckland Cape Town Dar es Salaam Hong Kong Karachi
Kuala Lumpur Madrid Melbourne Mexico City Nairobi
New Delhi Shanghai Taipei Toronto

With offices in
Argentina Austria Brazil Chile Czech Republic France Greece
Guatemala Hungary Italy Japan Poland Portugal Singapore
South Korea Switzerland Thailand Turkey Ukraine Vietnam

Published by Oxford University Press, Inc.
198 Madison Avenue, New York, NY 10016

www.oup.com

Oxford is a registered trademark of Oxford University Press

Library of Congress Cataloging-in-Publication Data

Smith, Christian, 1960–
Passing the plate: why American Christians don't give away
more money/Christian Smith and Michael O. Emerson, with Patricia Snell.
   p. cm.
ISBN 978-0-19-533711-2
1. Christian giving.   2. Christians—United States.
I. Emerson, Michael O., 1965–   II. Snell, Patricia, 1978–   III. Title.
BV772.S611 2008
248'.6—dc22   2008019801

9 8 7 6 5 4 3 2 1

Printed in the United States of America
on acid-free paper

For Emily, generous without measure
C.S.S.

To my father Neil and in loving memory of my mother Fran
M.O.E.

For my family, for your unending support and guidance—you are my heroes
P.A.S.

ACKNOWLEDGMENTS

KYLE LONGEST PROVIDED invaluable service in survey data analysis. A generous grant from Atlantic Philanthropies made the collection of the Indiana University's Center on Philanthropy Panel Study possible; special thanks to Mark Wilhelm of the Center for assisting us with analysis of COPPS data. We are indebted to John and Sylvia Ronsvalle, of empty tomb, inc., for permission to reprint from their report, *The State of Church Giving through 2003* (Champaign, IL: empty tomb, inc., 2005, p. 36), their figure 6 as figure 2.12 in our chapter 2. Discretionary resources from the University of North Carolina at Chapel Hill Stuart Chapin Distinguished Professor Chair research fund, the University of Notre Dame William R. Kenan, Jr., Professor of Sociology Chair research fund, and the Rice University Center on Race, Religion, and Urban Life research fund helped make possible analyses for this book. Chris Morrissey and Lisa Schwartz, both from Notre Dame, were important helps in conducting interviews in multiple states for this project and in helping to analyze our thematic findings. At Rice University, Nina Mayes conducted interviews, and Valeria Gutierrez helped with various administrative tasks. Friends, colleagues, and students who helpfully read and critiqued part or all of this manuscript were Steve Vaisey, Stan Gaede, Thomas Tyson, Allan Poole, Ron Sider, and Peter Mundey. Others who provided important assistance and advice include Jessica Collett, Shawna Anderson, Mark Chaves, Sylvia Ronsvalle, Corwin Smidt, John Evans, Dan Myers, Omar Lizardo, Rory McVeigh, Lyn Spillman, Lisa Pearce, Melinda Lundquist Denton, David Sikkink, John Bartkowski, Chris Morrissey, Ryan Lincoln, Jud Carlberg, Stephen Smith, Jean Tyson, various members of the

Chicago Area Group for the Study of Religious Communities, organized by Fred Kniss, and members of the social science faculty at Brigham Young University, who critically discussed chapter 3 with the authors. Thanks, as always, to our editor, Cynthia Read, for her interest in our work and her contribution of helpful ideas.

CONTENTS

*"Don't let the car fool you.
My treasure is in heaven."*

*—Bumper sticker seen by author on a $41,500 SUV
parked at a bank in Chapel Hill, NC*

Passing the Plate

The Riddle of Stingy
Christian Giving

THIS BOOK ATTEMPTS to help solve a riddle: why is it that American
Christians give away so relatively little of their money? Contemporary
American Christians are among the wealthiest of their faith in the world
today and probably the most affluent single group of Christians in two thousand years of church history. They have a lot of money—as we will see in
chapter 1. Nearly all American Christians also belong to churches that teach
believers, as stewards of the belongings with which God has blessed them,
to give money generously for the work of God's kingdom, as we will see
in appendix A. Most Christians belong to churches that teach tithing—the
giving of 10 percent of one's income. Most American Christians also profess
to want to see the gospel preached in the world, the hungry fed, the church
strengthened, and the poor raised to enjoy lives of dignity and hope—all
tasks that normally require money. And yet, despite all of this, American
Christians give away relatively little money to religious and other purposes.
A sizeable number of Christians give no money, literally nothing. Most of the
rest of American Christians give little sums of money. Only a small percent
of American Christians give money generously, in proportion to what their
churches call them to give. All of the evidence, we will see, points to the
same conclusion: when it comes to sharing their money, most contemporary
American Christians are remarkably ungenerous.

The goal of this book is not to morally chide or condemn American
Christians for their tightfistedness. We do not need to. The numbers speak
for themselves. And many other previous books and journal articles have also

already done that. There is little use in our repeating what numerous others have already well expressed.[1] The primary goal of this book, rather, is to try to better *understand and explain* American Christians' lack of generosity, from a sociological perspective. Very many incisive analyses, prophetic reproofs, and articulate pleas to give money more faithfully appear to have altered very little in how much money American Christians give away. For that reason we suspect that some kind of other mechanisms, besides mere moral and theological ideas, must be at work among American Christians to keep their financial giving at low levels. One of our goals here is to try to better identify those mechanisms as a means of helping to explain the riddle.[2] We do not here much engage biblical teachings or doctrinal statements about wealth, stewardship, and tithing.[3] Rather, we use the investigative approach that we know best—sociological analysis—to try to make some progress into better understanding the underlying reasons for the illiberal financial giving of most American Christians.

Such an analysis could prove to be valuable in many ways. If successful, it might help to shed light on reasons explaining how and why religious faith is practiced more or less faithfully, by its own standards, in different social contexts. More broadly, it might enrich our general understanding of fundamental processes involved in charitable giving, private philanthropy, and other-regarding behavior.[4] It might also challenge readers to think in new and hopefully helpful ways more generally about what makes people tick and how social and institutional life works. And, more practically, it might help religious leaders to better address what has recurrently been for many of them a vexing problem of inadequate financial support by ordinary believers. If this book is successful, it might help to change American Christians' financial giving. But we are also just as interested in enriching our theoretical sociological understanding of the workings of human social life generally as we are in possibly helping to change people's giving behaviors.

Looking for Better Explanations

Some readers might immediately say that the answer to the riddle is obvious: people, including Christians, are simply often selfish and greedy. Perhaps. But we think that hardly solves the riddle, finally, for a few reasons. One reason the "selfishness and greed" explanation may not entirely work is that Americans in general and religious Americans specifically are often widely thought to be quite generous, in attitudes at least—sometimes to the point of gullibility and credulity.[5] Rarely does a disaster strike when Americans all over the country do not seem to scramble to write checks, collect donations, and send flowers and teddy bears in sympathy and hopes of reducing suffering. Little of this may in fact amount to the kind of sacrificial giving that many Christian churches call their believers to practice. But to dismiss the low levels of Christian financial giving documented in this book as the mere product of raw selfishness and greed seems to oversimplify matters, to fail to take account of some of the complexities of real human thinking, intentions, and behavior.

More generally, selfishness and greed are rarely autonomous and consistent powers that straightforwardly determine the outcomes of people's lives. Rather, tendencies like selfishness and avarice are normally mediated through the routines, habits, expectations, mental categories, interactions, norms, cultural practices, and organizational processes that shape human selves, communities, and institutions.[6] Solving the present riddle with the simple answer of "selfishness and greed" fails to trace out the various ways that these motivational tendencies do and do not work through social-psychological, interactive, and organizational processes to produce the ungenerous results we observe.

Furthermore, not all groups of American Christians or even different groups of non-Christian religious believers in the United States give away the same amounts of money.[7] Different groups in fact tend to give at different levels. Mormons, for example, appear to give more than seven times the amount of money as a percentage of income than do Catholics.[8] Unless we are prepared to believe that these different levels of financial charity are simply caused by different levels of greed and selfishness in different groups, then we have more explaining to do. Thinking sociologically, we begin instead with the suspicion that differences in religious giving are at least partly explained by mechanisms operating through social-psychological and institutional processes. Those are what we try to get at in the analyses of subsequent chapters, particularly chapter 3.

Measuring and Explaining Charitable Giving

How do we even know how much money Christians and others give? Personal income and family money issues are considered private matters by most Americans. People can be quite touchy about others knowing their earnings, wealth, spending, and giving. So how can we accurately know the amount of money American Christians give to churches and other religious and nonreligious charities?

Scholars who study U.S. religious and charitable giving rely on a number of kinds of sources of data to determine people's financial giving. The most often used sources of information are individual and household surveys, religious denomination financial records, Internal Revenue Service charitable contribution reports, and government reports based on U.S. Department of Labor Consumer Expenditure Surveys and similar information. Using these data to determine people's financial giving can be tricky. Some data sources refer to all charitable giving, while others refer only to religious or congregational giving. Some report on individual giving, some on household giving, some on "consumer units," and some on giving by tax return filer units. Sometimes giving is calculated as a percentage of total (gross) income and sometimes of after-tax (net) income. Furthermore, none of the available data on religious and charitable giving is perfect. For example, people's informal, spontaneous giving of cash—to a homeless person or hastily dropped in an offering plate during a special religious service—may be left out of totals of money that people report donating. Then again, these donations may in people's minds be inflated when they are asked to report on giving. Some tax filers also do not itemize deductions for every amount of money or dollar value of material gifts they have donated. Also, people taking surveys sometimes cannot remember the various donations they have given in the previous one or two years. And survey nonresponse biases themselves may under-represent low givers, high givers, or both. At the same time, a "social desirability bias" encourages many people to *over*estimate the total amount of money they have donated when asked for dollar figure valuations of giving on surveys—it turns out that people have a tendency to say they give more money than it appears they actually do. The financial giving records of denominations can be useful, but they do not tell how much para-church and nonreligious giving their members do. And the denominations that publish their financial records represent less than one-half of all congregations in the United States. So nobody has entirely complete and flawless data with which to work.

Nevertheless, despite these complications, we can carefully put together the many sources of data about financial giving and come up with a pretty clear picture of how much money different kinds of people in the United States give. Relying on one single source of information alone can raise doubts about the reliability of findings. But combining information from surveys, church records, tax records, and government household finance studies greatly helps to "cross-reference" findings and vastly increases our confidence about their reliability and validity—especially when the different data sources produce roughly similar results. For the purposes of this book—that is, for understanding the financial giving of American Christians—we will see that available data sources do provide more than enough solid information on which to base reliable observations and firm conclusions.

In addition to using existing data to measure levels of religious and charitable giving, we also collected some original data of our own in order to try to better understand the perceptions, motives, and influences involved in Christian financial giving. First, we fielded focused survey questions on our Tithing Experiment Survey in 2006 about how American Christians would respond if their churches raised giving expectations by making tithing a normative expectation of membership.[9] Our questions asked respondents to engage in a mental experiment, which we think provides another perspective to help answer our ungenerous giving riddle. We also asked questions about perceptions of what percent of income churchgoing Christians thought their churches expected members to give, and questions about their personal support for or opposition to their churches increasing expectations of financial giving. In chapters 3 and 5 we report findings from our 2006 Tithing Experiment Survey on American Christians' various responses to the prospect of being expected by churches to give ten percent of their after-tax income. We think the results are illuminating. In addition, we conducted 77 personal interviews with a sample of Christian church pastors and members representing a variety of theological traditions, races, and social classes.[10] We quote from these interviews throughout the book to help put a human face on our survey findings. Chapter 4 also systematically analyzes our interview findings.

Caveats and Cautions

Before moving forward, however, a few caveats and considerations of context are in order. First, this book ought not to be read as implying that money is *the* most important issue in human life, in the Christian's life, or in the church. Nor should it be read as suggesting that a failure of financial generosity is American Christianity's absolute greatest vice. Those types of judgments are not the point of this kind of book. We will leave to theologians and ethicists the evaluation of the moral gravity of the lack of generosity analyzed in these pages. Furthermore, from a Christian perspective, as we understand it, to overemphasize the importance of money in life is itself to wrongly attribute to it a centrality that might theologically be labeled "idolatry." We do not want to go there. Our general position, therefore, is simply that American Christians' lack of financial generosity is a consequential matter well worth trying to better understand.

Second, along similar lines, the argument of this book should not be read as suggesting that an ample supply of money is the sufficient solution to all of the world's problems. Neither Christians nor sociologists ought to subscribe to that view. Many of the former would surely point to spiritual considerations, besides mammon, for rightly explaining the woes of the world and considering approaches to change. Most sociologists and many others also know that a great deal of suffering in the world is not the direct result of a lack of money alone, but of many other, complicated forces—including intractable civil wars, administrative corruption, political callousness and ineptitude, tribal conflict, endemic social structural inequalities, elite nepotism, counter-productive tax policies, bureaucratic red tape, and other forms of bad economic, public policy, and bureaucratic decision making.[11] Material resources are often immensely important, but—we trust most people also know—money is not everything. Particularly with regard to the next chapter, nobody ought to suppose that we are suggesting that Christians or anyone can simply *buy* the world that they want. However, neither should that fact minimize the importance of financial resources for achieving the kind of goals that many people, including many Christians, view as good and worthy of accomplishing.

A third, more analytically focused point concerns the importance of *making the right kind of comparisons* in our analyses of financial giving for properly understanding the giving situation. It is sometimes observed that Americans give to charity more generously than citizens of other advanced industrial nations, and that American religious believers give more generously than nonreligious Americans.[12] Both of those observations are true, important to know, and well worth keeping in mind. But these are not really the most important or revealing comparisons to observe. In fact, in certain ways they may be quite misleading. From the perspective of Christian faithfulness, for example—that is, from the point of view most relevant to the population that this book concerns—it is hardly a cause for celebration to be giving somewhat more generously than religious unbelievers or other more secularized nations. What matters is not that the Christian glass is a bit more full than the nonreligious glass or the glass of more secular nations. What matters more is that the Christian glass is *nearly empty* relative to its normal capacity. And we shall see in chapter 2 that the American Christian glass *is in fact* nearly empty, even if it is a bit fuller than many of the even emptier nonreligious and non-American glasses.

To keep generosity of giving in proper perspective, therefore, the primary analytical focus of this book will not be financial giving in absolute dollar amounts, but rather financial giving *relative to one's capacity to give*. In most cases this means measuring giving as a percentage of income. The Bible and Christian teachings, incidentally, are clear about this—what really matters is not an absolute amount of money given, but the amount given as a proportion of the total that one has to give. Thus, the poor widow who gave a pittance, Jesus said, actually gave more than the rich man who gave a bundle.[13]

Some readers may wonder why we focus here specifically on Christians, rather than all religious Americans or all Americans generally. Good question. The answer is that we wish to keep our argument focused. We do not want to be pulled in myriad directions trying to do justice to the variety of teachings and practices of diverse religious (and nonreligious) communities and traditions. Nor do we want to lose the stark contrast between specific Christian teachings about giving and American Christians' actual giving behavior. Other religious groups in the United States—Jews, Mormons, Muslims, and more—well deserve full research projects and books devoted entirely to understanding financial giving in their communities.[14] Meanwhile, this book focuses on Christianity, touching on the religious giving of other groups only briefly for comparison. On these kinds of matters, we think, it is preferable to do a better analysis of a more restricted scope than to produce a seemingly comprehensive yet more superficial investigation of too much. American Christianity itself is plenty big enough to try to make sense of. So that is our focus here.

Finally, to be clear, by saying above that prior scholarship on religious giving appears to have changed very little actual giving behavior, we are not suggesting that this scholarship itself has been worthless. Much previous thinking, research, analysis, and writing on this topic has been very important for helping to lay out the dimensions and complexities of the problem. This book is clearly indebted to and builds directly upon the impressive work of Robert Wuthnow, Dean Hoge, Mark Chaves, John and Sylvia Ronsvalle, Andrew Greeley, Charles Zech, Stephen Hart, and others. But, having digested their research and studied subsequent trends in giving, it appears that ordinary American Christians as a group have not as a result of this good prior work actually changed their financial giving patterns. In any case, our intention is not to discount or trump the prior work of these scholars, but rather to continue the trajectory of their scholarship—by not only updating their substantive findings with some more recent statistics, but also by continuing to press toward illuminating sociologically informed understandings of religious giving.

What Is at Stake

Until recently, the topic of financial giving seemed to us to be a boring area of research. Church budgets, denominational maintenance, and routine charitable giving all looked to us pretty dull. But we have come recently to see things differently. The financial giving of American Christians is not simply about offering plates, church treasuries, and uncomfortable sermons delivered on "Stewardship Sundays." We are talking about many tens of *billions* of dollars per year here—quantities of money that could, if well deployed, make an enormous impact in the world. And—if Christian teachings about money are to be taken seriously at all—we may also be talking about an important part of the soul of American Christianity. Something is at stake here that touches a nerve in every Christian household and affects the world far beyond. Far from being boring and humdrum, understanding people's charitable dealings with money seems rather to open a large window on understanding the workings of the human mind and heart, which itself may hold the potential to help make a real difference in the world.

Giving to Change the World

L ET US BEGIN on a positive note. The up-side potential for good in
U.S. Christian giving is immense, almost unimaginable. If American
Christians were to give from their income generously—not lavishly, mind
you, only generously—they could transform the world, starting right away.
Ordinary American Christians have within their power the capacity to foster
massive and unprecedented spiritual, social, cultural, and economic change
that closely reflects their values and interests. In order to achieve such dramatic, world-transforming change, ordinary American Christians simply
need to do one thing: start giving reasonably generously from their incomes,
let us say 10 percent of post-tax income. Fostering such changes could begin
immediately. It would not require getting Congress or the United Nations
to act. It would not require a military mobilization or waiting for a majority
turnover in the Supreme Court. It would only require ordinary Christians
from one country to start doing something that seems entirely within their
power and that most of them, according to the teachings of their own faith
traditions, ought to already be doing anyway: giving generously from the
financial resources with which they have been blessed.

Fully grasping the capacity of ordinary American Christians to transform
the world through generous financial giving requires comprehending the
vast financial resources that are in fact at their disposal. Americans, curiously,
often do not view themselves as living in abundance. Most Americans—even
among the uppermiddle class—often see themselves as "just getting by."
But any comparative study of the number of Christian believers in different
countries of the world and of the financial incomes at their disposal reveals
that *ordinary American Christians as a group are sitting on utterly enormous monetary*

resources, both relatively and absolutely. In 2005, the United States contained approximately 226,624,000 professing Christians, adults and their children, of various levels of commitment. About 140,070,000 Americans are members of Christian churches. About 138,090,000 Americans report attending Christian church at least two times a month or more often or describe themselves as strong or very strong Christians. At least 192,080,000 Americans are Christians who report that their faith is very or even extremely important in their lives. About 149,822,000 Americans report that religion provides a great deal of guidance in their day-to-day life. In short, well more than one hundred million Americans are professing and practicing Christians. The 2005 average U.S. household income was $47,290 for Protestants and $52,918 for Catholics. For regularly churchgoing Protestants and Catholics, average annual household income was even more, $50,138 and $57,791, respectively.[1] Calculated out, self-identified Christians in the United States earned a total collective income in 2005 in the *trillions* of dollars. Christians in the United States who are actually members of churches earned a total collective 2005 income of more than $2 trillion. Christians in the United States who actually attend church twice a month or more often or who consider themselves strong or very strong Christians earned a total collective 2005 income of also more than $2 trillion. Needless to say, more than $2 trillion earned every year is a huge amount of money. It is more than the total Gross Domestic Products of every nation in the world except, at most, the six wealthiest—United States, Japan, Germany, China, the United Kingdom, and France.

Let us imagine, then, that, from their abundance, American Christians began to give an average of 10 percent of their after-tax personal income to causes of their choosing. To sustain this average, let us assume for now that Christians in more fortunate financial circumstances would give more than 10 percent in order to compensate for others in truly difficult financial circumstances who genuinely could not afford, at least during tight spells, to give 10 percent. What specifically might American Christians accomplish with their shared resources? The short answer is: enough to transform the world.

Committed Christians, for Starters

Realistically, things might be more complex than what we just described, since not all Americans who consider themselves Christians may not be actually serious enough about their faith to start giving away 10 percent of their income.

Because different kinds of professing Christians might give or not give more money when the financial "rubber hits the road," the answer to how much more money U.S. Christians could generate if they tithed depends in part on which Christians we are talking about. Let us begin, then, with a conservative estimation, imagining that only those American Christians would begin to give 10 percent of their after-tax income who either attend church regularly (a few times a month or more frequently) or profess to be "strong" or "very strong" Christians. Let us call these "committed" Christians. Below, we will consider how much more money less committed Christians could contribute by increasing their giving. But for now let us only consider what might happen if only the more highly religious American Christians—who already give at higher levels—would begin to give 10 percent of their after-tax incomes. What might they accomplish with those financial resources? What difference might their generosity make in the world?

We estimate that if committed Christians in the United States gave 10 percent of their after-tax income—fully but no more than 10 percent—that would provide an *extra* $46 billion per year of resources with which to fund needs and priorities.[2] That represents nearly an additional 25 percent of what *all Americans*—Christians or otherwise—currently give in *all* types of private philanthropy. We will adjust this number upward below, but for now it provides a good starting point. What follows is an estimation of the changes that such an increase in giving could help affect. In actual practice, some of the following expenditures might turn out to be higher or lower, but the overall picture presented here ought to be largely reliable. If the households representing more committed American Christians—again, those who attend church a few times a month or more frequently or who say they are strong or very strong Christians—were to begin giving 10 percent of their after-tax income, what might that accomplish? By our reckoning, with $46 billion they could—in addition to sustaining all currently funded churches, organizations, ministries, and programs—achieve the following.[3]

Cost	Description
Global Missions	
$330,000,000	Sponsor 150,000 new indigenous missionaries and pastors in nations most closed to foreign religious workers
$2,200,000,000	Triple the resources being spent by all global Christians on Bible translating, printing, and distribution to provide Bibles in the native languages

of the 2,737 remaining people groups currently without Bible translations

$350,000,000   Provide 50,000 needs-based scholarships of $7,000 each per year for deserving Christian seminary and Bible school students in Africa, Asia, and Latin America

$30,000,000   Translate into four different languages (Spanish, Portugese, Chinese, Japanese), publish, and distribute 20,000 copies of 100 new titles per year of the best English-language Christian books for reading in Asia, Africa, and Latin America

$120,000,000   Hire 1,500 new Christian ministers to work in hospitality, evangelism, and discipleship with foreign students studying in U.S. universities

$9,000,000   Finance the organizational infrastructure of a major Christian research and advocacy organization fighting against contemporary economic and sexual slavery worldwide

$75,000,000   Provide funds to help build, expand, or upgrade 75,000 church and ministry buildings in Africa, Asia, and Latin America

$9,000,000   Finance the organizational infrastructure of a major Christian research and advocacy organization fighting for religious freedoms worldwide

$95,000,000   Finance 350 new Christian radio stations broadcasting Christian programming into the least evangelized regions of the world

$50,000,000   Finance 1,000 new interreligious study groups and travel tours per year to promote grass-roots mutual understanding and communication, particularly between Christians and Muslims around the world

$1,000,000,000   Quadruple the total resources being spent by all Christians globally on missions to evangelize the unevangelized world

Global Development and Relief

$2,000,000,000   Finance 5,000,000 grass-roots, micro-enterprise economic development projects per year in poor countries worldwide that employ revolving loan

	funds for needy entrepreneurs to purchase tools, materials, and equipment to start or expand micro businesses, which they pay back as their businesses grow
$500,000,000	Completely close the funding gap on resources needed by the current global campaign to eradicate polio worldwide before 2010
$2,000,000,000	Fund 1,000,000 new clean water, well-drilling projects per year in the poorest nations (25% of the world's population drinks unsafe water), dramatically improving the health of tens if not hundreds of millions of people per year
$1,000,000,000	Finance 10,000 comprehensive faith-based programs of AIDS/HIV prevention, education, and medication in sub-Saharan Africa
$3,900,000,000	Provide full resources needed for a global campaign to prevent and treat malaria worldwide
$2,000,000,000	Supply 1 heifer or 4 hogs (as needed and appropriate) to 4,000,000 needy Christian or other families worldwide per year
$4,550,000,000	Provide food, clothing, and shelter to *all* 6,500,000 current refugees in all of Africa, Asia, and the Middle East
$9,000,000	Finance the organizational infrastructure of a major Christian think-tank and advocacy organization working on creative means to reduce poverty and hunger worldwide
$480,000,000	Quadruple the current annual operating budget of Habitat for Humanity
$1,600,000,000	Double the current annual operating budget of World Vision, which serves 100 million people in 96 nations
$200,000,000	Boost funding to Christian organizations worldwide that provide free and subsidized eye exams, vision care, glasses, limb braces, and prosthetics to 1,000,000 of the poorest and neediest people of the world
$10,000,000,000	Sponsor 20 million needy children worldwide through Christian organizations providing them food, education, and healthcare

| $810,000,000 | Quadruple all resources currently being spent by all Christians globally on medial missions work |

U.S. Christian Ministry and Church Finance

$750,000,000	Hire 10,700 new Christian youth ministers to evangelize, disciple, guide, and counsel U.S. teenagers
$750,000,000	Raise the salaries of 50,000 of the most needy U.S. church pastors by an average of $15,000 each, to provide for proven needs and to increase incentives encouraging the best and brightest young adults to consider callings to ministry
$75,000,000	Fund 500 new Christian Prison ministry organizations providing evangelism, discipleship, and education to prison inmates
$10,000,000	Translate into English 200 per year of the best Christian articles and books by foreign language writers for publication and sale in the United States and other English-speaking nations
$1,800,000,000	Finance the refitting of the heating, cooling, and electrical systems of 20,000 of the most desperate and inefficient U.S. church buildings per year, including the installation (where appropriate, in 1/3rd of the cases) of new PV solar electric generating systems
$1,100,000,000	Fund 5,500 new Family Counseling and Support organizations in the United States and major cities worldwide to bring affordable Christian support and counseling to families, marriages, and individuals in trouble
$4,000,000,000	Hire 50,000 new, trained, church-based adult Christian educators for the re-education of U.S. Christians in theology, discipleship, and ministry
$9,000,000	Finance the organizational infrastructure of a major Christian think-tank working on Christian perspectives and moralities of new biotechnologies and emerging medial ethics
$9,000,000	Finance the organizational infrastructure of a major Christian research and training center

addressing Christian views on mass media and media production and consumption

$3,375,000,000   Provide the hiring of 45,000 church-based U.S. ministers to the elderly whose mission would be to provide Christian friendship, care, and support to millions of the most isolated, abandoned, disabled, and lonely aging Americans in their homes, nursing homes, or apartments

$75,000,000   Launch 300 cross-race immersion programs around the United States to provide Christians opportunities to live for 2 weeks in different race environments, to learn and build relationships toward more profound racial reconciliation

U.S. Economic Stewardship & Diaconal Ministry

$150,000,000   Provide financial and debt management training to 200,000 U.S. Christians per year who are deeply in debt, to help them get on solid financial ground in order to be able to make positive financial contributions in the future

$100,000,000   Provide church-based jobs training and career counseling to 100,000 unemployed or welfare-dependent Americans per year

$50,000,000   Finance 25 new U.S. regional faith-based organizations that would provide assistance and subsidies to pay heating and utilities bills to the most needy of the poor and elderly in the United States

U.S. Christian Educational and Scholarship Development

$15,000,000   Pay down the mortgages of 500 Christian middle and high schools by $30,000 each to reduce debt burden and interest payments

$150,000,000   Provide needs-based scholarships of $15,000 each per year for 10,000 needy U.S. Christian college students

$45,000,000   Provide needs-based scholarships of $15,000 each per year for 3,000 needy Christian seminary students preparing for ministry

$12,000,000	Provide research and writing fellowships to 150 of the best Christian scholars per year to work on scientific and humanities scholarship informed by Christian perspectives that holds promise for influencing higher education and academic scholarship
$202,000,000	Provide 101 $2 million contributions per year to Christian seminaries, divinity schools, colleges, and Bible schools for building campaigns, capital improvements, endowment building, or other demonstrated needs
$6,000,000	Provide graduate school scholarships for 300 of the most promising Christian Ph.D. students per year in various fields of study

$46,000,000,000	= GRAND TOTAL

Different readers will of course find themselves attracted and not attracted to various of the proposals suggested above. Fine. These ideas are merely suggestive of possibilities different kinds of American Christians might find attractive. We are not suggesting we would personally support all of these proposals. We are simply trying to show a range of possibilities that might appeal to a range of different kinds of Christians. Readers can imagine their own lists with different sorts of spending items. Liberals could lean in certain directions, conservatives perhaps in other directions. No problem. With personal financial giving, each giver can choose to donate to the organizations and causes that fit their own values and commitments. What matters for present purposes, therefore, is not different people's support for or questions about the individual ideas we proposed above. What really matters is grasping the *absolutely immense scope and scale of the possible goods that ordinary American Christians could accomplish in the world every year if they simply began to give away 10 percent of their after-tax income.* The possibilities are staggering.

Note too how very well the kind of world transformation through faithful Christian financial giving described in this chapter fits the beliefs, values, and interests of most ordinary American Christian believers. This strategy does not require government programs, centralized bureaucracies, or building group consensus on priority allocations in order to succeed. In fact, those might hinder success. Rather, world transformation through faithful Christian financial giving is radically decentralized, empowers individual givers, is fully reliant on private initiative, and is responsive to new needs and giving opportunities. This approach does not rely on government and taxation or the decision making of high powered committees meeting behind closed doors. Instead, it leaves decision making about the distribution and targeting of resources in the hands of ordinary giving Christians spread all around the country according to their consciences. Each contributing person or household can choose to devote the resources they give to the specific churches, ministries, programs, causes, needs, and commitments that are their own priorities by conviction, interest, or association. Through regular channels of communication and accountability, Christian givers can also monitor how their money is being used and adjust their giving targets accordingly. This decentralized process naturally generates a highly responsive and efficient system of financial allocation, sustaining good stewardship of resources. And, on top of all that, the United States Internal Revenue Service and state tax offices reward Christians for their generous charitable giving by reducing their tax liabilities. How then—to foreshadow our central question—do we explain the actual ungenerous financial giving of most American Christians that we will see in the next chapter?

The Increased Results of More Equitable Giving

In reality, committed Christians as a group could actually give much *more* than $46 billion if responsibility for giving were distributed more evenly among them. In the following chapter, we will see that the top few percent of Christian givers contributes much more than 10 percent of their income, accounting for the majority of all dollars given. These contributors are truly giving sacrificially, digging deep into their income or savings.[4] It is reasonable to believe that in any given year a small percent of Christians will be willing and able to contribute at these higher levels. But should their very generous giving automatically "fill in" for the relatively ungenerous giving of the majority of Christians (which they do, in the numbers calculated above)?

Suppose we count the generous contributions of these sacrificial givers as "freewill bounty giving" and do not allow the dollar value of those contributions above 10 percent of income to figure into calculations of mean averages to compensate for the lower giving levels of so many others—precisely as the mathematical estimations informing the prior section did? In our previous calculation leading to the estimate of $46 billion, we essentially estimated the total dollars that committed U.S. Christians *would* give if they gave away 10 percent of after-tax income, subtracted from that the total amount of money that U.S. Christians actually *do* give, and found the difference to be approximately $46 billion. But the amount of money we subtracted that U.S. Christians actually do give includes this "freewill bounty giving" mentioned here. If we remove this "freewill bounty giving" from the equation, the difference between the total amount U.S. Christians *would* give and what they actually *do* give would increase significantly. Suppose, then, that we adjust one assumption that we made in the prior discussion of potential Christians giving—namely, that Christians in fortunate financial circumstances can give more than 10 percent in order to compensate for others in truly difficult financial circumstances who genuinely cannot afford, at least during tight spells, to give 10 percent. Let us relax this assumption on the basis of having good reason to believe that few, let us say about one-tenth, of those Christians who give less than 10 percent would like to give more generously but do not simply because they are truly in difficult financial circumstances that genuinely prevent them from giving more. Let us assume that the other 90 percent could give 10 percent if they were truly committed to doing so, and so do not give for other reasons. So as not to lose the realism originally intended in this assumption, then, let us suppose that, during any given year, 10 percent of committed Christians are, for whatever reasons—unemployment, family disruption, illness—legitimately unable to give away any money at all. We can adjust this assumption in our calculations in exactly this way. We simply need to reestimate potential Christian giving at the 10 percent level after, first, *removing dollars given by the relatively few extra-generous Christians in excess of 10 percent of their income* (their dollars up to 10 percent remain) and, second, removing the contribution of the 10 percent on hard times who we assume legitimately cannot give anything. How much money could committed Christians then generate every year if 90 percent of them gave fully 10 percent of their after-tax income, *without being compensated for by the big donations of the relatively few who are willing and able to contribute more than 10 percent?* The answer, we estimate, grows from $46 billion to $85.5 billion per year.[5]

What could $85.5 billion per year of generous Christian contributions accomplish in the world? Once more, the possibilities are staggering. First, we can count and build upon all of the accomplishments that the first $46 billion achieved in the previous section. *In addition to all of those accomplishments described above,* what more could the leftover $39.5 billion per year achieve? Again, different Christians would have diverse giving priorities. Here we merely suggest a variety of possibilities that we estimate would cost $39.5 billion, different ones of which we imagine many committed Christians in the United States would consider worthy investments and contributions. Here, then, is one scenario estimating what committed American Christians could accomplish every year—*in addition* to the $46 billion worth of accomplishments per year listed above, and *not* counting the dollar value of the "freewill bounty giving" by those few who are willing and able to give more than 10 percent of their income—simply by 90 percent of committed Christian households giving fully 10 percent, no more and no less, of their after-tax incomes.

Cost	Description

Global Missions

Cost	Description
$220,000,000	Sponsor *another* 100,000 new indigenous missionaries and pastors (now totaling to 200,000) in nations most closed to foreign religious workers
$150,000,000	Fund 1,000 new Christian "safe houses" in cities throughout Latin America to minister to hundreds of thousands of Latin American street children, urban orphans, glue sniffers, and petty thieves
$600,000,000	Start eight new Christian colleges in Eastern Europe, states of the former Soviet Union, and Southeast Asia to provide the alternative of Christian education for young people in those nations

Global Development and Relief

Cost	Description
$2,000,000,000	Finance *another* 5,000,000 grass-roots economic development projects (now totaling 10 million) per year in poor countries worldwide that employ revolving loan funds for needy entrepreneurs to purchase tools, materials, and equipment to start or expand micro businesses, which they pay back in subsequent years as their profits grow
$1,000,000,000	Fund *another* 500,000 new clean water, well-drilling projects (now totaling to 1 million) per year in the poorest nations (25% of the world's population drinks unsafe water), dramatically improving the health of tens of millions of people per year
$800,000,000	Hire 10,000 Christian literacy workers to teach reading and writing to the illiterate in the United States and around the world

$480,000,000	Quadruple *yet again* the current annual operating budget of Habitat for Humanity
$1,600,000,000	Double *yet again* the current annual operating budget of World Vision, which serves 100 million people in 96 nations
$11,000,000	Establish an Institute of Christian Peacemaking to help negotiate political and military conflict resolutions around the globe
$2,000,000,000	Provide basic medical treatment through Christian clinics for 5,000,000 infants and toddlers around the world suffering dehydration from simple diarrhea, thus dramatically reducing the easily preventable deaths of millions of children
$1,125,000,000	Provide vitamins, antibiotics, and simple medical supplies to 100,000 Christian medical clinics in poor countries around the world

U.S. Christian Ministry and Church Finance

$3,750,000,000	Pay down the mortgages on 75,000 U.S. church buildings by $50,000 each, thus freeing up hundreds of thousands of new dollars of mortgage interest money as well as the principal paid off itself
$800,000,000	Raise the salaries of *another* 80,000 of the most needy U.S. church pastors (now totaling 120,000) by an average of $10,000 each, to provide for proven needs and to increase incentives encouraging the best and brightest young adults to consider callings to ministry
$100,000,000	Send 40,000 U.S. teenagers on short-term missions trip to the Third World to serve and learn
$100,000,000	Finance 200 Christian organizations and associations networking and supporting Christian creative artists in film, television, the theater, writing, and the visual arts
$6,000,000,000	Hire 50,000 new domestic Christian evangelists to lead churches in effective ways to share the Christian gospel with unbelievers

$1,000,000,000	Hire 10,000 new Christian evangelists and pastors dedicated to ministering to people working in the arts, media, and upper levels of business management
$1,000,000,000	Establish 5,000 new crisis pregnancy centers around the United States to counsel and support pregnant women in need
$18,000,000	Finance the organizational infrastructure for two different major Christian research and advocacy organizations working on issues of environmental stewardship from a Christian perspective
$2,000,000,000	Finance 10 new feature-length theater movies reflecting the best in Christian artistic abilities in the film arts
$3,000,000,000	Finance the leading of 300,000 new lunchtime Bible studies in offices and factories around the United States
$2,000,000,000	Establish 10,000 new local Christian Centers for Restorative Justice around the nation, in order to help reform the current U.S. justice system's emphasis on retribution and inmate-warehousing
$400,000,000	Establish 2,000 new local Immigrant Ministry Centers to provide Christian ministry and services to the millions of documented and undocumented new immigrants to the United States
$1,000,000,000	Pay for the hiring of an additional 10,000 military chaplains to evangelize and minister to U.S. military personnel overseas
$68,000,000	Send 20,000 disadvantaged inner-city children to Christian summer camps for two weeks

U.S. Economic Stewardship & Deaconal Ministry

$600,000,000	Provide 2,000 new urban ministry programs in inner cities across the United States offering Bible study, evangelistic outreach, jobs training, and social and economic support for the most disadvantaged Americans

$600,000,000	Provide 2,000 new rural ministry programs in poor rural counties across the United States offering Bible study, evangelistic outreach, jobs training, and social and economic support for the most disadvantaged Americans
$100,000,000	Provide church-based jobs training and career counseling to *another* 100,000 unemployed or welfare-dependent Americans per year (now totaling to 200,000 per year)
$80,000,000	Sponsor 40,000 U.S. teenagers to work on 2-week Christian summer service projects in service to the poor and elderly
$1,000,000,000	Establish a medical care trust fund to pay for $50 million per year of tests, treatments, and medications for poor U.S. AIDS patients
$1,000,000,000	Establish a Christian diaconal trust fund to pay for $50 million per year toward the housing, utilities, and educational needs of America's neediest widows and orphans
$68,000,000	Fund shelter, food, substance abuse counseling, job training, and life skills support for 17,000 of America's estimated homeless population
$1,000,000,000	Establish a medical care trust fund to pay for $50 million per year of major medical expenses of poor and uninsured Christian Americans

U.S. Christian Educational and Scholarship Development

| $2,000,000,000 | Establish 1,000 grassroots Centers for Continuing Christian Education around all 50 states to foster biblical, theological, and ministry education for tens of thousands of Christian laity around the United States |
| $80,000,000 | Finance 8 major Christian think-tanks in New York City, Washington, D.C., Chicago, and Los Angeles to promote reflection, writing, programs, and media relations to increase the presence of various traditions of Christian thought in public debates and popular culture |

| $1,600,000,000 | Establish 20,000 new Christian college student ministers at public and private non-Christian universities around the United States |
| $150,000,000 | Establish new Christian Studies Houses at America's top 500 secular universities to help Christian students integrate their faith and academic learning during college |

$39,500,000,000   = GRAND TOTAL

Again, we repeat, different readers will no doubt find themselves attracted and not attracted to various of the proposals suggested above. That is fine. We are not personally endorsing all of these suggestions merely by including them here. These ideas are simply proposals, ideas to stimulate the imagination. Readers can think of their own lists with alternative spending items for which they would most want to give money. The point is not that all Christians must support exactly these ideas. The real point is that Christians could accomplish incredible things if they began to give reasonably generously of their financial means.

Adding Back in the "Freewill Bounty Giving"

We have seen that, simply by 90 percent of committed Christian households giving away strictly 10 percent of their after-tax income—no more and no less—committed Christians in the United States could raise $85.5 billion each year on top of what is currently given. Recall, however, that to estimate that amount we eliminated from our calculations the dollars that the most generous givers contributed over and above 10 percent of their income. The $85.5 billion does not include the dollars from what we called "freewill bounty giving." Excluding this money was necessary for our calculations above. But it is not necessary in real life. Rather, it might be reasonable to believe that in any given year a small percent of Christians will be willing and able to give at levels higher than 10 percent of their income. They already do so now, and we have no reason to think that they would need to stop doing so into the future. What happens to our projections, then, when—on top of the faithful 10 percent giving of 90 percent of committed Christians—we add back into our estimations the extra money of the minority who is willing and able to give more than 10 percent of their income? By our calculation, that would add an additional $34.6 billion in giving by committed American Christians each year.[6]

What might Christians achieve with *another* $34.6 billion—*on top of* what American Christians are already *currently* funding *and* what the $85.5 billion could accomplish that we *added* in the previous two sections? The mind becomes giddy, almost weary, imagining further possibilities for world transformation through Christian financial generosity. Our point, we think, has been already made above. So we will not continue to describe specific scenarios estimating possible goods that American Christians could accomplish with an extra $34.6 billion. Again, different Christians are welcome to imagine lists that reflect their own values and commitments. The fact we want to continue to drive home is simply that the reasonably generous financial giving of ordinary American Christians would generate staggering amounts of money that could literally change the world. And the more generously American Christians were to give, the more they could do to change the world.

Less Committed Christians

So far we have focused on the potential giving of more committed Christians in the United States, those who attend church a few times a month or more often plus those who may not attend so frequently but who say that they are strong or very strong Christians. We have found that this group of believers alone could give more than enough money to dramatically transform the world—an extra $120.1 billion per year total, by our reckoning. But committed Christians, as we have defined them, represent only about 47 percent of the U.S. population. There remain, in addition, other Americans who think of themselves as Christians but who attend church less than a few times a month and who do not consider themselves strong believers. This group comprises another approximately 30 percent of the U.S. population. How much money could this other group of less committed Christians contribute—on top of the $120.1 billion already raised from committed Christians above—if some of them got more serious about financial giving?

Let us again allow realism to temper expectations of this group. Let us assume, through an increased challenge by churches to give generously, that only *one-third* of typical households in this less committed Christian group responds only *half-way* to the challenge to give fully 10 percent and thus begins giving *five percent* of their after-tax income—leaving two-thirds of this group resistant to the challenge and so maintaining their current low giving levels. Given this nonutopian scenario, how much more money would one-third of currently less committed Christians produce by increasing their giving to only one-half of the 10 percent that committed Christians above contributed? By our calculations, they would produce an additional $13.3 billion.[7]

Once again, we ask: what of value could Christians accomplish with an additional $13.3 billion? We have already by now established our fundamental point, that the amount of money that committed American Christians could generate merely by giving reasonably generously—at the level that most of their own traditions already teach they ought to give anyway—is simply colossal, and that the good they could accomplish with it is stunning. An additional $13.3 billion is a lot of *additional* money that could accomplish even more. Again, for present purposes, at this point in the chapter, we will leave it up to individual readers to imagine how, on top of all that has been proposed above, to use this extra money.

Conclusion

This chapter has shown simply that, if American Christians could somehow find a way to move to practices of reasonably generous giving, they could generate, over and above what they currently give, a total of another *$133.4 billion a year* to devote to whatever purposes and needs they would choose. What good in the world U.S. Christians could do with an additional $133.4 billion, year after year, is almost unimaginable, simply astonishing, nearly beyond comprehension.

In the next chapter we turn to examine the more sobering question of what U.S. Christians actually do give financially. In a quite different way, what we find there is also, in light of the potential for good examined here, quite astonishing and nearly beyond comprehension.

| Failed Generosity

W E SAW IN the previous chapter that American Christians could give a colossal amount of money if they chose to. How much money, then, do American Christians actually give in religious and other donations? How financially generous in fact are American Christians? This chapter mines numerous data sources on charitable giving in the United States to establish six crucial facts about the giving of U.S. Christians.

> Fact #1: At least one out of five American Christians—20 percent of all U.S. Christians—gives literally *nothing* to church, para-church, or nonreligious charities.

No less than one out of five U.S. Christians gives away *no* money to charity whatsoever, whether to religious or secular causes. Zilch. All of their money they appear to spend on themselves. This lack of giving of even $1 per year by 20 percent of U.S. Christians overall varies in extent among different American Christian groups. General Social Survey (GSS) data collected in 1998,[1] presented in the first column (on left) in table 2.1, show that 19 percent of all self-identified Protestants and 28 percent of all Catholics give *no* money to charity. Nothing. Not giving any money to religious or nonreligious causes also varies in extent among different self-identified types of Protestants (shown in table 2.1 in italics as subcategories of Protestant). Twenty percent of self-identified liberal Protestants and 13 percent of mainline Protestants give no money to charity. Twelve percent of fundamentalist and 4 percent of evangelical Protestants also give no money. These rates of Christian non-giving are comparatively much lower than the 50 percent of nonreligious Americans who do not give any money. But they are also generally

TABLE 2.1 Self-reported financial giving by U.S. religious types (in %).

All U.S.	% giving $0 in previous year	% of income given by average (mean) giver	% of mean dollars given by median giver[a]	Gives less than 2% of income	Gives 10% or more income
Christians	22.1	2.9	13.6	71.7	9.4
Protestants	19.2	4.1	13.5	63.9	12
fundamentalist	11.5	6.2	29.6	40.4	17.6
evangelical	4.4	8.2	29.8	36.4	27.3
mainline	12.6	4.6	18.5	59.1	13.6
liberal	19.8	2.7	17.3	68.4	11.2
other	24.4	3.1	10.6	75	7.5
Catholics	28.2	1.8	13.7	80.8	4.4
non-Christian	9.4	3.3	24.7	69	13.8
nonreligious	50.5	.7	<1	89	.6
Regularly attending[b]					
Christians	4.5	6.2	27.7	44.7	17.9
Protestants	3.2	7.4	34.3	37	22.5
fundamentalist	5.6	8.3	54.3	21.9	21.9
evangelical	<1	9.5	36.9	28.3	30.2
mainline	3.8	7.1	28.1	40	22
liberal	7.5	5.2	55.8	36.8	23.7
other	1.5	7.1	23.2	47.7	16.9
Catholics	7.8	3.7	30.9	55.9	7.8

[a]The result of dividing the median (average denoted as numerically middle position among all Christians) dollars given by U.S. Christians by the mean (average calculated by summing all dollars and divided by total number of Christians) dollars given by U.S. Christians, showing how the median reveals much lower levels of giving than do means.

[b]Regularly attending is defined as attending religious services two to three times per month or more often.

Source: General Social Survey, 1998.

much higher than the 9 percent of non-Christian religious believers in the United States—Jews, Mormons, Hindus, Muslims, Buddhists, and so on—who give no money. Thus, while higher proportions of U.S. Christians than nonreligious Americans give at least $1 per year to religious and nonreligious charities, non-Christian religious Americans as a group are much more likely than Christians to give at least some money away. We would expect American Christians who are more involved in their churches to be more likely to contribute at least some money, and that is what the data show. The bottom half of the first column in table 2.1 reports on the financial giving of different types of U.S. Christians who attend church two to three times per month or more often. There we see that, among regularly attending Christians only, 3 percent of Protestants and 8 percent of Catholics give away no money.

Overall, then, we see that Catholics display the highest rates of financial non-giving among U.S. Christian groups. Nearly one out of three American Catholics—which obviously includes many nominal Catholics—gives no money to church or charity. More remarkably, more than one out of every 13 Catholics who regularly attend church also gives away no money whatsoever to any religious or secular cause.

Data from the Center on Philanthropy Panel Study (COPPS), conducted by the Indiana University Center on Philanthropy in association with the Panel Study of Income Dynamics, help to fill out this picture of Christian non-giving with a slightly different measure. Here we use data from the 2001 COPPS survey, which asked respondents, "During the year 2000, did you or anyone in your family donate money, assets, or property/goods, with a combined value of more than $25 to religious or charitable organizations?" Figure 2.1 shows the percent of different religious groups who, according to COPPS data, did not donate anything to anyone worth $25 or more. There we see that between 16 and 38 percent of different kinds of American Christians contributed nothing above a token $25 amount in either money or belongings. Note that giving at least $25 or more does not mean giving a lot of money or a large percent of one's income. It simply means giving at least a nominal amount.

Figure 2.1 also suggests that the all-inclusive "non-Christian" category used in table 2.1 comprises different types of givers who, when possible, are worth separating from each other. The vast majority of Jews and Mormons give away at least $25, whereas half of Jehovah's Witnesses and other kinds of non-Christians—on this survey, Muslims, Buddhists, Hindus, etc.—do not.[2] Apparently not all kinds of "non-Christian" Americans are the same when it comes to charitable giving.

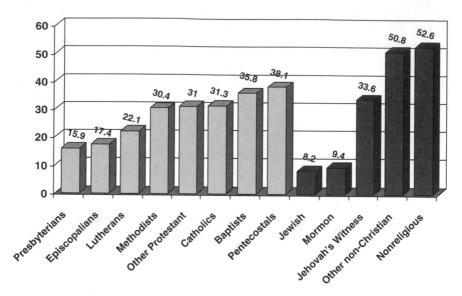

FIGURE 2.1 Percent not donating $25 or more in money, assets, or property, by U.S. religious group. (Source: Center on Philanthropy Panel Study, in PSID, 2001.) Note: Results for Mormons, Jehovah's Witnesses, and other non-Christians should be treated with caution due to low Ns (25, 21, and 46, respectively).

The 1996 General Social Survey also asked respondents about charitable giving. Figure 2.2 shows the percents of different U.S. religious groups who reported giving no money or property at all to health, educational, religious, human service, environmental, public benefit, recreational, arts, cultural, humanities, work-related, political, youth, private community foundation, or international or foreign charities or purposes in 1996.[3] In figure 2.2, we see that 35 percent of all U.S. Christians, 34 percent of Protestants, and 38 percent of Catholics gave no money or property to any of these kinds of charities.[4] Between 17 and 40 percent of different kinds of self-identified Protestants gave nothing—with evangelicals the least likely and theological liberals the most likely to have given nothing. Non-giving by members of specific Protestant denominations ranges between 14 and 46 percent, with most reflecting about 30 percent of non-givers.

The percents in figure 2.2 represent all affiliated or self-identified members of the noted religious groups. As we found above, however, we would expect those who attend religious services regularly to give at higher rates—and they do. But the differences (not shown) are still not huge. In the 1996 GSS sample, 26 percent of all Christians, 26 percent of Protestants, and 25 percent of Catholics who attend church at least two times a month report giving nothing on a more formal basis to religious or charitable causes.

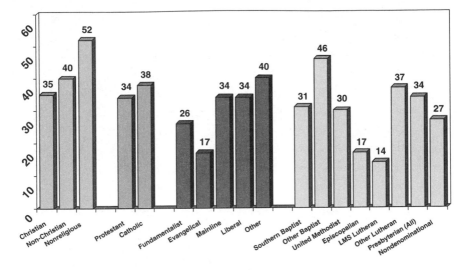

FIGURE 2.2 Percent contributing no money or property to charitable purposes, by religious group. Note: Includes giving to health, educational, religious, human service, environmental, public benefit, recreational, arts, cultural, humanities, work-related, political, youth, private community foundation, or international or foreign charities or purposes; does not include informal giving to needy relatives or neighbors. (Source: General Social Survey, 1996.)

Among self-identified Protestant types, 10 percent of evangelical, 28 percent of mainline, 33 percent of fundamentalist, and 40 percent of liberal Protestants gave nothing. Even among regularly churchgoing Christians of various kinds, then, significant proportions report giving absolutely no money or property to religious, educational, medical, human service, cultural, political, youth, and other similar charitable needs and causes—not even a token $5.00 per year.

Our findings here based on GSS and COPPS data about non-giving are corroborated by analyses of other data sources.[5] For example, the Giving USA Foundation estimates that in 2004 about 25 percent of Americans did not make any charitable contributions. A 2004 review of four U.S. survey datasets by scholars at the Indiana University Center on Philanthropy shows that between 12 and 29.7 percent of Americans report giving no money to charity, and that 31.3 percent of Americans gave no more than $25 a year. Examining the percentage of U.S. households that are religious that give no money at all, the Independent Sector's 2001 "Giving and Volunteering in the United States" survey shows that 43 percent of U.S. households that give no money are members of a religious organization, 45 percent attend religious services monthly or more often, and 25 percent attend less than once a month but more often than never. Given the numerical dominance of Christianity in the United States, most of these religious households are clearly composed of various types of Christians. United States Internal Revenue Service tax returns data show that 26.5 percent of all 1994 tax returns reported no charitable contributions. Independent Sector surveys of household giving in 1993, 1991, 1989, and 1987 show that about one-quarter of U.S. households contributed no money to any charitable causes—including 24.3 percent of Catholics and 25.9 percent of Protestants in 1993. General Social Survey data from 1987 to 1989 analyzed by Dean Hoge and colleagues show that at least 20 percent of Americans—including Catholics and Protestants—self-reported as making no charitable contributions. And a 1988 General Social Survey question on religious giving shows that 30.9 percent of all Americans reported giving nothing to religion. Even 22.4 percent of 1998 General Social Survey respondents who said they believe "the Bible is the actual word of God and is to be taken literally, word for word" also reported giving no money to any religious or nonreligious purpose or cause. Different findings from diverse data sources, in sum, all point to the same conclusion: a significant minority of American Christians gives away no money at all to any organizations, needs, or causes.

Fact #2: The vast majority of American Christians give *very little* to church, para-church, or nonreligious charities.

If a significant minority of Christians in the United States gives away no money at all, as we have just seen, what about the rest of the Christians? How much money do the majority of Christians give? Very little, it turns out.

First, let us examine the average percent of household income given to all religious and charitable causes. According to 1998 General Social Survey data (table 2.1, second column), the amount of (pre-tax) household income contributed by the *mean* average American Christian is 2.9 percent. Protestants give slightly more and Catholics slightly less than that, as a percent of household income. Examining the different types of self-identified Protestants, conservative Protestants generally give higher percentages of income than mainline and liberal Protestants. Non-Christian religious believers in the United States give a mean average of 3.3 percent of income. Nonreligious Americans tend to give the least, less than 1 percent of income here. What about giving by Christians who attend church regularly? The percent of income given by Christians who attend church two to three times per month or more often increases noticeably, as we would expect, over all Christians, to 6.2 percent. Again, Protestants, especially conservative Protestants, give more than Catholics and liberal Protestants.

Figure 2.3 reports findings from the 2001 COPPS survey on the average giving of different religious groups as a percent of their average household income. Here the proportions of giving to religious versus nonreligious causes is shown by horizontal splits in the bars for each group—the top portion of each bar represents giving to nonreligious causes and the bottom portion giving to religion. The total percent for combined giving by households in each group is noted above the bars. Figure 2.3 shows that most Christian groups give away only about 1.5 to 2 percent of their income. Above that, Baptists give 2.5 percent of income, and Pentecostals and "other" Protestants—most of who are likely fundamentalists, evangelicals, and other conservative Protestants—give about 3.5 percent. By contrast, Mormons give 5.2 percent of income and Jews and other non-Christians about 2.3–2.8 percent of income. Nonreligious Americans as a group are, as usual, among the least liberal givers. All groups, we see, contribute to a mix of religious and nonreligious purposes. Mormons, Pentecostals, and Baptists devote the highest proportions of

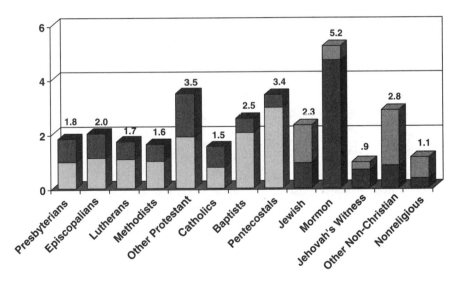

FIGURE 2.3 Total, religious, and nonreligious giving as a percent of household income, by U.S. religious group. Note: Bottom of bars is religious giving portion, top of bars is nonreligous giving portion, percent is mean total giving as percent of income. Results for Mormons, Jehovah's Witnesses, and other non-Christians should be treated with caution due to low Ns (25, 21, and 46, respectively). (Source: Center on Philanthropy Panel Study, in PSID, 2000.)

their giving to religion, while Jewish, other non-Christian, and nonreligious Americans give the lowest proportions of contributions to religion.[6]

But reliance on mean averages to tell us about central tendencies in giving money is optimistically misleading. Understanding why requires noting a key point about the calculation of averages. There are two kinds of averages often used to calculate central tendencies in data distributions: means and medians. Means, as most people know, calculate mathematical averages by summing and dividing. That is what most people mean by "the average." Medians, by comparison, identify the numerically middle position in a distribution as representing the most representative status among all cases. When distributions of things like dollars given to charity are skewed at one end—as they in fact are in U.S. charitable giving—medians generally provide more accurate measures of central tendency than means, since a few contributors giving many dollars can significantly and misleadingly increase a mean by natural mathematical calculation.[7]

How, then, does average Christian giving look when viewed as medians instead of means? In 1998, the amount of money given by the *median* U.S. Christian giver was $200 and the median income of U.S. Christians was $32,500 (not shown in the table). The median American Christian giver thus gave only 0.62 percent of the median Christian annual income—a little more than one-half of one percent of income. That percent of incomes increases to 2 percent of income for regularly church-attending U.S. Christians, but these are obviously still much lower levels of giving than mean calculations provide.

Another way to examine this more realistic view of median giving is to calculate the percent of mean contributions given by median givers. These results are shown in the third column of table 2.1. There we see that the median Christian financial giver contributes only about 14 percent of the mean Christian contribution, and the median Christian who regularly attends church gives about one-third of the mean contribution of that group. Again, then, the "typical" American Christian gives much less money than mean calculations suggest because of the highly skewed distribution of Christian giving overall.

Yet another way to assess the generosity of American Christians is to examine the percentage of givers who contributes less than 2 percent of their income. The fourth column of table 2.1 reveals that 72 percent of all Christians, about two-thirds (64 percent) of all Protestants and four-fifths (81 percent) of Catholics, give less than 2 percent of their income to all causes, religious and not religious. Different proportions of diverse subtypes of Protestants give less than 2 percent of their incomes, ranging from 75 percent of "other"

Protestants (those who do not consider themselves fundamentalist, evangelical, mainline, or liberal Protestants, but something else) on the high end, to 36 percent of evangelical Protestants on the low end. United States Catholics here, as above, are the most likely group of U.S. Christians to give less than 2 percent of their income—Catholics are only a bit less likely than nonreligious Americans (81 compared to 89 percent) to give away less than 2 percent of their incomes. At the same time, non-Christian religious Americans as a category are more likely than U.S. Christians to give less than 2 percent of their income—that is, higher proportions give away less than 2 percent of their incomes—just as they are more likely to be non-givers, as we saw above. In sum, financial giving by U.S. Christians is dramatically skewed toward zero.

What about regular churchgoers, whom we would expect to give more? They do. Even so, large proportions of U.S. Christians who regularly attend church still give less than 2 percent of their incomes. Forty-five percent of all Christians, 37 percent of Protestants, and 56 percent of Catholics who attend church two times a month or more often give away less than 2 percent of their income. On the high side, 48 percent of regularly churchgoing "other" Protestants (again, those who do not consider themselves fundamentalist, evangelical, mainline, or liberal Protestants, but something else) gives away less than 2 percent of their incomes. On the low side, 22 percent of regularly attending fundamentalist Protestants gives away less than 2 percent of their income. In short, even among Christians who frequently attend church, nearly half overall give away less than 2 percent of their income to religious and nonreligious causes.[8]

An alternative approach to assessing American Christian financial generosity is to calculate the percent of U.S. Christians who tithe—that is, who give away 10 percent or more of their income. Results are shown in the fifth column of table 2.1, where we see that only 9.4 percent of all Christians, 12 percent of Protestants, and 4 percent of Catholics give 10 percent or more of their incomes. As seen above, among all Protestants, fundamentalists and evangelicals tend to tithe in higher proportions than do mainline, liberal, and other Protestants. Only about one-half of 1 percent of nonreligious Americans gives away 10 percent or more of income. On the other hand, about 14 percent of non-Christian religious believers in the United States gives away 10 percent or more of income, more than any Christian group in this comparison, except evangelical and fundamentalist Protestants. The percent of tithing Christians rises among those who attend church regularly, but not dramatically so. Twenty-three percent of all Protestants and 8 percent of Catholics who attend church regularly give 10 percent or more of their income. Particularly for the Protestants, these are relatively larger numbers, but they still fall far short of the normative expectations about generous financial giving that these Christian traditions teach (see appendix A).

These findings about low levels of giving are corroborated by analyses of other data sources.[9] A 2000 Bureau of Labor Statistics Consumer Expenditure Survey, for instance, found that Americans give only 2.87 percent of after-tax income to charity, of which only 1.43 percent is given to religious organizations. The Urban Institute's analysis of 2003 and 2002 IRS tax return data to estimate Americans' charitable contributions shows that the average contribution per return was 2.3 percent of reported adjusted gross income. An analysis of 2003 Bureau of Labor Statistics Consumer Expenditure Survey data shows per capita charitable contributions of Americans to be 1.12 percent of disposable personal income, of which giving to religion is .8 percent. John and Sylvia Ronsvalle's analysis of church member giving data estimates per member contributions at 2.59 percent of income. A 1993 Independent Sector survey of charitable giving found that U.S. Protestants gave 2.5 percent and Catholics gave 1.2 percent of their annual incomes. Stephen Hart's analysis of 1984–89 General Social Survey data found that American Catholics give an average of 1.2 percent, mainline Protestants give an average of 2 percent, black Protestants an average of 2.5 percent, and white conservative Protestants an average of 3.1 percent of their income. Hart also found that Americans who attend religious services weekly or more often give an average of only 3.9 percent of their income, that only 9 percent of them gives 10 percent or more of their income, and that the percent of income given by Americans who attend religious services less often is even lower. A Barna Research Group survey conducted in 2002 reports that only 3 percent of all adults and 6 percent of "born again" Christians give away 10 percent or more of their income.

The reader should bear in mind, as a nontrivial aside, that when people are asked by surveys, such as most of those reported on in this chapter, to estimate the number of dollars they give to religion and charity, they may *over*estimate the number of dollars they contribute. Giving to charity is generally considered a good thing in American culture. So a social desirability bias seems to induce many people to think optimistically of themselves and give themselves the benefit of the doubt when it comes to remembering or estimating the amount of money they have contributed. They are not necessarily being consciously dishonest—they are often simply letting good intentions cloud their memories and estimations. More detailed or objective measures, such as real denominational income and tax returns, sometimes find somewhat lower levels of giving than surveys that ask directly about estimates of dollars given. For instance, 1998 General Social Survey respondent reports of giving to religious causes average to 1.69 percent of household income, whereas equivalent contributions to religion reported on the much more detailed Bureau of Labor Statistics 2000 Consumer Expenditure Survey show Americans contributing 1.43 percent of their income—a seemingly small discrepancy that actually represents billions of dollars of difference in total.[10]

Furthermore, survey respondents who refuse to answer giving-to-charity questions—whose cases are therefore normally simply dropped from analyses for containing missing data—are likely to disproportionately represent people who give little or no money.[11] That is often precisely why they do not want to answer the survey question. Consequently, as ungenerous as the numbers reported in this chapter make American Christians appear, it is possible if not likely that the true statistical facts about the generosity of actual financial giving, if those facts could ever be fully and accurately known, are *even lower* than the numbers from surveys reported here. If anything, the statistics on financial giving reported here may be somewhat on the optimistic side.

Finally, it is worth repeating that not only do American Christians give away relatively little of their income, but they are also out-given by at least some American non-Christian religious groups. We have seen in table 2.1 that non-Christian religious believers in the United States—Jews, Mormons, and other minority religious groups taken together—tend to give more of their means than do American Christians as a group. Non-Christian religious believers in the United States as a group are less likely than Christians to give no money at all and to give away less than 2 percent of their income. They are also the most likely among compared groups to give 10 percent or more of their income to charity and give a higher average percentage of their income than do Christians. Their giving is also more equitably distributed among their members, as measured by median giving as a (larger) percentage of mean income given.[12] Much of this high level of U.S. "non-Christian" giving appears to be led by Mormons and Jews. By comparison, American Christians—particularly Catholics—are clearly on the lower side of charitable giving among diverse groups of American religious believers. If financial giving were a competition among different types of religious believers in the United States, American Christians would be among the definite losers of the contest.

> Fact #3: American Christians do not give their dollars
> evenly among themselves, but, rather, a small minority
> of generous givers among them contributes most
> of the total Christian dollars given.

Were it not for a relatively small group of Christians who give of their money generously, American Christianity would go financially bankrupt and most of the ministries that Christian charitable giving supports would fold. That is because most of the dollars that are given by Christians are contributed by a fairly small percentage of Christian givers. This third fact is the reverse side of the other facts already noted above, namely, that the majority of American Christians gives either nothing or very little of their resources. If the majority gives little or nothing, then the bulk of what is given must come from a minority.

Most studies of religious giving as a percent of income, as we noted above, calculate means instead of medians for average percents of income given. For example, the 2001 Independent Sector "Giving and Volunteering in the United States" survey report shows that Americans as a whole give a (mean) average of 2.7 percent of household income in charitable contributions, Americans who belong to religious organizations give a (mean) average of 3.9 percent of household income, while Americans who do not belong to a religious organization give a (mean) average of 1.6 percent.[13] Mean percentages of income contributed, however, convey a brighter picture of religious giving than do median percentages. That is again because, typically, as explained above, the generous giving of a small group of contributors dramatically skews giving distributions and significantly drives up the mean averages. Calculating median averages (the midpoint in a distribution) instead removes this distorting effect. This difference we noted in column three of table 2.1, which reports on the percentage of the mean dollars given for different groups that are contributed by the median giver in each group. There we saw that the median Christian giver contributes only 13.6 percent of the total dollars given by the mean average Christian giver. For a concrete example of dollar figures, consider Protestant givers specifically: the *mean* average Protestant giver in 1998 contributed $1,803.75 (not shown in table), whereas the *median* Protestant giver contributed only $224 (13.5 percent of the mean contribution). Clearly, again, the mean contribution was increased dramatically over the typical Protestant giver by the large dollars contributed by a few very generous Protestant givers. By reporting means instead of medians, we repeat, most prior studies have portrayed a more optimistic picture of religious giving in the United States than is warranted. The reality is that if a relatively small group of the most generous religious givers were removed from contributing, the mean average of percent of income given would plummet—more closely reflecting what we suggest is the more revealing median average. In other words, a small group of truly generous Christian givers are essentially "covering" for the vast majority of Christians who give nothing or quite little.

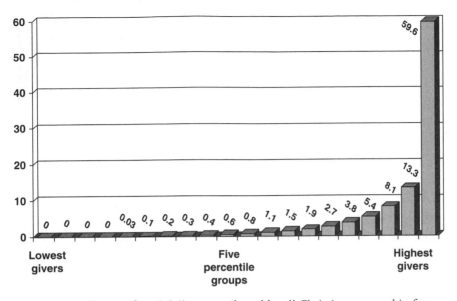

FIGURE 2.4 Pecent of total dollars contributed by all Christians grouped in five percentiles by increasing levels of generosity. (Source: General Social Survey, 1998.)

One way to better grasp this fact is to calculate the proportion of all dollars given that is contributed by the top givers. Figure 2.4 plots out the number of dollars contributed by successively generous 5 percent groups of all U.S. Christians, ranging left to right from the least to the most generous givers.[14] There we see that the vast majority of all dollars contributed are given by a relatively small group of more generous Christian givers. The top most generous 5 percent of givers contributes 59.6 percent of all dollars contributed. From there, the percent of all money given drops to 13.3, 8.1, and 5.4 for respectively lower five percentiles of Christian givers. The overall distributions for Protestants and Catholics (not shown) are nearly identical.

Figure 2.5 shows the same giving distribution for "committed" Christians, defined here as those who attend church two to three times a month or more often or who report themselves to be "strong" or "very strong" Christians. There we see only a slight shift toward more evenly spread giving—but the overall pattern is indistinguishable from that of figure 2.4. In both cases, between the small group of Christian givers at the top who contribute the lion's share of charitable dollars and the 20 percent of Christians who give essentially nothing exists a large middle range of givers who make up the final difference in total dollars with very modest levels of giving. Thus,

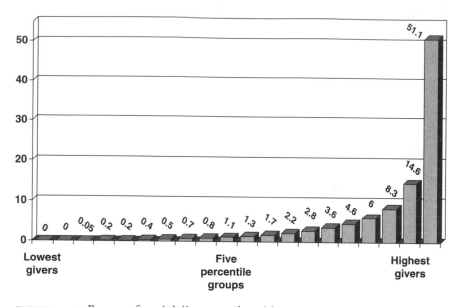

FIGURE 2.5 Percent of total dollars contributed by regularly church-attending and self-described "strong" or "very strong" Christians grouped in five percentiles by increasing levels of generosity. (Source: General Social Survey, 1998.)

we see that, below the top 20 percent of givers, the proportion of total dollars given by each 5 percent group falls below the 5 percent of all dollars that each group would have to contribute to make giving perfectly even. In other words, the bottom 80 percent of givers is giving well less than their proportionate share.

Figure 2.6 shows the percent of all dollars contributed by the top 5 percent of givers of different religious groups. There we see that the top 5 percent of givers among all Protestants gives 56 percent of all dollars given, and the top 5 percent for Protestants who regularly attend church gives 46 percent. That is, about half of all of the money that U.S. Protestants give away is contributed by only 5 percent of givers. The proportions given by the top 5 percent of Catholics is even higher: 59 percent of all U.S. Catholic giving in dollars is contributed by the top 5 percent of contributors. Those numbers drop only slightly for Catholics who attend church services regularly, to 55 percent of all dollars given. That the top 5 percent of givers contributes large proportions of all charitable dollars given remains true for all Protestant subtypes, at 34 for fundamentalists at the low end, 51 for evangelicals, 57 for mainliners, 52 for liberals, and 64 for other-identity Protestants at the high end. Again, we also see that the giving of non-Christian believers appears more equitably distributed.

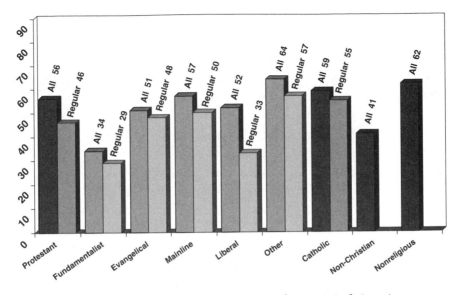

FIGURE 2.6 Percent of all charitable dollars given by top 5% of givers in religious group. (Source: General Social Survey, 1998.)

Another way to make this general point is to calculate the percentage of all dollars given that are contributed by those relatively few generous givers who contribute 10 percent or more of their income. To sharpen the point, let us focus here only on committed Christians, of whom we might expect more. Let us again define committed Christians as those who attend church regularly (two times a month or more often) or who say that they are "strong" or "very strong" Christians. Among these committed Christians in the United States, the small minority who give at least 10 percent of their income contribute 62.3 percent of all dollars given. In truth, a relatively small group of faithful financial contributors is pulling two-thirds of the giving weight for everyone.

At this point, many readers may assume that the most generous givers must at least also be the wealthiest givers, those who are most *able* to give most generously. If this were true, then we would expect to see income and generosity of giving strongly correlated. In fact, as the following shows, we do not.

Fact #4: Higher income earning American Christians—like Americans generally—give *little to no more money* as a percentage of household income than lower income earning Christians.

For American Christians, as with Americans more broadly, a greater capacity to give does not generally result in higher levels of financial giving. This is remarkable, indeed. But it is true. To verify the fact, we rely on multiple kinds of analyses using three different data sets, focusing on numerous types of financial givers and giving. Since here relative comparisons across income groups, not absolute representations of giving, are most important, most of the following numbers rely on means, not median averages. To begin, figure 2.7 shows the mean percent of household income given specifically to religious organizations by all Americans—most of whom, it bears remembering, given America's religious demography, are certainly Christians—separated out into different income brackets. These data come from the Bureau of Labor Statistics Consumer Expenditure Survey, conducted in 2000. Here we see a trend showing that the more (mostly Christian) Americans earn, the lower percentages of their income they give to religious organizations. Americans who earn less than $10,000 gave 2.3 percent of their income to religious organizations, for example, whereas those who earn $70,000 or more gave only 1.2 percent, nearly half the proportion of income contributed by the poorer group. Despite higher earners enjoying more income from which to give, in other words, earning higher salaries actually *decreases* Americans' share of giving to religion.[15]

Another way to examine the relationship between income earned and the proportion of income contributed to charity is to calculate the percents of households in different income brackets that give more or less than a certain

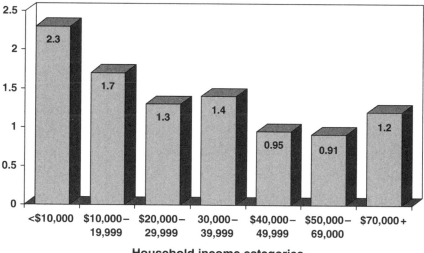

FIGURE 2.7 Percent of household income given to religious organizations by income level, all Americans. (Source: Bureau of Labor Statistics Consumer Expenditure Survey, 2000.)

percent of their income to charity. Figure 2.8 shows this for U.S. households measured at the level of financially giving more than 3 percent of household income. These numbers come from the Independent Sector's "Giving and Volunteering in the United States" survey, conducted in 2001. Here we see that households' earning more money is associated with smaller proportions of households giving more than 3 percent of their income to charity. The drop slips 13 percentage points from the lowest to the highest income earning groups, from 40 to 27 percent giving more than 3 percent of income. Similar investigations of giving data by Independent Sector analysts that measured the average incomes of all U.S. households that gave at different levels reveal the same findings. For instance, the average household income of Americans who gave 5 percent or more of their income was $50,257, compared to an average income of $59,353 for households who gave more than nothing but less than 1 percent of income. Likewise, the average income of those who gave at least 3 percent of household income was $52,503, compared to $58,840 as the average income of those who gave *less* than 3 percent of household income.[16]

Figure 2.9 uses the same survey data to examine the mean percent of income given by all financially *contributing* households (nongiving households

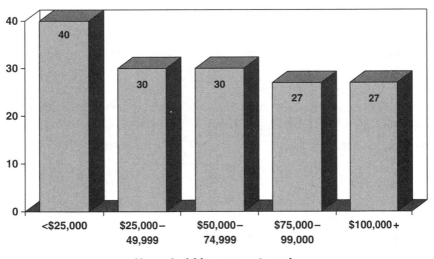

FIGURE 2.8 Percent of U.S. households giving more than 3 percent of income, by household income level. (Source: Giving and Volunteering in the United States, 2001.)

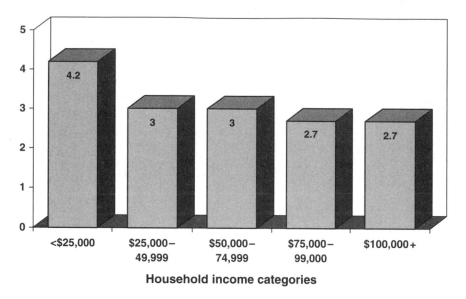

FIGURE 2.9 Percent of household income in total charitable giving by income level, contributing households only. (Source: Giving and Volunteering in the United States, 2001.)

are excluded), separated out into five income brackets. Once again, we see that the higher the household income, the lower the percentage of that income is given away. The decline from lowest to highest income brackets is 1.5 percent, a greater than one-third drop by the highest earners compared to the lowest in the percentage of income given to charity.

What about U.S. Christians specifically? Figure 2.10 reports on mean average Christian total charitable giving as a percent of income, separated into six income groups. The taller columns on the left of each pair represent regularly attending Christians; the shorter columns on the right represent all U.S. Christians, both regularly attending and less frequently attending. Among American Christians, the general pattern is similar to that observed in the findings above, except that, for regularly attending Christians at the highest income bracket, giving as a percentage of income takes a noticeable turn up. That up-tick at that highest level should not be exaggerated, however, as those earning $90,000 or greater give only 1.8 percent more of their income than those earning less than $12,500. And, other than that significant upturn in the last income bracket, the general observable trend for Christians is similar: higher income is associated with lower giving as a proportion of income.

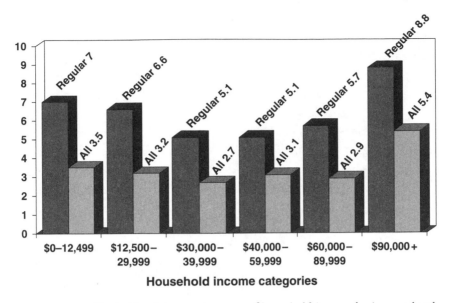

FIGURE 2.10 Charitable giving as a percent of household income by income level, U.S. Christians. (Source: General Social Survey, 1998.)

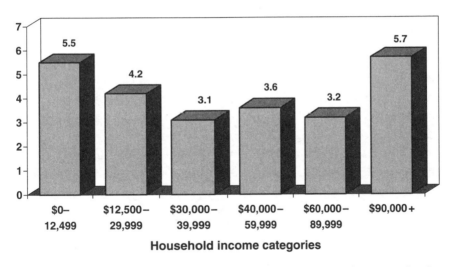

FIGURE 2.11 Charitable giving as a percent of household income by income levels, giving U.S. Christians (nongivers excluded). (Source: General Social Survey, 1998.)

Figure 2.11 shows a similar analysis for financially giving Christians only (excluding nongivers). There we see again the trend that giving as a percent of income actually drops as income increases, up until the highest income category. At that point we see that giving Christians in households earning

$90,000 or more, however, does not significantly surpass but instead simply returns to essentially the same level of giving as those in households earning less than $12,500—the difference between 5.5 and 5.7 percent, comparatively, being substantively insignificant. In short, even among U.S. Christians who are financial contributors, the giving advantage of larger incomes does not translate into increased generosity in actual financial giving, measured as a percent of income contributed. The highest income earners give away the same or lower proportions of their financial means than the lower earners.

Finally, in order to confirm with more sophisticated statistical analyses that higher income earners do not give more generously than lower earners, despite their vastly increased capacity to give, we ran multivariate regression analyses of income differences' associations with higher levels of giving. These more sophisticated results are reported in the tables in appendix C. In table C.1 we find among American Christians *no* statistically significant association for earning higher income with charitable giving as a percent of income, whether as a bivariate association or in a multivariate model. The same finding emerges for all Americans, in table C.2. Even more amazing, reporting on American Christians, table C.3 shows that—once we control for region, religious service attendance, and differences among Protestant self-identities or denominations (models 4 and 5)—higher income is also not associated with more generous giving *even when measured in absolute terms as total dollars given,* except for those at the highest income bracket. The same finding emerges in table C.4 for all Americans (models 4 and 5). In sum, those American Christians and Americans generally with greater financial resources from which to give are, once the influence of simple religion factors is removed, in fact *not* particularly more generous in their financial giving. It is true that higher income earners pay higher tax rates but that could hardly explain the lack of more generous giving observed here. Differences in generosity of giving are evidently driven by factors other than the capacity to give generously.[17]

> Fact #5: Despite a massive growth of real per capita income over the twentieth century, the average percentage share of income given by American Christians not only did not grow in proportion but actually *declined* slightly during this time period.

The twentieth century was a time of amazing economic growth in the United States, producing a more than quadrupling of real (inflation-adjusted) per capita disposable personal income. Figure 2.12 depicts this standardized income growth between the 1920s and century's end with shaded vertical bars, growing in size from left to right. One might reasonably expect this real growth in personal expendable income to be paralleled by an associated growth by American Christians in financial giving as a percent of their income. Systematically collected historical religious-giving data from the *Yearbook of American and Canadian Churches* enables analysts to track giving trends for numerous Protestant denominations over much of the twentieth century. Figure 2.12 graphs a solid black line to show the religious giving—measured here as financial contributions to churches in denominations—per church member as a percent of real income over time by members of 11 major U.S. Protestant denominations.[18] What we see is that the generosity of the members of these Protestant denominations in fact did *not* grow along with the increase in real income between 1921 and 2003. Indeed, overall, the generosity of these Christians actually *declined* slightly from the 1920s to the century's end. The trend line is wobbly, not straight, due to a dramatic decline in giving during the Great Depression of the 1930s and an equally dramatic rebound in financial giving between the Second World War and 1960. But the century's overall trend is clearly one of modest decline. In

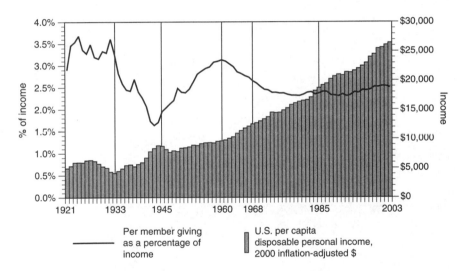

FIGURE 2.12 Giving per church member as a percent of income in 11 Protestant denominations, and U.S. per capita inflation-adjusted income 1921–2003. The 11 denominations analyzed are American Baptist (Northern), Christian Church (Disciples of Christ), Church of the Brethren, the Episcopal Church, Evangelical Lutheran Church of America (and subsidiaries that merged), Morvaian Church in America, Presbyterian Church U.S.A., Reformed Church in America, Southern Baptist Convention, United Church of Christ (and subsidiaries that merged), and United Methodist Church (and subsidiaries that merged). (Source: empty tomb analysis; *YACC* adjusted series; U.S. BEA.)

the 1920s, the members of these 11 denominations were as a whole giving 3.0–3.5 percent of their income to their churches. By 2003, despite the national economy producing a fourfold increase in real personal income, the per capita religious giving to these churches by members dropped to about 2.5 percent of personal income. The two trends' clearly heading in opposite directions—declining religious giving in the context of rapidly growing incomes—is remarkable.

What, then, about U.S. Catholics? How has Catholic religious giving changed over time? To answer this, we build on previous analyses by sociologists Andrew Greeley and Stephen Hart that employed two other data sources to track Catholic giving.[19] To their work we added data from Independent Sector surveys and the 1998 General Social Survey. Figure 2.13 depicts Catholic religious giving as a percent of income marked at multiple years between 1960 and 1998, as found by a variety of surveys. There we see a parallel to changes in the giving trend line shown for Protestants in figure 2.12 for the years between 1960 and 1989, namely, a modest but definite trend downward. The percents reported in figure 2.13 jump around a bit after 1984, probably primarily because of different methodologies used by different surveys. By imagining an averaging trend line moving from left to right, however, we can notice a drop in Catholic giving from 2.2 percent of income during the 1960s to approximately 1.4 percent after the 1970s. The absolute percentage differences here might seem slight, but the apparent .8 percent drop between the two time periods actually represents a one-third proportion (36.4 percent) reduction from the original level of Catholic giving as a percentage of income in the 1960s. In short, Catholic giving as a share of income

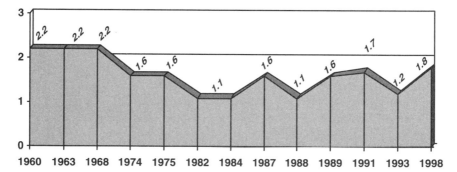

FIGURE 2.13 U.S. Catholic religious giving as a percent of income, 1963–1998. Note: Years not to scale. (Source: Greeley and McManus, 1987; Hart, 1990; GSS, 1998; Independent Sector, 1994.)

did not increase in the last decades of the twentieth century. If anything, it appears to have declined.[20]

Other studies come to similar conclusions. The report *The State of Church Giving through 2003*, for instance, publishes the results of an analysis of religious giving by members of 31 Protestant denominations, comprising about 100,000 religious congregations, covering the years 1968 and 2003. This analysis represents a larger number of religious givers but over a shorter period of time, compared to the analysis of figure 2.12. This analysis also finds that religious giving to churches by these members as a proportion of real income declined, from a mean average of 3.11 percent of income given in 1968 to 2.59 percent given in 2003, a 17 percent drop from the baseline number.[21] Scholars at the Indiana University Center on Philanthropy have also analyzed U.S. data on religious giving that are compiled in the national philanthropy report, *Giving USA*, covering the years 1963 to 2000. Their analysis finds that national religious giving as a percent of income dropped from 1.2 percent in 1963 to .9 percent by 2000. Some of this decline they attribute to the less generous religious giving of baby boomers moving into middle adulthood, due in part to baby boomers' lower levels of general religious involvement compared to older cohorts of Americans.[22] These data and analyses are different, but the findings remain the same: religious giving in the United States as a proportion of income has actually declined over the last decades and century, despite an overall massive increase in real income and wealth.

> Fact #6: The vast majority of the money that American Christians do give to religion is spent in and for their own local communities of faith—little is spent on missions, development, and poverty relief outside of local congregations, particularly outside the United States, in ways that benefit people other than the givers themselves.

Determining how and on what the money that is given by American Christians for religious and other charitable purposes is spent is no easy matter. Multiple targets of giving and the ambiguity of some expenditure categories make precise and direct determinations of spending impossible. Nevertheless, all available evidence suggests the conclusion that most of the money that American Christians give away actually ends up turning around to get spent essentially on themselves, directly or indirectly—to supply their own pastoral staff, educational programs, church buildings, supplies, denominational support infrastructures, and so on. Relatively little donated money actually moves much of a distance away from the contributors to primarily benefit others. In other words, while most of the financial giving of American Christians is indeed charitable and tax-deductible, relatively little of it is genuinely altruistic or reflective of what Christians call *agape* (completely self-giving) love, since the givers turn out to be among the primary beneficiaries of most of the money given.

What evidence exists to support this claim? First, at a broadest level of global Christianity, researchers calculate that the vast majority of all income that Christian churches and ministry organizations around the world receive is spent on local pastoral ministry to Christian believers. Barrett and Johnson, for instance, calculate that 97 percent of total income in 2000 was spent on costs benefiting Christians who mostly live in highly Christianized societies. Three percent, by their reckoning, was dedicated to expenses serving non-Christians. According to their data, in comparing specific expenditures, greater than 106 times more money was spent on the salaries of full-time ministers serving Christians than on the salaries of ministers working with non-Christians. Furthermore, 30 times more dollars from Christian organizations' income around the world was lost due to mismanagement than was spent on Christian medical missions. The multiple sources and global nature of these data mean they likely involve inexactitudes. But even taken merely as a broad-brushed picture, the relative differences in proportions of types of financial expenditures are enormous.[23]

What data exist concerning the United States specifically? In 1996, Independent Sector conducted a nationally representative survey of 271 U.S. religious congregations.[24] Included in the survey were questions about the congregations' financial budget expenditures the previous year. Figure 2.14 portrays the percentage breakdown of the congregations' 1996 average expenditures by major category. There we see, first, that more than 70 percent of congregational income is spent on local operations, on things like wages, salaries, benefits, supplies, and services needed to maintain current operations. Another 13 percent is spent on acquiring and improving local church buildings. Eight percent of income is contributed to denominations, most of which is then spent on regional and national level organizational operations. Four percent of income is put into savings. About 3 percent (2.8 percent to be exact) is donated to other organizations—ones, note, in which we have reason to believe that congregational members are not infrequently also involved. And about 1 percent (1.4 percent to be exact) is given directly as assistance to individuals in need, many of whom are often needy members of congregations. For some of these categories, it is not clear whether the resources are being expended primarily for the benefit of local church members or for ministry and service to the outside world. The same church build-

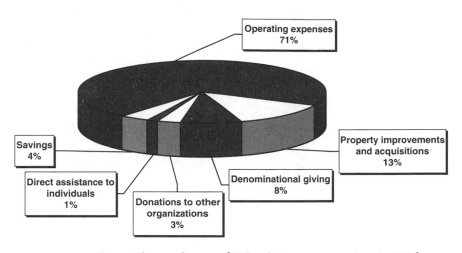

FIGURE 2.14 Financial expenditures of U.S. religious congregations in 1996. (Source: Independent Sector, 1996.)

ing, for instance, can of course be used for Sunday school meetings and for community Alcoholics Anonymous meetings. The same clergy member may attend to the pastoral needs of church members as well as engage in evangelism and social service ministries well beyond their congregation. Some proportion of denominational contributions certainly goes to world missions and humanitarian assistance. But even if we count all of the money donated to outside organizations, one-half of the direct assistance money, and one-tenth of denominational contributions as expenditures dedicated to serving needs beyond members of giving congregations, that still only totals to about 4 percent of income expended for purposes not primarily benefiting the givers. Thus, nearly all of the money that religious givers—which in the United States comprises mostly Christians—give to their congregations appears to end up getting spent directly or indirectly on themselves. Although these data are now more than a decade old, we know that the organizational features that generate such financial expenditure patterns—salary structures, mortgages, benefits systems, denominational obligations, and so on—are highly stable over time, such that the structure of church spending today is therefore likely very similar.

These findings are confirmed by an Independent Sector and Gallup Organization nationally representative survey of 1,353 U.S. religious congregations conducted a decade earlier.[25] Included in that 1987 survey were also questions about the congregations' financial budget expenditures the previous year. Figure 2.15 portrays the percentage breakdown of the congregations'

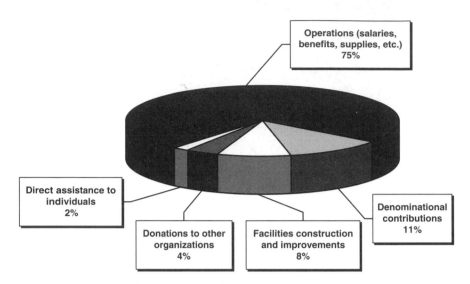

FIGURE 2.15 Financial expenditures of U.S. religious congregations in 1986. (Source: Independent Sector, 1987.)

1986 average expenditures by major category. We see, again, that the vast majority of budgeted money appears to be spent to maintain the personnel, programs, and facilities of local congregations that primarily serve the contributors. It is difficult to interpret this budget in any way that apportions significant dollars for ministry, service, and missions to people well beyond the local worlds of those giving the money that funds the budget. Again, the evidence suggests that the vast majority of the money that religious givers—which in the United States comprises mostly Christians—give to their congregations appears to end up getting spent directly or indirectly on themselves. Research by Mark Chaves on congregational resources also reinforces this conclusion.[26]

Information from other sources also confirms these findings. Data on 28 U.S. Protestant denominations, for example, show that an average of less then 2 percent of dollars given to local churches is devoted to overseas missions through denominations.[27] According to 1998 National Congregations Survey data, only 5.3 percent of U.S. religious congregations have programs that give cash to the needy; only 2.7 percent have programs to provide needy people furniture, household items, or money for rent and utilities; and only 14 percent give or loan money to individuals or organizations. National Congregation Survey data also show that 57.6 percent of reporting U.S. Christian congregations give no money to any social service program (if we assume the nonreporting congregations also give nothing, that rises to 64.5 percent giving no money to social service programs); a few very generous Christian congregations among them skew the *mean* dollars given by the average congregation up to $7,040.53, but the *median* dollars contributed to social service programs per congregation are $0. Furthermore, one national study of more than 120 African American churches found that the average congregation spent at least 77 percent of its income "to maintain basic operations and programs," and that "the median giving to global missions of those same churches comprised only .6 percent of their budgets." Other significant portions of their church budgets, in addition to the 77 percent, were also spent simply to maintain local congregational life.[28]

Thus, other available evidence again points to the same conclusion: most of the money that U.S. Christians currently do give away to congregations ends up getting spent essentially on the givers, primarily for maintaining their own local congregations and communities of faith from which they directly and indirectly benefit. Relatively little money actually gets spent to meet the needs of other people who live outside of the local worlds of American Christian financial givers. From what we have seen above, this is mostly because the illiberal giving of most American Christians appears to provide only enough money to sustain, sometimes barely, their own local congregations, and so not enough to devote to needs and purposes beyond—however pressing or worthy they may be.

Conclusion

This chapter has reviewed a great deal of empirical evidence testifying to the reality of ungenerous American Christian financial giving. If what we have presented here is indeed not a misreading of the data, but rather a set of facts verified by a sensible interpretation of the best available empirical evidence, then it would appear that American Christians have much soul searching to do about the question of money. More relevant sociologically, the findings of this chapter give us an *explanandum,* an interesting and important fact about social life that needs to be explained. Ungenerous American Christian financial giving needs to be explained because of three other points that bear on the question. First, American Christians appear to posses the financial resources to give generously if they so desired. Second, nearly every tradition in American Christianity explicitly teaches its followers to give liberally, if not to tithe 10 percent of income (see appendix A). Third, as we saw in the previous chapter, generous financial giving promises to help achieve so many things that American Christians profess to desire to accomplish, and to achieve them through means consistent with their core values and standards. Here, then, is the confounding riddle: why, in light of these three points, do Christians in the United States not give away their money much more generously than they do? Why are most American Christians so remarkably stingy in their financial giving? Helping to unravel and answer this riddle will be the purpose of the next chapter.

| Toward Explaining Ungenerous Giving

HOW MIGHT WE explain the lack of financial giving by U.S. Christians found in chapter 2? Previous studies of religious financial giving in the United States have identified a number of variables that statistically correlate with more and less giving. For instance, more generous giving has been found to be associated with variations in age, income, church attendance, and other factors.[1] But discovering statistical correlations is not the same thing as explaining causes. In order actually to *explain* something, we must move beyond mere statistical associations to identifying and describing the operation of real causal mechanisms through which particular factors or conditions actively produce specific outcomes or consequences.[2] That is what we attempt to do in this chapter. This book's introduction acknowledged that basic human selfishness and greed are no doubt involved in U.S. Christians' inadequate generosity. But we also suggested that the reality is more complicated than that. The capacity if not tendency to be selfish and greedy may be universal among human beings. But such predispositions and motivations are also always worked out through specific causal mechanisms operating in the context of particular cultural and social systems that can reinforce, resist, or override them. If we want to understand differences in the generosity of people's giving, we need to examine possible, more proximate social and social-psychological causal influences on charity.

This chapter suggests and evaluates to the best of our ability nine such hypotheses seeking to better explain the ungenerous financial giving of U.S. Christians. We first simply state the hypotheses together, so the reader understands the terrain that this chapter will cover. We then consider each hypothesis singly, relying on the best available empirical evidence to test their explanatory value to the best of our ability. In some cases, we have fairly strong evidence with which to evaluate the hypothesis. In others, our ability to test the hypothesis is more tenuous. What follows, then, is not a completely thorough and definitive analysis of the reasons for American Christians' lack of financial giving. We have here no proof to provide an irrefutable argument. Rather, here we offer the outlines of a general framework for understanding ungenerous giving, some partial evaluations of what could be possible explanations of lack of religious and charitable giving, and suggestions for further research that might better establish some of the causal factors behind the observed financial stinginess of American Christians. Some readers may find some of the hypotheses incredible, but we wish to err on the side of taking nothing for granted and so consider a range of possibilities that come to mind, however elementary or remote they might seem to some.

To begin, then, the nine hypotheses that this chapter examines and attempts to evaluate are the following:

Hypothesis 1—Resource Constraints: Despite American affluence generally, many American Christians simply do not possess the discretionary financial resources to give 10 percent of their income, given the many fixed costs of living in American society.

Hypothesis 2—Subjective Resource Constraints: Many American Christians, whatever their objective financial capacities, *subjectively believe* that they do not possess the discretionary financial resources to give 10 percent of their income.

Hypothesis 3—Unperceived Needs: Most American Christians do not give their money generously because they simply do not perceive existing legitimate needs that their money could address and meet.

Hypothesis 4—Normative Ignorance: Low levels of financial giving by American Christians are due in part to believers' simple lack of awareness that the faith traditions of most teach either 10 percent tithing or generous, sacrificial, proportionate financial giving as the norm of Christian stewardship.

Hypothesis 5—Administrative Distrust: Most American Christians do not give their money generously because they are suspicious of waste and abuse by non-profit administrators, especially those with access to too much surplus wealth.

Hypothesis 6—Low Leadership Expectations: American Christians do not give generously because their *churches hold low expectations* of financial giving—insecure church leadership and congregational cultures oriented toward avoiding possible offense soft-peddle expectations of faithful, generous giving.

Hypothesis 7—Collective-Action Shirking: American Christians do not give money generously because they lack confidence that other American Christians are also contributing generously and do not want to be individually responsible for achieving collective goods.

Hypothesis 8—Issue Privatization: Most American Christians do not give their money generously because matters of personal and family finances are highly privatized in American culture, effectively removing religious giving from any public discussion or accountability.

Hypothesis 9—Non-Routine Giving Process: American Christians give relatively little money because much of their giving tends to be occasional and situational, not a consistent, structured, routine practice.

None of these hypotheses are mutually exclusive, of course. Do any of these possibilities help to explain the ungenerous financial and charitable giving of American Christians? What empirical evidence might we find to assess these hypotheses? It is to answer these questions that we now turn.

> **Hypothesis 1—Objective Resource Constraints: Despite American affluence generally, many American Christians simply do not possess the discretionary financial resources to give 10 percent of their income, given the many fixed costs of living in American society.**

On the face of it, this seems a rather implausible hypothesis. Contemporary American Christians, we noted in the introduction, are among the wealthiest of their faith in the world today, and probably the most affluent single group of Christians in two thousand years of church history. Chapter 1 also showed that Christians in the United States have a lot of money, that, for instance, they earned a total collective 2005 income of approximately $2.6 trillion. Indeed, far from being financially tight, some scholars argue that most contemporary Americans suffer from a social disease of prosperity, aka "affluenza" or "luxury fever," and so in fact actually possess plenty of financial resources to give more generously if they so desired.[3] At the same time, some other scholars—Harvard economist Elizabeth Warren in particular—suggest that, although middle-class income has indeed risen over time, the proportion of income consumed by fixed costs (e.g., taxes, health insurance, child care, automobile, mortgage) has increased significantly, leaving less discretionary income available, for instance, to give to charity.[4] Warren claims that between the early 1970s and the early 2000s, the proportion of family income spent on fixed costs rose from 54 to 75 percent. Furthermore, according to the 2001 Giving and Volunteering in the United States survey, by far the most common reason offered by Americans who did not make any charitable contribution in the previous year—offered by 65.2 percent of noncontributing households—was that they "could not afford to give money in 2000."[5] Moreover, according to one study of 593 randomly selected Evangelical Lutheran Church of America members who attend church regularly, 35.8 percent agreed with the statement "Tithing...is an unrealistic expectation of current [church] attendees." Only 25 percent disagreed with the statement, suggesting that tithing was not unrealistic, and 39.4 were neutral or unsure.[6] Could it be that American Christians do not give more money to religious and charitable causes because they simply do not have the discretionary funds to do so?

To answer the question of resource constraints properly, it is necessary to first distinguish between objective reality and subjective perceptions. The former concerns people's actual financial abilities to give money. The latter concerns people's personal, subjective beliefs about their ability to give money. The two are not necessarily the same, and so we need to answer the resource constraint question from both angles. We address the objective reality issue first, considering hypothesis 1 here. We then consider the matter of subjective perceptions separately, with hypothesis 2.

So, first, might it be that American Christians do not give money to religious and charitable causes more generously because they simply do not have the funds to do so? Objectively speaking, in most cases, we think not. Some Christians may truly be financially strapped and unable to give. For instance, some respondents in our 2006 Tithing Experiment Survey wrote in an open-ended part of the survey that they could not give more money for what appear to be potentially legitimate resource constraint reasons. Some mentioned ups and downs in income. "I used to give 10 percent," reported one, "but am unable to now." Another replied, "I have too many bills, but I plan on giving 10 percent once they are paid off." Others said, "I don't work," or "Living on retirement income," and "I was active and we paid more than our share when my three children went to Catholic School, but now I am alone, a widow, and couldn't afford to give 10 percent of my income." Another who implied that she was willing to give more reported that "[m]y husband would not agree to giving that much money to the church." Yet another simply wrote, "I'd give 10 percent if I had it."

But statistically we know that these cases are not the majority. It may be that the macro economic changes that scholars like Elizabeth Warren observe have made it somewhat more relatively painful for American Christians to give generously. But little evidence indicates that it makes generous giving impossible. That is, if Christians in the United States find themselves after paying fixed taxes and bills with proportionately less discretionary income leftover, then generous financial giving might indeed cut into their purchases of discretionary consumer items. But that is another matter altogether from being literally unable to afford to give money more generously to religious and other charitable causes. Available evidence suggests that, with some exceptions, if and when Christians want to give generously, they are able to do so.

Recall, first, from the previous chapter that, generally, there appears to be no correlation between ability to give as measured by household income and the percent of income given by households. If anything, the correlation is negative. Earning more money, and thus normally enjoying more discretionary money, does not increase the proportionate amount people give to charity. In fact, according to the tables in appendix C, after controlling for the effects of only a few simple religion variables, earning higher incomes does not even increase the absolute dollar amount given to charity, at least until households reach the $90,000+ income level. So we have little reason on this count to think that simple lack of money explains the relatively ungenerous giving of American Christians.

Does any other evidence support our conclusion? We think so. According to the 2001 Giving and Volunteering in the United States survey, 59 percent of Americans say they "worry about having enough money in the future." However, 57.5 percent of households that give money also worry about having enough money in the future—a statistically insignificant difference. Furthermore, worrying and not worrying makes only a 1 percent difference in amount of income given: those who worry about having enough money in the future give an average of 2.7 percent of income to charity, compared to 3.7 percent of income for those who do not worry. Moreover, those who worry about having enough money in the future are only slightly more likely to belong to households that do not give money than those that do give. In addition, according to the GVUS 2001 survey, 40.3 percent of Americans reported having less money left over after paying bills in 2001 compared to 2000. However, this one-year decline in discretionary income is not associated with less charitable giving, as those who reported having less (as well as those having about the same) money left over compared to the year before gave 3.2 percent of their household income to charity, compared to only 3 percent of income given by those who say they have more left over this year compared to last. Furthermore, households that reported having less money left over in 2001 compared to the previous year were only slightly less likely to give money than those that did not.[7] Thus, we see a very weak association between worrying that one will not have enough money in the future and avoiding giving some money to charity. And we see that a one-year reduction in the amount of discretionary income is not strongly reflected in less readiness to give money. In sum, the link between ability to give and actual giving seems weak to nonexistent.

Consumer spending data collected by U.S. government agencies also belie the idea that more than a minority of American Christians are not more financially generous because they simply cannot afford to be. For Americans—the majority of whom are self-identified Christians—turn out to have plenty of money to spend on other discretionary consumer items. For instance:[8]

- In 2005, Americans spent $27.9 billion on candy.
- In 2004, Americans spent $92.9 billion on refreshment beverages such as soda and bottled water.
- American consumers spent $59.4 billion in 2005 buying jewelry and watches.
- In 2000, Americans spent $203.7 billion on entertainment products and services, $67.9 billion of which was spent on televisions, radios, and sound equipment; and $56.3 billion of which was spent on fees and admissions for theater and amusement park tickets and the like.
- Americans spent $36.5 billion in 2000 on pets, toys, and playground equipment.
- In 2004, Americans spent $288.7 billion on domestic travel and tourism, including $30.5 billion on consumer (not business or government) domestic air travel, $7.7 billion on cruise vacations and other passenger water transportation, $283 million on RV vehicle rentals, and $59.9 billion on travel and tourism-related gambling.
- American consumers (not business or government) spent an additional $48.3 billion on travel and tourism abroad in 2004.
- In 2005, American consumers spent $24.1 billion on movie DVDs, not counting VHS rentals and purchases.
- In 2005, Americans spent $15.2 billion on boats, engines, and other marine products.
- In 2004, Americans spent $29.7 billion in sporting goods stores.
- In 2003, Americans spent $45 billion in state lotteries.
- Americans spent more than $100 billion per year on fast food in the early twenty-first century.
- In 2000, Americans owned more than 3.6 million second residences as vacation homes.

- Between 1978 and 2005, the average square footage of new single family houses in the United States rose from 1,750 to 2,414—a 40 percent increase in the size of single family homes in 27 years; the percentage of all new single-family houses sized 3,000 square feet or greater more than doubled between 1988 and 2005, from 11 to 23 percent.
- In 2000, Americans ages 21 and older spent $29.8 billion on alcoholic beverages, while underage drinkers added significantly to that figure. That legal-age figure breaks down to $372 spent on alcohol per legal-age consumer unit—which is $172 more than the median charitable dollars donated by American Christian households in 1998.
- In 2002, moreover, the average American consumer unit spent $320 on tobacco products, a 25 percent increase over 1996, while the average tobacco-purchasing consuming unit spent $1,321 on tobacco in 2002—totaling to $35.9 billion spent on tobacco for all Americans.
- Generally, between 1959 and 2000, while the financial giving by American Christians was *declining,* the personal consumption expenditures of Americans *increased* for eating out in restaurants, toys, sports supplies, live entertainments, foreign and domestic travel by U.S. residents, lottery tickets, casino gambling, photography, sports and recreation camps, and other entertainment expenses.

We could continue with such statistics, but these should suffice to make the point. In fact, in general, it appears that the overall U.S. consumer market is increasingly tilting not toward products meeting basic needs but spending by ordinary Americans on luxury goods.[9] Of course, because government agencies, such as the Bureau of Labor Statistics, do not collect data on religion, we are unable to determine what percent of these expenditures are by Christians. But we do know that the majority of Americans are self-professing Christians, and so Christians must account for a major proportion of this spending in most categories.

Our point, of course, is not that any of these things are necessarily bad, that people should not spend money on vacations and pets and toys and golf clubs. Our point is simply that Americans—the majority of whom are self-professing Christians—have plenty of money to spend on all sorts of discretionary and luxury goods, and do in fact spend it in vast sums. And if Americans have that kind of money to spend on those kinds of goods, then it would seem the Christians among them could also figure out a way to come up with more money to give to religious and other causes if they so chose to adjust their spending priorities. If anything, it is likely that the fact that they do not give away more money is related to the fact that they spend so much money on such consumer items. For most, it appears that there would be enough money to give more generously after fixed expenses were paid. It is only after the many discretionary consumable goods are purchased, and debt sometimes incurred, that there may not be much left over to give away. Thus, if a sizeable chunk of Evangelical Lutheran Church of America members, who are largely middle class, believe that "tithing is an unrealistic expectation," that probably has less to do with their fixed expenses than their larger lifestyle expectations. If there is any financial deprivation going on, then for most it is not likely an absolute deprivation but rather a relative deprivation—the deprivation being relative to the other felt wants and "needs" that may have to be given up if one's means are given to others generously.[10]

It is worth, at this point, taking a look at the specific question of credit card debt. Might it be that American Christians cannot afford to give more money away because they are drowning in credit card liability? One commonly cited statistic in the media is that the average American owes more than $8,000 in credit card debt. That kind of liability, if it were true, would certainly get in the way of more generous religious and charitable financial giving. The evidence, however, suggests instead that, while a fairly small minority of Americans really is in serious credit card debt, the majority are not. Numbers like $8,000 are inflated in the calculation of *mean* averages by a relatively small number of people who are in huge debt. Such numbers are also driven up when they are calculated only for those carrying credit card debts, not for all Americans. As we saw in the previous chapter, however, when distributions like this are skewed, a better average calculation than the mean is the *median,* the midpoint in the distribution. The best data on U.S. credit card debt come from the Federal Reserve Board's Survey of Consumer Finances (SCF), which reveals the following facts for 2004.[11] Twenty-five percent of American families in 2004 did not even own credit cards. Those that did owned a median of two cards. Another 28.7 percent of Americans owned credit cards but were regularly paying off their monthly balances and so owed no credit card debt. That leaves 46.2 percent of American families that carried some credit card debt from month to month. For them, while the *mean* balance of credit card debt *for those carrying any balance* in 2004 was $5,100 (driven up by a few very deeply in debt), the *median* balance was only $2,200. That itself represents only three percent of all debts held by American families, the vast majority of which (83.8 percent) is held in home mortgages, home improvement loans, and other real estate investments. Finally, credit card debt in higher amounts is held disproportionately by higher-earning income families, those more capable of paying their bills. In short, while many Americans are no doubt "overspent,"[12] the possibility of most people drowning in credit card debt as the explanation for lack of generous religious and charitable financial giving lacks empirical support. Rather, in the words of financial journalist Liz Pulliam Weston, "Conventional wisdom is that we're all hooked and struggling. The reality is, in fact, quite different and less frightening."[13] Thus, if consumerism is preventing generous financial giving by American Christians—as we think it often is—it is a consumerism of a quite manageable kind, the sort about which people make ongoing choices and pay for month by month, *not* a consumerism of debilitating debt that has spiraled out of most people's control. Therefore, primary obstacles to most American Christians giving away more of their money are their own ongoing spending priorities and patterns, which are well within their control, not mountains of accumulated debt out from which people can hardly dig.

Before moving on, a final note on Elizabeth Warren's argument deserves mention. It may be true that fixed expenses as a proportion of household incomes have increased in recent decades. And some fixed expenses, such as taxes and health care, are largely beyond people's control. But other, major "fixed" expenses are in fact determined by people's voluntary consumption choices. A house mortgage, for instance, is fixed only after one selects and buys a house. But nothing says that everyone must buy nearly the most expensive house they can possibly afford. And yet that is what most people appear to do.[14] Likewise, automobiles are a legitimately fixed expense in American society, insofar as most plausible lifestyles simply require the ability to drive a car. And yet the automobile market in the United States affords consumers a wide range of products from which to buy. Americans are in fact able to "fix" the cost of their automobile transportation at widely varying ranges of expense.[15]

In short, most Americans, including most American Christians, have a significant amount of control through their consumption decisions over time about exactly how much of their overall income their fixed costs will consume. If American Christians were committed *a priori* to giving money much more generously—perhaps even considering financial giving itself to be a fixed cost—then very many of them should be able through house and automobile purchase decisions alone to adjust even their fixed costs to make that possible. Thus, in response to the survey respondent above who reported, "I have too many bills," one might ask for what the bills are due—this might be a case of genuine hardship or it might be one of too much spending on consumer items. In short, the larger relevant issue would seem to be less people's financial capacities and more people's financial priorities. We therefore reject, in most cases, our first hypothesis viewed in terms of objective reality as significantly explaining American Christians' ungenerous financial giving.

> Hypothesis 2—Subjective Resource Constraints: Many American Christians, whatever their objective financial capacities, *subjectively believe* that they do not possess the discretionary financial resources to give 10 percent of their income.

When it comes to people's financial behavior, objective reality is not the only or perhaps most important influence. Subjective perceptions about money can be as or more important than objective reality. So, besides the question of objective financial ability, we also have to address the question of subjective belief: might some American Christians not give more money to religious and charitable causes because they *believe* they do not have the discretionary funds to give more generously? If so, their subjective perceptions of inability to give more may override their objective ability to give more.

Evidence from our 2006 Tithing Experiment Survey suggests that, for very many American Christians, this is exactly the case. In our survey, we asked a nationally representative sample of U.S. adult Christians whether they would give 10 percent of their after-tax income if their churches directly asked them to do so, requiring it for membership in good standing. We then asked those who said they would *not* give 10 percent of their after-tax income the most important reasons why they would not do so. In chapter 5, we examine the overall pattern of their responses to these questions in detail. For present purposes, we focus on some of the specific reasons offered by those unwilling to give 10 percent. Our 2006 Tithing Experiment Survey shows that *more than one-half of U.S. Christians who would not give 10 percent of their after-tax income say they cannot do so because they cannot afford to give that much money.* Specifically, 52 percent of respondents reported as one of their most important reasons for not giving more, "I could not afford to give 10 percent of my income."[16] This perceived inability was the second most frequently reported reason offered for not giving more, accounting for a substantial proportion of all the reasons offered. Thus, regardless of American Christians' possible *objective* ability to give more generously, their *subjective* perceptions of financial constraint appear to be one important factor limiting their giving money more liberally. About one-half of U.S. Christians who do not and would not give 10 percent of their income to religious and other good charitable causes believe that they simply do not possess the financial resources to do so, whatever other factors may also be influencing their decisions and actions. Some of the answers that respondents wrote in the open-ended section of the survey reflect this viewpoint. One remarked, "I do not mind giving that much, but there are times that a family can not give so much." Another wrote, "I don't have the money to give to any church or organization." "The church has more money than I do," reported one. And another simply wrote, "Dentist!" presumably meaning they had big dentist bills to pay.

Our evaluation of hypothesis 1 concluded that most American Christians, objectively speaking, in fact do possess the financial resources to give more generously, if such generous giving were a priority to them. But half of the less-than-generous givers view things differently, believing that they do *not* possess the financial ability to give more open-handedly. We thus confront here a major discrepancy between the objective and the subjective, a big contradiction that needs to be better understood and explained. The research we conducted for this book limits our ability to explore this discrepancy in great depth, so additional research guided in part by the findings here will have to explore these matters further. However, even the data we have available now suggest some interesting insights on the matter. Our analysis of our 2006 Tithing Experiment Survey data—which we will examine in much greater detail in chapter 5—shows that objective ability to give more generously (higher income) is *negatively* associated with both supportiveness of church efforts to encourage members to give more generously and readiness personally to actually give money more generously. That is, American Christians who earn *higher* incomes are statistically significantly more *opposed* to the idea of churches directly asking members for more money, and they are significantly *less* likely to give more money than they do now if their churches were to ask them to do so. This is consistent with previous findings in this book: increased financial resources actually appear to decrease financial generosity.[17] This, by itself, only scratches the surface of the matter of the discrepancy between objective ability and subjective perceptions concerning financial contributions. But it does suggest that an important part of the answer to the riddle of ungenerous giving lies in many U.S. Christians' *subjective* beliefs about their inability to give. In short, hypothesis 2 appears in part to explain the riddle of this book. We believe that subjective resource constraints on financial giving operate primarily through social-psychological processes of "relative deprivation," driven by status-discontent producing self-evaluations encouraged primarily by advertising and other media in the United States' affluent, mass-consumerist society.[18] We will have more to say about that in the conclusion. For now, we simply observe that by accounting for the subjective resource constraint factor, some of the puzzle pieces begin to fall into place. What other influences may also help to explain our riddle?

> Hypothesis 3—Unperceived Needs: Most American Christians do not give their money generously because they simply do not perceive existing legitimate needs that their money could address and meet.

Could it be that U.S. Christians are not more financially generous in giving to religious and charitable causes simply because they are not aware of genuine needs that their money could help meet? There are a couple of different subvariants on this hypothesis. It might be that American Christians give so little money because they simply do not see that it is genuinely needed—there is a simple lack of perception at all. Stated in somewhat different terms, perhaps American Christians are not motivated to give generously because the needs that their giving would meet are not part of their everyday life-worlds but instead are remote and so feel unreal, abstract, and ethereal. We know from decades of studies in social psychology and social cognition that—among all the din of perceptual stimulation—it is concrete, everyday facts that impinge upon individuals in personal, direct ways, affect their selves, and are most likely to be given attention and responses. Maybe American Christians are theoretically or vaguely aware of needs that merit their financial responses, but those needs are too distant, abstract, or impersonal to motivate generous giving. A third possible spin on this hypothesis might be that American Christians are generally aware that the world is full of needs but believe that the government through taxation and spending is already using a large proportion of their incomes to meet the most pressing needs. Paying taxes then might substitute for voluntary financial giving as a means to believe the world's needs are being addressed. There are different ways to frame or consider this hypothesis. But to cut to its central idea by asking it in counterfactual terms: would U.S. Christians give of their money much more generously if they were simply more aware of the real opportunities and needs that their financial giving could make a big difference in addressing? Much could depend on what we mean by "aware" and "perceive."

This hypothesis on the face of it, like the previous one, seems hard to believe. But, in fact, we possess little empirical data with which to test this hypothesis. To our knowledge, no previous existing survey or interview data directly address American Christians' perceptions of the needs of the world in ways that could definitively help us to verify or reject this hypothesis. However, we did collect some survey data ourselves on this matter. In our 2006 Tithing Experiment Survey, we asked respondents who said that they would not give 10 percent of after-tax income to church or other good causes for membership in good standing exactly why they would not give. Again, respondents chose from a range of answer alternatives, including the option of explaining their reasons in writing if none of the given answers matched their own. Of all church-attending Christian respondents who would not give 10 percent of after-tax income, only 2 percent said they would not because they did not think there are enough legitimate needs in the world to require giving so much money. This finding strongly suggests that lack of financial giving by American Christians is *not* due to unperceived needs that given money could meet.

In addition, a few pieces of other survey data enable us to assess the hypothesis partially and indirectly. According to the 1993 American Congregational Giving Study, for instance, 47 percent of the Lutheran, 40 percent of the Presbyterian, 40 percent of the Assemblies of God, 39 percent of the Catholic, and 37 percent of the Baptist respondents reported that they believed that their churches had "serious financial needs."[19] According to the 1996 Religious Identity and Influence survey, among U.S. Protestants, 45 percent of self-identified evangelicals, 38 percent of self-identified fundamentalists, 43 percent of mainline Protestants, and 45 percent of theologically liberal Protestants say they believe that Christians giving money to charity is an important strategy for Christians who are trying to change American society.[20] Furthermore, according to the 2001 Giving and Volunteering in the United States survey, 67.2 percent of Americans who give money to religious organizations reported believing that "the need for charitable organizations is greater now than five years ago." And, according to that same survey, 91.4 percent of Americans who give money to religious organizations believe that "I have the power to do things that improve the welfare of others."[21] None of this directly and decisively assesses the posed hypothesis. But it lends weight to our inclination to reject this hypothesis, at least this version of it.

At a different level of awareness and perception, however, it could be that a particular way that needs might be unperceived might in fact help in part to explain ungenerous financial giving. What we mean is that, while many people may know *in the abstract* that the world has many needs that their money might help to meet, abstractions do not often motivate people to act in costly ways. What most people may really need in order to increase their financial giving is to recurrently or regularly confront real, *concrete* needs in their lived experiences which they see that they can address. Yet we have good reason to think that the organization of most Americans' lives does not provide for such regular presentation of or confrontation with tangible needs calling for their financial resources. Here is why. Most people by nature tend to gravitate toward the similar and the familiar (the so-called homophily principle). Most people also tend to try to make the most of their scarce resources, with the consequence that people with roughly similar resources at their disposal tend to end up grouped together in similar settings and institutions with people like them, socially separated from others with significantly fewer and greater resources. Thus, people tend to live in relatively socially homogeneous neighborhoods. They tend to make friends with people a lot like themselves. They tend to send their children to schools with other children socially similar to their own (and, within schools, children tend to associate with other children more socially like themselves than dissimilar). People also usually attend religious congregations composed of other people very similar to themselves, not only in religious beliefs but also with regard to social characteristics such as race, ethnicity, education, income, and lifestyle.

What all of this means is that, although most Americans may know in the *abstract* that the world is full of needs and causes that their money could help to meet and fund, in their daily lived experiences many people—especially those financially better off—actually run up against few *concrete* needs that press for their financial generosity. And so they do not give much. Most everyone around them seems to be in socio-economically similar circumstances. And most institutions seem to be managing to function adequately. We expect this dynamic to operate all the more powerfully for those with more money to give, as those enjoying higher socio-economic statuses tend to live their daily lives in social worlds that appear in their concrete experience to be places of ample resources and functionality. Nobody here is necessarily being malicious or hard-hearted. It is simply that hunger, disease, disaster, famine, health crises, and myriad other forms of suffering, injustice, and opportunity for change that money could address simply remain insubstantially abstract. Never actively denied, yet never fully real, the many concerns to which generous financial giving might respond exist in the limbo-land of abstraction. And that is often not enough to motivate generous financial giving.

At least that is the theory. Do we have empirical evidence to evaluate it? When it comes to the general principles at work, a great deal of existing research and theoretical elaboration supports the idea that conceptual abstractions do not motivate costly behaviors the way that lived concrete experience does.[22] And so we have good reason to think that this version of this hypothesis likely helps to explain the ungenerous giving of so many American Christians that we observed in the previous chapter. Unfortunately, we are not aware of focused empirical evidence that tests this hypothesis specifically with regard to the social psychology of voluntary financial giving, especially among U.S. Christians. This is unfortunate. More research simply needs to be conducted to determine whether stingy financial giving results in part from the mere abstract knowledge of needs and causes, and whether regular encounters in concrete, lived experience with human needs and worthwhile causes tend to increase financial generosity. There are many ways this could be studied. One would be simply to measure whether people whose ordinary lives are organized in ways that expose them to greater varieties of social difference and need tend to give more money. The possible social-psychological mechanisms at work, however, may be very subtle, requiring careful measurement and observation to detect. Here, in any case, is one promising avenue for future research on the subject of charitable giving.

In sum, available evidence does not suggest that a lack of *stated* perception of legitimate needs in the society or the world exists, much less causes U.S. Christians to be ungenerous in their financial giving. Some evidence suggests that American Christians at least profess to be well aware of the existing needs and opportunities that charitable giving could address and meet. Until and unless other scholars present more solid data in support of this particular version of this hypothesis, we believe we are justified in rejecting it. Sheer ignorance of need does not seem to explain the riddle of this book. However, we also suspect that a more subtle version of hypothesis 3 concerning the lack of perception of needs—centered on the difference between a general awareness of abstractions versus lived experiences of concrete realities—may help to explain some of the lack of financial generosity of American Christians noted in the previous chapter. It seems to us, therefore, that hypothesis 3 itself needs to be further developed and differentiated into more specific ideas and tested with more precision. Future research could well prove the importance of concretely encountered, and not simply abstractly known, needs.

Hypothesis 4—Normative Ignorance: Low levels of financial giving by American Christians are due in part to believers' simple lack of awareness that the faith traditions of most teach either 10 percent tithing or generous, sacrificial, proportionate financial giving as the norm of Christian stewardship.

Before exploring more complicated explanations of ungenerous giving, we should consider next the simple possibility that most U.S. Christians simply do not know any better that they ought to give. Pastors and denominational officials may be fully aware not only of the financial needs but also the official teachings of the church with regard to giving. But that does not mean that ordinary believers and churchgoers are. Studies often find significant discrepancies between official church doctrines and norms and the actual beliefs and understandings of the laity. Could it be that the low levels of giving by American Christians is more the result of ignorance than stinginess?

To our knowledge, no research has examined this hypothesis systematically and thoroughly. To try to help respond to this situation, we asked respondents in our 2006 Tithing Experiment Survey what percent of after-tax income they thought their own churches expected members to donate in religious and charitable giving, based on local teachings and general expectations.[23] The results for American Christians who attend church at least once or twice a year are presented in table 3.1. There we see that 16 percent of church-attending U.S. Christians believe that their churches expect members to give no income at all. Another 27 percent say their churches expect members to donate between one and nine percent of after-tax income. Fifty-three percent of survey respondents report that their churches expect 10 percent of income, and another five percent of respondents said that their churches expect more than 10 percent. The results, then, are mixed. On the one hand, the churches of 58 percent of respondents expect members to donate to religious and other charitable causes at least 10 percent of after-tax income. On the other hand, nearly one-third report their churches expecting less than 10 percent and another 16 percent of respondents say their churches expect no giving at all.

Other pieces of evidence might support this explanation as a possibility. Prior research has shown that very many pastors and priests are uncomfortable in communicating with the members of their congregations about their responsibility to give money generously. Clergy discomfort with talking about and training for handling money is a well-established fact.[24] One national study of clergy, for instance, showed that 77 percent of U.S. clergy are very or extremely satisfied with their seminary training on theological and liturgical issues, but a mere 7 percent are similarly satisfied with their seminary training on financial duties. The same survey revealed that while 83 percent of U.S. pastors are very or extremely satisfied with their experience of pastoral duties, only 33 percent are similarly satisfied with their experience in handling financial matters. When asked about their level of interest in taking continuing education courses on various subjects, courses on finances ranked the lowest in clergy interests among all continuing education possibilities.[25] Furthermore, according to Loren Mead, a clergyman and church management consultant:

> Most congregations live with an unspoken rule: The clergy will not address personal spiritual issues about money. The clergy are allowed to talk—a *little*—about church budgets and contributions to the church; but everything else concerning money and people's personal dilemmas about it is off limits. The laity will respond by trying to make sure there is enough money to run the show.... Everyone knows there is nothing the pastor dislikes more than having to pay attention

TABLE 3.1 Perceived percent of income churches expect members to give by church attendance and Christian denomination type, church attending Christians (in %).

% income churches expect to give	Church attendance			Denomination				
	Total	Regularly	Sporadically	Catholic	Baptist	Pentecostal	Other Protestant	Other Christian
0	16	11	17	13	12	10	15	20
1–2	9	7	12	15	6	2	7	4
3–4	5	4	6	7	2	~	6	2
5–6	10	9	11	20	2	~	7	6
7–9	3	4	1	4	1	~	2	1
10	53	59	49	38	68	75	59	63
11–12	1	2	1	~	4	10	~	~
12+	4	4	3	3	3	3	4	4
Total	100	100	100	100	100	100	100	100

Source: Tithing Experiment Survey, 2006.

to finances. Some pastors make a virtue of being "above" all that concern for filthy lucre.... Under the rubric that money is "secular" and that the pastor's work has to do with the "sacred," clergy have written a brief that permits them to avoid leadership in the financial management and leadership of the congregation. They have accepted a functioning job description that excludes any concern for what I contend is one of the dominant spiritual issues every parishioner has: how to deal with material resources. This means that clergy not only give little leadership to the financial life of the congregation, but also set up a climate that sets little value on the functions of financial management carried out by others.... It means pastoral abdication of one of the most troubling dimensions of living in our society.[26]

Has this discomfort and reluctance of clergy to communicate clearly, directly, and regularly with their congregations about tithing or generous financial giving perhaps had the consequence of leaving many ordinary Christians in the dark about what their faith demands of them as financial stewards? According to 1998 National Congregations Survey data, only 21 percent of Christian religious congregations in the United States have "special rules regarding how much money individuals give to the congregation."[27] Other national surveys have also asked certain questions that do help us to begin to evaluate this "normative ignorance" hypothesis, at least indirectly. The Economic Values Survey of 1992 asked a national sample of working adult Americans what they believed was "the best definition of stewardship." Figure 3.1 displays their responses. Here we see that only 11 percent of working Americans define stewardship primarily as giving a certain percentage of money to church. Stewardship as giving money is the least answered response category among the entire sample. Nearly four times the number think of stewardship instead as the responsible use of individual talents. Many more working Americans (19 percent) say that they simply do not know what stewardship means than define stewardship as giving money.

Understanding stewardship in financial terms is only slightly affected by respondents' religious tradition. Different types of American Christians, for example, do not answer this question very differently. Figure 3.2 shows that the same percent of working adult Catholics and mainline Protestants— 11 percent—take a distinctly financial approach to stewardship as do all working adult Americans. Evangelical Protestants, at 14 percent, are only slightly more likely to define stewardship in financial terms.[28]

What might we conclude from these findings? First, we must realize that we need to interpret these results with caution, for numerous reasons. The

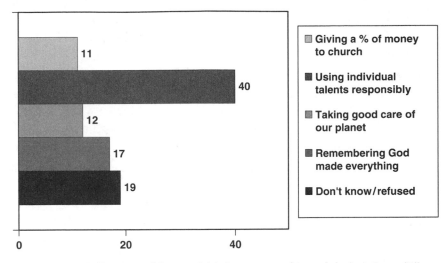

FIGURE 3.1 Definitions of "stewardship" among working adult Americans (%). (Source: Economics Values Survey, 1992.)

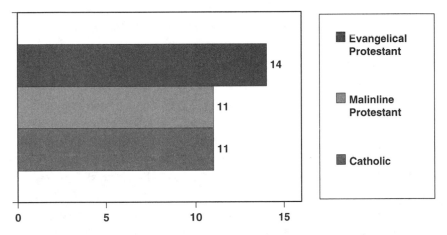

FIGURE 3.2 Defining stewardship as "giving a certain percentage of money to the church," by Christian tradition, working adult Americans (%). (Source: Economics Values Survey, 1992.)

survey question's response categories, let us note, are not mutually exclusive—Christians can very well believe both logically and theologically that stewardship means *all* of the answers given in the survey question. Few Christian traditions teach that the *most* important dimension of stewardship is giving a certain percentage of money to the church, even if that is a very important dimension. Thus, a Christian could very well have responded to this question by saying that stewardship means the responsible use of individual talents, say, and still believe that a faithful Christian should tithe or give money generously. Nevertheless, the results here do suggest that only a rather small minority of U.S. Christians associate faithful stewardship with financial giving. Giving money does not appear to be the primary expression of good stewardship in the minds of most American Christians. This itself is hardly definitive confirmation for the current hypothesis. But it does support the possibility that, when U.S. Christians think about their faithful stewardship of God's resources, few of them associate this with generous financial giving. It may be that in their efforts to teach an expansive understanding of Christian stewardship, church leaders have allowed the financial aspects of stewardship to fall through the cracks. These findings may thus provide partial, indirect support for the "ignorance" hypothesis under consideration.

How else might we empirically evaluate the current hypothesis? One possibility would be to measure people's knowledge of the meaning of tithing. The God and Society in North America survey in 1996 asked respondents directly what it means to tithe. The exact survey question was, "Churches often encourage their supporters to donate a 'tithe' of their income to the church—to the best of your knowledge, what percent of one's income would be a 'tithe'?" Respondents were asked to choose one of four forced-choice answer categories. The results are presented in figure 3.3. Among respondents in the American Christian sample (Canadian respondents are excluded), 76 percent, the vast majority, answered correctly that a tithe is 10 percent of one's income. Nineteen percent of respondents answered (incorrectly) that a tithe is less than 10 percent. More than 5 percent of respondents answered that a tithe is more than 10 percent. In short, the vast majority of all U.S. adults (81.5 percent) appear to know that to tithe means giving at least 10 percent of one's income, leaving a significant minority of Americans (19 percent) who apparently think that tithing means giving less than 10 percent. Whether they believe that they themselves are obliged to tithe, however, is itself another matter.[29]

One last bit of empirical evidence sheds light on this hypothesis from yet another angle. Independent Sector's 2001 Giving and Volunteering in the United States survey asked its respondents from households that did give money what their motivations are for giving money. Respondents were able to report more than one answer. Figure 3.4 shows the results. There we see that only about one-half of charitably giving Americans were motivated to donate in order to fulfill religious obligations or beliefs. Since we know that well more than one-half of American financial givers are Christians, we can conclude that religious obligation or teaching is not an important moti-

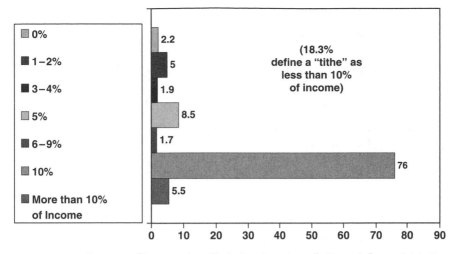

FIGURE 3.3 Percent of income that Christian Americans believe defines a "tithe" (%). (Source: God and Society in North Amrica Survey, 1996.)

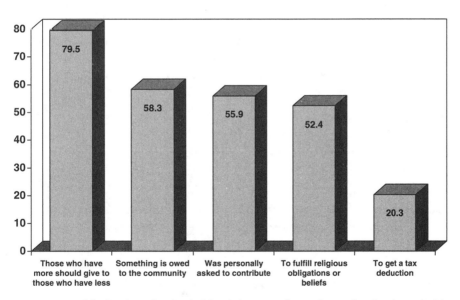

FIGURE 3.4 Motivations for charitable giving, members of contributing households only. (Source: Giving and Volunteering in the United States, 2001.)

vation for a substantial minority of financially giving Christians. Instead, respondents tended to report being motivated more by a not-specifically-religious ethic of giving to the needy or the community, or simply because somebody personally asked them to give some money. In fact, the only answer category smaller than the specifically religious motivation was the motive of getting a tax deduction. This finding does not speak directly to the current hypothesis, but indirectly it suggests that a sizeable minority of U.S. Christians who do give money to religious and charitable causes do not primarily do so for any specifically religious motives. And this may reflect some lack of awareness of—although it could just as easily reflect an actual resistance to—the normative religious teachings of their own Christian tradition about generous financial giving.[30]

What, then, might we conclude about this hypothesis from these limited empirical findings? We cannot conclude anything definitive, because we have not directly measured U.S. Christians' knowledge or ignorance of their own religious traditions' teachings and expectations regarding faithful financial giving. More research needs to be conducted. However, we think we can at least observe the following related points. On the one hand, the vast majority of U.S. Christians do seem aware that the "tithing" that many churches encourage of their members does mean giving 10 percent or more of their income. Few American Christians can plead ignorance on that point, it appears. On the other hand, however, when it comes to understanding the broader idea of Christian "stewardship," the majority of American Christians tend to think first in terms of use of personal talents, acknowledgment of God as Creator, and taking care of the earth, rather than in terms of financial giving. Insofar as these are theologically legitimate aspects of Christian stewardship, this does not itself prevent generous financial giving. However, it could also be that a primary teaching focus on these other nonfinancial dimensions of stewardship has the unintended consequence of displacing financial giving from the minds of many ordinary believers as another crucial aspect of faithfulness in Christian stewardship. As Robert Wuthnow suggests, "Paradoxically, trying to get people to focus on other things than money also has the effect of diminishing the importance of actually talking about money."[31] If so, then many American Christians might, through lack of clear and consistent instruction, be confusing or underestimating the central importance of generous financial giving in the teachings of their churches, denominations, and traditions. In this case, the "normative ignorance" hypothesis may explain some of the lack of generous giving by U.S. Christians.

It is unlikely, however, in view of the evidence above, that ignorance alone explains most of the ungenerous giving we observed in the previous chapter. In our judgment, ignorance of normative theological expectations for giving is likely only one factor explaining *some* of the lack of giving by *some* American Christians. It is, we think, a safe supposition to believe that if all U.S. Christians were to become fully educated in the teachings and expectations of their specific faith traditions regarding financial giving, that alone would *somewhat* increase the giving of *some* U.S. Christians. But it would not by itself bring financial giving up to levels that their own Christian traditions would consider faithful. Other factors are very likely also at work depressing Christian giving.

> **Hypothesis 5—Administrative Distrust: Most American
> Christians do not give their money generously because they
> are suspicious of waste and abuse by non-profit administrators,
> especially those with access to too much surplus wealth.**

Perhaps American Christians do not give money generously because, whether they like it or not, they simply distrust the non-profit organizations to which they would give money, if they gave more generously. Maybe U.S. Christians would give more money if they trusted the recipients of their donations to spend their money well. Perhaps, however, they are concerned that their money would be wasted, pilfered, abused, or spent ineffectively—and so they give sparingly. Numerous recurrent financial scandals, involving both religious leaders in denominations and in para-church ministries as well as leaders in organizations such as the United Nations, may have fostered a sense of suspicion among ordinary Christians in the United States of feeding too much money into non-profit organizations that operate beyond their oversight. Perhaps American Christians actually view giving money to organizations and causes that they do not entirely trust a practice of bad stewardship and so avoid it in the name of a regrettable kind of financial faithfulness. This is a rather odd possibility, but far from out of the question.

What does available evidence suggest about this possible explanation? Again, data that might give definitive answers are lacking. For now, we must rely on sparse evidence to make tentative judgments. Some survey data, however, do suggest some possibilities. For instance, as described above, we asked our 2006 Tithing Experiment Survey respondents who reported that they would not give 10 percent of their after-tax income, even if their churches required it for membership in good standing, whether lack of trust in recipients of religious and charitable giving was a reason that they would not give. Of church-attending U.S. Christians in this case, 9 percent reported that one of the most important reasons for their lack of giving is that "I do not trust those to whom I would give money to spend it wisely, there would be too much waste and abuse of donations." This is not a large number, but neither is it trivial. Some of the written answers in the open-ended section of our survey also reflect this suspicion. For instance, one reported, "The church I go to was one of the ones that allowed those priests to molest those alter [*sic*] boys and they aren't getting my money to cover any of this up. The church was wrong in doing this and in my opinion they should have been held accountable." Others said, "I may not agree with the church's use of the money" and "I would have to see exactly where the money is needed." Lack of trust, then, appears to be one factor reducing the financial giving of some American Christians, though it does not appear to be a major factor in that regard. It may also function as a mere rationalization for lack of giving for other reasons.

General Social Survey data collected in 2004 by the National Opinion Research Center show that 27 percent of Protestants and Catholics express a "great deal" of confidence in "organized religion," 54 percent of each express "only some" confidence, and about 17 percent express "hardly any" confidence in "organized religion." Such confidence in organized religion increases, as we would expect, with higher levels of church attendance—with 38.2 percent of Americans who attend weekly or more often expressing a "great deal" of confidence, and 47.7 percent of Americans who never attend religious services expressing "hardly any" confidence in organized religion. Note that this question only measures general confidence in "organized religion." It does not measure confidence specifically in religion's trustworthiness with donated funds, nor confidence in respondents' own religious congregations or favorite para-church organizations to which they would presumably give their money—we can assume that those numbers would be higher. Still, these statistics suggest a range of levels of confidence in religious organizations. A sizeable minority of American Christians expresses a lot of confidence and a smaller minority expresses very little confidence in institutional religion. Between them, the majority of Protestants and Catholics express "only some" confidence in organized religion. If we assume that this lack of full confidence by the majority is partly related to religious organizations' trustworthiness with donated money, then these data may indirectly suggest a possible partial reason for a hesitation on the part of at least some American Christians to give their money generously to religious organizations and causes.

To further assess this possibility, we do have a bit more survey data on the trustworthiness of religious organizations. According to Independent Sector's 2001 Giving and Volunteering in the United States survey, 70.4 percent of Americans who give money to religious organizations believe that "most charitable organizations are honest in their use of donated funds." The majority of Americans, then, do not express suspicions about the trustworthiness of those organizations to which they give money. But a significant minority, 30 percent, does express reservations or suspicions. Furthermore, according to the same survey, when it comes to views of the effectiveness of religious congregations and organizations in the spending of donated money, 89 percent of all Americans (not only Christians) believe that local religious organizations are very or somewhat effective in alleviating hunger, 78 percent believe they are very or somewhat effective in reducing homelessness, and 82 percent believe they are very or somewhat effective in providing care for the elderly.[32] Those numbers are likely to be higher for church-going Christians. Still, a minority of respondents do not view local religious organizations as particularly effective in using their resources to meet community needs. Finally, according to the 1993 American Congregational Giving Study, 31 percent of the Lutheran, 28 percent of the Presbyterian, 26 percent of the Assemblies of God, 47 percent of the Catholic, and 19 percent of the Baptist respondents did *not* agree with the statement, "The budget priorities of my congregation are appropriate." The same survey found that 19 percent of the Lutheran, 15 percent of the Presbyterian, 16 percent of the Assemblies of God, 18 percent of the Catholic, and 13 percent of the Baptist respondents did *not* agree with the statement, "Overall, I approve of the decision-making processes in my congregation." The numbers of disagreement with such statements were much larger when it came to trust in denominational treatment of money. For example, 53 percent of the Lutheran, 57 percent of the Presbyterian, 32 percent of the Assemblies of God, 54 percent of the Catholic, and 57 percent of the Baptist respondents reported that they did not have high levels of trust in "the handling and allocation of funds by the leaders of [their] denomination." Between 39 and 56 percent of members of these denominations did not agree with the statement, "The leaders of my denomination are sufficiently accountable to members regarding how church contributions are used."[33] Thus, a not-insignificant portion of active mainstream American Christians express reservations if not some distrust about the financial dealings of their congregations and denominations.

In sum, the survey evidence we have provides mixed indications about U.S. Christians' possible distrust for religious and charitable organizations and causes. Some express a lot of trust, many express some trust, and some express little trust. The lack of trust evident among some Christians in the religious organizations to which they might donate money may be part of what compels them to give less money than they otherwise would if they believed them to be more trustworthy. We therefore tentatively conclude that one factor among others that likely contributes to the low financial giving of some American Christians may be a lack of full trust in the organizations to which their money would be given. Stated counterfactually, we think that if more U.S. Christians had much more confidence in the trustworthiness of the religious and charitable organizations to which they might give money, at least some of them would give more generously.

> Hypothesis 6—Low Leadership Expectations: American Christians do not give generously because their *churches hold low expectations* of financial giving—insecure church leadership and congregational cultures oriented toward avoiding possible offense soft-peddle expectations of faithful, generous giving.

Perhaps the ungenerous financial giving of American Christians is not so much a supply problem, so to speak, as it is a demand problem. Perhaps for various reasons leaders of churches and religious organizations are simply too tentative in asking for generous giving. Does evidence exist to evaluate this hypothesis?

First, again, as noted above, we asked our own survey respondents what percent of income they thought their own churches expected members to give, based on local teachings and general expectations. The question concerned not churches' actual expectations but respondents' perceptions of their churches' expectations. What is clear, as noted in table 3.1, is that nearly one-half of church-attending Christian respondents (43 percent) think that their churches expect members to give something less than 10 percent of after-tax income. Sixteen percent think their churches do not expect them to give any money at all. Thus, a very large minority of church-attending Christians do not believe they are being asked by their churches to give at a tithing standard. This of course may reflect highly selective listening by Christians who may prefer to think that their churches expect not too much of them. But it may also reflect genuine low expectations for giving or lack of clear teaching about giving offered by timid church leaders.

We have already noted above the ambivalence and hesitation many clergy feel about teaching boldly about generous financial giving. Previous studies suggest that the majority of U.S. clergy do not feel confident about maintaining high expectations in their congregations for financial contributions.[34] Perhaps many clergy would rather have one percent of something than 10 percent of nothing—if higher expectations were to turn parishioners off and away. Survey numbers support this impression. In 1993, for instance, Dean Hoge and colleagues conducted a survey of Baptist, Assemblies of God, Catholic, Lutheran, and Presbyterian congregations in which they asked about church programs for teaching about religious giving. Among their many findings, the majority of churches in four of the five denominations reported emphasizing the biblical concept of stewardship not regularly but "only occasionally" during the year, or less often. Eighty-four percent of Catholic, 77 percent of Presbyterian, 73 percent of Lutheran, 64 percent of Baptist, and 46 percent of Assemblies of God congregations emphasized stewardship either never, once a year, or only occasionally during the year. Across the five denominations studied, between 6 and 16 percent of the churches actually reported having no program at all to encourage giving.[35] According to another study conducted in the mid-1990s, only 32 percent of American church members reported that they had heard a sermon on the relationship between faith and personal finances in the previous year. The majority, it seems, are not being taught. Even so, "what," asks the study's author, Robert Wuthnow, "do people hear? Both from talking with clergy about what they say and from examining the transcripts of their sermons, we must say that clergy often tiptoe around the topic of money as if they were taking a walk through a minefield."[36]

But do lower cultural expectations about giving actually result in less giving? It appears so. Our own Tithing Experiment Survey found a strong correlation between perceived expectations and readiness to give money. As we will see in multiple tables in chapter 5, American Christians who attend churches they perceive as holding higher expectations of financial giving are more likely to give generously than those who attend churches holding lower expectations. For instance, we will see in table 5.1 that only 1 percent of Christians tithe who are in churches that they perceive expect members to give 1–4 percent of income, while 25 percent of Christians tithe who are in churches that they perceive expect members to give 10 percent or more of their income. Those in churches holding higher expectations are also more supportive of the idea of their churches asking all members to give more money and are significantly less likely to say they would drop out of church life altogether if churches did ask all members to give more. While the association merits more investigation, we think there is good evidence to think that low expectations in Christian churches for financial giving contributes toward the unimpressive financial contributions of American Christians.

One other related fact reinforces this conclusion. That is that, in other American religious traditions that maintain higher common standards of financial giving, members of those traditions give significantly higher than do American Christians. Most American Jewish temples and synagogues, for instance, collect membership dues and, as we saw in figures 2.1 and 2.3 in the previous chapter, American Jews as a group are much less likely than most American Christian groups to give no money and overall give more money as a percent of income than do U.S. Christians. We do not attribute this greater generosity to membership dues alone, but believe it also reflects an underlying attitude about money and giving embodying higher expectations than those held in many American Christian churches. Similarly, the U.S.-based Church of Jesus Christ of Latter-day Saints (Mormons) requires all of its members to give one-tenth of income to the Church. This tithing is required for temple attendance and so has direct consequences for members' participation in sacred marriages and other key religious events. Accountability for tithing takes place through an annual "tithing settlement" between the Mormon believer and his or her bishop, in which the latter asks the direct question, "Are you a full tithe payer?" The Church also keeps specific records of financial contributions for each member.[37] Again, as we noted in figures 2.1 and 2.3 of the previous chapters, American Mormons contribute significantly more money than do U.S. Christians. The associations here between high expectations, accountability, and generosity of financial contributions are not spurious, we think. American Christians may have theological objections to the financial giving systems of American Judaism and Mormonism. But that itself does not negate the sociological observation that higher expectations of financial giving clearly appear to be correlated with greater actual financial giving. The relatively ungenerous financial giving of so many U.S. Christians, then, may reflect in part low expectations of giving held by their churches.

> **Hypothesis 7—Collective-Action Shirking: American Christians do not give money generously because they lack confidence that other American Christians are also contributing generously and do not want to be individually responsible for achieving what are collective goods.**

One central problem in social science analysis is known as "the collective action problem." The problem is how to motivate and coordinate rational, self-interested individuals to contribute in costly ways (e.g., time, money, energy, safety, reputation, etc.) to the achievement of collective goods. Collective goods are shared benefits that all involved can enjoy, from which it is not possible to exclude non-contributors. The essential problem behind the collective action challenge is the assumption that rational, self-interested people will prefer to let other people make the costly contributions to achieve the collective good from which they cannot be excluded from benefiting. Stated differently, the problem is how to overcome the tendency of presumed rational, self-interested actors to "free ride," that is, to allow others to pay the costs of accomplishing or maintaining a public good that they can then enjoy for free.

Take, for example, the civil rights movement of the 1950s and 60s. Challenging and overturning racist, segregationist institutions of that era required many African-Americans to participate in marches, sit-ins, demonstrations, freedom rides, and boycotts. But such involvements were often costly. Participants not only spent time and energy, but sometimes lost their jobs, risked their safety, and, on occasions, lost their lives. Yet when the civil rights movement succeeded, nearly all African-Americans benefited from the elimination of legal segregation and enhanced voting rights, *whether or not they had contributed to achieving them*. New civil rights were a collective good from which non-contributors could not be excluded. In such a situation, the collective action problem concerned how to motivate and coordinate widespread contributions involving real costs from people who have rational, self-interested reasons to withhold contributing and instead allow others to pay the costs, since in the end they will benefit equally from the achieved collective good anyway.

A similar situation can characterize the matter of voluntary religious and charitable giving. Assuming (in this context not unreasonably, we think) some degree of rationality and self-regarding consideration on the part of potential givers, the question is how to motivate and coordinate individual contributors to donate money when in fact they will likely be able to enjoy the benefits achieved by others' financial contributions whether or not they themselves contribute. As long as any individual potential giver believes that enough other people will contribute to secure the collective good—their prosperous church, for example, or an effective ministry—then those individuals automatically face the continual temptation to "free ride," that is, to enjoy the collective benefit without having to pay for it. In the words of Charles Zech, Professor of Economics at Villanova University, "People sit in their pews and say 'What's the difference—they're not going to miss my money.' When you have a whole parish saying that, you've got a problem."[38]

Note that certain solutions to the collective action problem are difficult and sometimes not available to Christian churches. One solution is to find ways to exclude non-contributors from benefiting from the collective good. In theory, churches might only allow dues paying members in good standing to have access to worship services, potluck dinners, choir recitals, Sunday school lessons, vacation Bible schools, pastoral counseling, and other collective goods found in religious communities. This of course is precisely the equivalent of what most tennis clubs, exercise gyms, amusement parks, movie theaters, and a host of other income-dependent institutions do to maintain their finances. But for theological reasons, this solution is not an option for Christian churches, which believe on theological grounds that they should be open and unconditionally inviting communities, not fee-based services.

Another possible solution to the collective action problem is to eliminate rational self-interest from potential contributors' considerations. To some degree, most churches partially succeed in this, by emphasizing themes of good stewardship, sacrificial giving, service, gratitude, unconditional love, care for the needs of others, and so on, which override pure self-interest.

Nevertheless, the reality of human life on earth, whether redeemed or not, is that there are definite limits to anyone's capacity to eliminate rational self-interest from most people's considerations, perhaps especially those concerning money. Any approach to generous Christian financial giving simply must take seriously the bounded reality of rational self-interest and work with or around it.

A third possible solution to the collective action problem is to redefine for people what *is* in their self-interest. Despite what some economists teach, few self-interests are ever absolutely fixed, uniform, and consistent. Self-interest can be shaped in multiple directions. So, if, for instance, a person comes to see her family's participation in a vibrant, well-endowed community of faith as more in their self-interest than, say, building an immense DVD library, that person may be motivated precisely by a kind of enlightened self-interest to contribute generously to their church.

Having thus unpacked the idea behind our sixth hypothesis, we propose for consideration the possibility that one explanation for the relatively ungenerous financial giving of American Christians is not a principled unwillingness to give money per se, but rather a reluctance to give liberally in face of the belief that others are not also likewise giving liberally. In short, the problem may have less to do with innate stinginess than with lack of communication of information, the miscoordination of action, and the lack of mutual assurance of collective investment in the shared good. Suspecting, whether rightly or wrongly, that others are shirking their obligations to give money generously, perhaps the average American Christian chooses to shirk their own obligation to give generously as well? In this way, according to this hypothesis, the majority of U.S. Christians mutually adjust down their financial giving to very modest levels to avoid, even if perhaps only semiconsciously, the possibility that they are being taken advantage of by much less generous givers.

This is an interesting possibility. But does empirical evidence exist that might actually help test this hypothesis? Again, the evidence on this matter is very thin. The only data we know of that explicitly addresses the possibility come from our 2006 Tithing Experiment Survey. Again, we asked respondents who do not give and say they would not give 10 percent of after-tax income if their churches made that a normative expectation to tell us their most important reasons for not giving at that level. Respondents replied with many answers. But only *one percent* of respondents mentioned as one of their important reasons that "I doubt that other church members would give 10 percent of their income and I would not want to give 10 percent of mine unless I knew everyone was doing so." Furthermore, no respondent who wrote out open-ended answers mentioned this reason for why they would not give 10 percent of their income. This provides only one test of hypothesis 7. But it is an explicit test designed for the very purpose, and its findings are clear: collective-action shirking does not appear to help explain the low levels of American Christian financial giving. If U.S. Christians do not give money more liberally, it does not seem to be because they are concerned that other Christians are not giving equally generously. More research is needed on these questions. But until further evidence arises to the contrary, therefore, we believe that we can remove this possible explanation from the table as not explaining our riddle of ungenerous giving.

> Hypothesis 8—Lack of Accountability: Most American Christians do not give their money generously because matters of personal and family finances are highly privatized in American culture, effectively removing religious giving from any public discussion or accountability and so eliminating any potential consequences or costs to stingy or no giving.

One of the reasons that people do various things is because they have internalized the beliefs that they should do them. Sometime in the past, they learned or decided that certain things are good, right, honorable, just, or proper. And, accordingly, people do them simply because they personally believe that they should. Nobody must compel them to do so. Nobody must punish them if they do not do so. People simply act certain ways whether or not anyone else is encouraging them or even paying attention. Not stealing possessions from strangers even when one is certain to be able to get away with it is one example of such an action. Suppressing hateful thoughts toward others who may even deserve them, showing small kindnesses to animals, and picking up other people's litter in a deserted park are other examples.

But most human behaviors and actions are not entirely of this kind. The majority of human actions, even the noblest, in fact involve interactions with other people that comprise variable consequences for different actions. And those consequences partly shape those actions. That is, most human actions spring from both internal personal motivations and external social cues, encouragements, sanctions, conditioning, and rewards. It is the interactive combination of the two that sets the direction of most human courses of behavior. To be clear, none of this endorses any kind of stimulus-response behaviorism that denies real human freedom and choice in life. All we are observing here is that, in human life, social interactions give rise to interpersonal accountability and consequences for actions that often significantly shape people's behaviors—particularly when it comes to behaviors that baser motives (e.g. greed, selfishness, malice) may recommend otherwise. Many times, social influences operating through personal relationships will help to give a final "push" for someone to actually do something that they mostly want to do or believe that they ought to do, but which inertia, other desires, or mixed motives might have otherwise prevented them from doing. Of course, in few circumstances are people's behaviors absolutely determined by others. But the influence of other people nevertheless typically exerts important impacts shaping individuals' actions. In short, people normally rely a lot on each other to figure out in different situations how it seems they ought to and ultimately will act.

This being the case, all other things being equal, the more a person is accountable to significant others in stable relational networks of interaction, the more those others will exert influence on that person's actions. This is what sociologists mean by ideas like social influence, social coordination, and the social control of deviance. Behaviors that are highly subject to observation by and accountability to others will be more influenced by those others. Those that are less subject to observation and accountability will be less influenced. Most people thus want to do things in secret, when they do, precisely because they do not want the consequential influence of others to impinge on their actions.

Our eighth hypothesis uses these facts as a springboard to consider the consequences of the reality that, in American culture, money is one of the most personal, private, protected subjects going. Most Americans guard information about their financial conditions and behaviors behind strong walls of intense secrecy. Few Americans ever discuss with anyone, beyond perhaps their closest intimates, matters concerning income, savings, investments, debts, spending patterns, and—importantly for us—amounts of charitable giving. Most Americans would be as or more shocked and offended by an acquaintance probing for details about their financial status than about their religion, politics, or sex lives. Information about one's own money is strictly a private matter, nobody else's business. It might not go too far to suggest that in American culture money is sacred and improper social dealings with it are therefore taboo. These attitudes were certainly expressed in some of the open-ended written responses of our 2006 Tithing Experiment Survey respondents, as the following quotes illustrate: "It is a personal decision how much to give," "The church has no business in my pockets," "It's between the individual and God if they don't give," "It's not my church's business what I do with my money," and "I decide what I have to give."

How, then, should we expect this situation to affect practices of religious and charitable giving? If the sociological observations we made above about social visibility, accountability, consequences, and influences are correct, then we should expect the intense privacy and secrecy surrounding personal and family money in American culture to remove the question of financial giving from the influences of social interaction and accountability. The person sitting nearby in the pew cannot tell the denominations of the crumpled dollars one put into the offering plate. The church treasurer might be able to estimate from checks cashed how much money one did or did not donate, if they are paying attention; however, they do not know whether one also gave more freely in cash or whether one also contributes more generously to some other worthy charitable cause. Few church pastors are going to ask offensive questions about how much their parishioners are giving. As a consequence, whether and how much anyone gives to religious and charitable causes become influenced primarily if not exclusively by mere internalized normative beliefs about giving, however robust or weak those are. Rare will be the situations when the social influences of interpersonal interactions provide the final "push" to encourage people to give differently than they otherwise would have on their own. Strong of conviction will have to be the personal, internalized normative beliefs to counteract the power of advertising, the lures of mass consumerism, the press of other financial obligations and opportunities. By the logic of this hypothesis, it is little wonder that American Christians give so ungenerously. For very little in their *social relationships* holds the power to encourage truly generous giving.

But does empirical evidence match the theory suggested by the hypothesis? To get started, the 1992 Economic Values Survey tells a lot about how private a subject finances are to most adult Americans, including Christians. For instance, when the survey asked how often in the past year the respondent discussed their personal finances with other people, 97 percent of Christian respondents said they either never or hardly ever discussed finances with members of their church. The percents for never or hardly ever discussing personal finances with other types of people are 96 percent for a member of the clergy, 98 percent for a therapist or counselor, 92 percent for a financial expert, 88 percent for people at work, and 77 percent for friends. When it came to knowing the basic fact of the incomes of Christian respondents, only 18 percent of children (for those who had children), 23 percent of co-workers, 24 percent of their siblings, 24 percent of closest friends knew their incomes. Moreover, 81 percent of the Christian sample said that only a few or none of their close friends have told them how much money they earn. And 76 percent of Christian respondents reported that, when they were growing up, their parents discussed family finances only once in a while or never. Altogether, these data strongly suggest that the vast majority of working American Christians indeed view the subjects of income and finances as highly private matters not to be discussed with others.

But does greater openness about one's personal finances correlate with higher financial giving at the individual level? We do have suggestive evidence, noted above, indicating that those U.S. religious traditions that practice greater transparency and accountability on the matter of financial giving—Mormonism and Judaism, in particular—tend to produce higher levels of financial contributions from their members. But, beyond that evidence, the question posed here is a difficult question to answer, for three reasons. The first is that there appears to be very little variance among U.S. Christians with regard to genuine accountability about financial stewardship, and correlating factors when one has little variance is impossible. The second reason is that, perhaps because such little variance on accountability exists, no studies to our knowledge have obtained measures of genuine financial transparency and accountability toward better stewardship among Christians. Such individual level data simply do not exist. Third, the relationship between open discussions of personal finances and amounts of money given to religious and charitable causes is greatly complicated by the fact that greater transparency about money among American Christians appears to reflect not financial accountability toward faithful stewardship but rather financial difficulties that themselves may associate with different levels of giving. Our examination of limited available evidence suggests that the Christians most likely to talk with family, friends, church members, and others about their personal finances are those with particular financial troubles—not those seeking or able to give money at high levels. As a result of these three factors, it is very difficult empirically to assess whether a decrease in the privatization of financial matters among Christians would help to increase their financial giving. By our reckoning, that is a nearly impossible relationship to test with existing data. Future studies specifically focused on the question of accountability will have to try to examine the matter more closely.

However, we do think the following tentative conclusions on this point are reasonable. First, it may be that a widespread lack of financial transparency and accountability among American Christians generally depresses financial giving broadly. That is, the lack-of-accountability factor that applies to nearly everyone similarly may have a common influence decreasing giving, net of other factors that also shape giving. In other words, lack of accountability may not be an irrelevant factor at all, although its causal influence may affect most people roughly the same, so that detecting quantitative variations is difficult if not impossible. Second, however, whether or not future increased financial transparency among U.S. Christians would increase their financial giving, the fact is that great variance in giving already does exist now, meaning that other factors than transparency must explain the variance that exists. Third, given the very strong individualism in American culture and most of American Christianity, it is highly unlikely that transparency and accountability regarding income, finances, and charitable giving are ever going to sweep through U.S. churches and transform Christian religious and charitable giving. The radical privatization of money matters seems here to stay. So if anyone is interested in influencing the financial giving of American Christians, they would be unwise to rely on a significant increase in financial transparency and accountability. That is no more likely to happen among American Christians than their all becoming Hindus. In conclusion, the available evidence is sketchy, and reasonable arguments suggest treating the lack of accountability hypothesis as a general background factor framing, not as a proximate causal influence on, differences in financial giving.

> Hypothesis 9—Nonroutine Giving Process: American Christians give relatively little money because much of their giving tends to be occasional and situational, not a consistent, structured, routine practice.

There are two distinct ways that human beings can act to accomplish things. One is occasional and situational. The other is through structured habit or routine. Consider exercising at the gym. Some people do it when they think of it, when their schedule allows it, and when they feel like it. Others do it regularly, almost without thinking about it, at a predetermined time, whether they feel like it or not. The latter generally end up exercising a lot more than the former. That is because human actions that are costly or difficult are more consistently accomplished when they are systematically structured into established routines and habits that reduce reliance on memory, thought, and intention. There are reasons people schedule their next dentist appointment while in the dentist's office at the end of the previous appointment, rather than waiting to think of the need to visit the dentist sometime in the future. There are reasons that mortgage and credit card companies routinely send monthly bills with minimum payments as a systematic practice, rather than letting people send whatever payments they think they can afford whenever they happen to think about it. Structured routines and established habits and systems minimize the chances that a costly or demanding but important activity will be forgotten or delayed or avoided. They do this by minimizing dependence on conscious, recurrent remembering, deliberation, and desire. One simply makes a one-time reasoned decision and commitment to a certain activity, deliberately builds it as a methodical practice into an "automatic" routine, and then regularly performs the activity with little mental cost. We do this in myriad ways throughout our lives, from brushing teeth to picking up the mail to withholding taxes to driving particular routes to work.

Underlying the advantages of habits and routines are certain given facts about human capacities. Foremost among them is that people have limited mental ability to focus and remember. Even the smartest people can only keep so much on their mental radar screens. Even the most attentive can only remember to fulfill so many intentions and commitments. The human mind enjoys only a finite amount of "random access memory" that is free to anticipate, remember, coordinate, plan, and execute. People effectively cope with this cognitive limitation by establishing routines, habits, and systems that reduce mental expenditure while maintaining consistency and function. Habits and routines are also advantageous in view of the subconscious ways that human bodies can "remember" how to perform activities. Once people invest significant initial outlays of time, energy, and attention into learning certain behaviors, human bodies have the uncanny ability to "memorize" how they are done and routinely perform them later with little thought or concentration. Once a person learns how, they no longer have to pay much attention to what it takes to ride a bike, drive a car, type on a keyboard, take money from an ATM, or politely greet strangers to whom they are being introduced. It just happens "naturally," with little conscious awareness.

Not all human activities require or are effectively accomplished with such systematic regularity. Some activities are driven instead by observable needs and demands that vary across time. Most people, for instance, do not cut the grass at the same time every time, but only when the grass appears to need cutting—which often varies by season, amount of recent rainfall, and other factors—and when they are able to fit cutting it into their schedules. Other activities require high degrees of situationally specific focus and judgment. These include diagnosing serious injuries, adjusting ineffective game-plans at halftime, and proposing important first dates. Much of the challenge to living life well is learning how to expend our limited cognitive resources in different ways for different kinds of tasks.

Religious and charitable financial giving by Christian believers belongs, from a sociological perspective, in the general category of costly yet important behaviors that are more effectively accomplished through regular habit than situational decision. Like many activities of this nature, if religious giving is not made a systematic routine, it is highly likely to be sporadic, uneven, and relatively weak. It is therefore better to pass an offering plate than to simply have a donation box next to the exit door. It is even better in theory to provide congregants with dated, weekly offering envelopes as reminders for regular giving. Better yet is to ask church members to make annual pledges and to send them regular notices of their progress toward fulfilling them. Best yet, from this sociological viewpoint, at least, would be to have congregants voluntarily set up regular, automatic, electronic bank transfers of designated dollar amounts from personal to church accounts. All such mechanisms routinize intentional financial giving in ways that minimize the need for givers to remember, deliberate, and choose at each and every giving opportunity. In fact, some of the church members who we interviewed for this project—on whom we report more systematically in the next chapter—told us explicitly that systematizing their financial giving was important in their lives and so described their giving as "routine." "It's just a part of my life," they said, and, "It's a habit." These people reported that they "take it off the top first and then pay our bills." One parishioner elaborated, "It's easier for me to do that. I simply set aside in my budget, right now I'm doing 5 percent with the goal of increasing that as I get used to living on what I'm living on. I think that's the best way to do it, to do a percentage, because that way you can keep track of what you're doing and make sure you actually are giving what you want to give." Another noted the tracking advantages of more systematic giving, "I look at the end of the year and think, 'Oh, that wasn't as high a percentage as I would have liked.' So then I feel guilt and sort of a renewed commitment to [giving more]." Yet another told us, "It's more like tracking a lifestyle, where the money is going. I try to pay attention to that so there is more money for giving." Another parishioner we interviewed explained the usefulness of structured giving as follows:

> I really am not too interested in financial matters. I mean, it's a necessary component of life, but it's not something that I'm dwelling on or choose to spend my time on. [So] I treat this like I treat my investments. I mean put that stuff in a place, get a system, and stick with it, and don't even look at it. Money is just a vehicle. It's just a tool, just a means to an end. The ends are what I care about.

Certain theological considerations, however, may work against such systematic routinizations of religious giving. Some Christian traditions emphasize purposive, conscious awareness in giving, insofar as good charity is supposed to be "cheerful" and "from the heart." Some Christian communities emphasize the taking of "free will offerings," seemingly more compatible with spontaneous generosity than automatic bank transfers. Some Christian traditions are hostile to anything that seems ritualistic, rote, routine, or overly formalized—their institutionalized tradition is, ironically, to be anti-institutional and anti-traditional. Similar other Christian communities are suspicious of strong church authority, emphasizing instead the autonomy of individual conscience and decision. Yet other Christian groups construct practices of faith, including religious giving, as deeply personal matters, which then easily become intensely private matters, in which church communities are then thought to have little business inquiring or guiding. A number of our 2006 Tithing Experiment Survey respondents wrote answers in the open-ended section of the survey reflecting the non-routine giving process described above. Some stressed openness and spontaneity in giving: "I don't specifically allocate a percentage," "Jesus said to give as you are led," "If I see someone in need, I will help with what I have to give," and "The Lord would put it on your heart to give at any time." Others emphasized the personal "free will" aspect of giving: "I give from my heart," "I give what I feel, I do not like to be 'required,'" "My family does not believe in giving tides [sic], we go out and give help and money directly to those who need it," and "Give what your heart (the Lord/Holy Spirit) is leading you to give." Some appealed to the Bible against relying on a system or routine: "A specific percentage for all would violate scripture" and "The New Testament requirement is to give with a joyful heart, therefore the percentage varies. It's not percentage-based but based on a heart-felt joy in giving to the Lord." Whether or not such points of theology or religious culture are authentically Christian or biblical, which is not the concern of this study, we have good reason to think that they may work against systematic, routine religious giving.

What empirical evidence exists that might help test this "lack of routine" hypothesis? Evidence from three separate surveys clearly confirms hypothesis 9. First, a 1993 American Congregational Giving study of members of five mainstream U.S. Christian denominations by Dean Hoge and colleagues found that both the amount of dollars given and the percentage of income given to churches were significantly influenced by the degree of planning in the giving. For instance, sampled Lutherans who reported tithing gave 10 percent of their income, those who said they "decided [yearly] on a percentage of . . . annual income" gave 5 percent of their income, those who "decide on an annual dollar amount" gave 4 percent of their income, those who "decide on a weekly dollar amount" gave 3 percent of their income, and those who "give what I can afford each week" gave 2 percent of their income. Thus, the difference between giving what one thinks one can afford each week and deciding on an annual dollar amount to give *doubles* the proportion of income given. Deciding annually on a percentage of income to give increases the percentage given even more. In absolute dollar terms, the difference between the weekly chooser and the annual percentage decider was $561 versus $2,181 given on average, respectively—an enormous disparity. The same pattern held true across all five denominations studied. In every case, the more long-range planning the church member put into giving, the more money they gave both relatively and absolutely. These findings were confirmed by the same survey's research on financial pledging—another form of routinized giving process. Respondents in every studied denomination who filled out an annual giving "pledge card or commitment card" contributed significantly more money than those who did not. For instance, the difference in yearly church giving between pledgers and non-pledgers among Presbyterians was an average of $2,306 and $923, respectively; the same difference in yearly church giving among Baptists was $3,950 and $2,318, respectively.[39]

Second, a 1993 poll conducted by the Gallup Organization found identical results.[40] So, for instance, Catholics who reported tithing gave an average of $1,962 per year, those who decided annually on a specific yearly dollar amount contributed an average of $1,113 per year, those who decided on a weekly dollar sum to give contributed an average of $882 per year, while Catholics who said they gave what they could afford each week gave an average of only $456 annually. Again, the same pattern was found in the other denominations studied. Likewise, the Gallup poll found the same results when it came to pledging. Pledging Lutherans gave 45 percent more money than non-pledging Lutherans, pledging Catholics gave 77 percent more than non-pledging Catholics, and pledging Baptists gave 34 percent more money than non-pledging Baptists. The difference these kinds of numbers make across all such U.S. believers collectively amounts to many billions of dollars given or not given. Of course, some of these differences may be due to selection effects, meaning that those Christians who would already give more money anyway also tend to be more likely to complete pledges and give on a more long-range planning basis. But we also have excellent theoretical reasons, consistent with the observed empirical evidence, to believe that engaging in the process of annual planning, deciding, and pledging as a structured means of regular, deliberate, and consistent financial giving itself influences giving to higher levels.

Third, findings from the 1992 Economic Values Survey, conducted by the Gallup Organization for sociologist Robert Wuthnow, comprising a sample of 2,013 U.S. adults in the paid labor force, also confirm hypothesis 9. The survey asked respondents who gave money to charitable organizations whether they generally (1) give on a regular, planned basis (45 percent) or (2) give when they happen to feel there is a need (45 percent).[41] The survey also asked respondents how much money in dollar figures they gave in the previous year to religious organizations of all kinds. Our analyses show that Christian respondents who gave as they felt the need donated an average of

$943 in the previous year, while those who gave on a regular planned basis donated an average of $1,324 in the same time period.[42] This $381 annual difference in giving represents a 40 percent increase in donations over the amount contributed by the situational givers.

Nevertheless, many U.S. Christians seem to be averse to systematic annual planning and decision making in their financial giving. According to the 1993 American Congregational Giving survey, among the church-affiliated Christians sampled, 76 percent of Catholics, 64 percent of Lutherans, 41 percent of Baptists, 40 percent of Presbyterians, and 23 percent of Assemblies of God members either decide on a weekly dollar amount to give or only give what they can afford each week.[43] And according to the 1992 Economic Values Survey data, we noted, 45 percent of working American Christians generally give money not regularly and on a planned basis, but rather when they happen to feel there is a need. However, it appears that such unplanned, non-routinized giving decreases levels of monetary contributions to religious and other charitable causes. As Dean Hoge and colleagues say, "The way [Christians]...plan their giving is associated with the amount given. Persons who say they give 10 percent or more of their income of course give the most. But in addition, those who decide on a percentage of income or a dollar amount to be given in the next year give much more than those who decide on a weekly amount or decide week by week."[44] Not planning in a deliberate and systematic way for annual financial contributions makes it too easy to leave religious and charitable giving as a situational afterthought, subject to the constraints of leftovers of other prioritized spending, both fixed and discretionary. Given how little money most Americans seem to think they have to spend, it is not surprising that the leftovers are often meager. So, potentially completely apart from people's conscious intentions to be generous with their money, the evidence shows that exactly *how* they go about giving their money influences how much they actually give.

We are therefore persuaded that part of the explanation of the riddle of ungenerous American Christian financial giving demonstrated in the previous chapter is the lack of annual planning, prior budget decision making, and routinized practices of contributing in the approach of very many U.S. Christians to financial giving.

Conclusion

This chapter has considered numerous hypotheses potentially explaining the low levels of financial giving by U.S. Christians, using available empirical data to attempt to test the alternative hypotheses.[45] The unevenness of available and relevant empirical data means that some hypotheses can be better assessed than others. What have we learned?

Our best explanation, based on findings from sometimes inadequate data, for low levels of financial giving and the prospects of more generous giving by U.S. Christians is the following. We think most American Christians do possess the financial resources to give generously—say, 10 percent of after-tax income—if they were committed to doing so, although for many such giving would come at a real lifestyle cost to consumer spending. Such generous financial giving by American Christians would require an intentional, principled, up-front decision to give faithfully, consistently, and systematically and would require the support of local church cultures in which generous financial giving is collectively expected and honored. Most American Christians, we think, do not give generously for a combination of reasons. The first reason is that many have, for various reasons, simply *not seriously confronted and grappled with the theological and moral teachings* of their traditions to give generously—they are only vaguely aware of or perhaps even avoid those teachings. Second, we think most American Christians do not give generously because many of their *churches settle for low expectations* of financial giving—there is a simple cultural lack of strong community norms encouraging and celebrating generous giving. Third, some American Christians do not give generously in part because they *lack a complete confidence in the trustworthiness* of the churches and charitable organizations to which they do or would give money. Fourth, most American Christians do not give generously because, due to the total privatization and lack of accountability of such issues, there are *few or no real consequences or costs* to stingy, intermittent, or no giving. Fifth, most American Christians do not give generously because most tend to practice *giving on an occasional and situational basis,* not as a disciplined, structured, routine practice.

Stated counterfactually, we think American Christians would give money more generously under five conditions. First, if local congregational cultures maintained high expectations of and collectively honored generous financial giving, Christians would give more generously. Second, and as part of that, they would give more if Christian congregations confidently taught the normative instructions of their faith tradition regarding generous financial giving. Generous giving would also be increased by Christian leaders' strongly encouraging believers to make theologically informed, principled decisions about and commitments to generous financial giving. If Christian organizations provided multiple means by which Christians could follow through on their principled decisions to give generously in ways that were structured and routine, that too should increase giving. Finally, if religious and charitable organizations established better procedures, systems, and practices of transparency, communication, and accountability that systematically increased potential and actual donors' trust in their uses of their contributions, that would increase the financial giving of American Christians.

Our analyses thus far have relied primarily on available survey data to tell us how much money American Christians do and do not give and why they may give what they do. We believe this approach has shed helpful, if limited, light on the riddle of ungenerous American Christian financial giving. We would like next, however, to approach the question from another angle. The following chapter reports our findings from in-depth interviews we conducted with 26 Christian pastors and 51 parishioners in seven states around the United States. Through such extended conversations with various kinds of Christians about the issue of money and financial giving, we seek to further test our ideas developed in this chapter and to add greater insight into the meanings, feelings, values, complexities, and experiences that Christians have around the issue of financial giving. It is to that task that we turn next.

CHAPTER 4	The View from Pulpits and Pews
	Written with Patricia Snell

I N   O R D E R   T O better understand the issue of Christian financial giving from a different perspective than that offered by survey research, we conducted a number of personal, in-depth interviews about money and stewardship with a modest sample of Christian pastors and church members. Our goal in these interviews was to answer questions such as, What are the experiences and meanings of financial giving for American Christians? What are their motives and purposes in giving? How much of a "live" issue is financial giving in Christians' lives? How do pastors approach and talk about money matters in their congregations? How do church members respond to those approaches? How do ordinary Christians think and feel about the messages concerning money that they hear in their churches? And how do Christians explain the frequent lack of monetary giving that we have observed in this book? Our purpose in addressing these questions was to begin to understand the thoughts, feelings, experiences, and meanings of American Christians that might affect their financial giving behaviors, in order to help solve the riddle posed by this book. We believe our interviews help us make a good step in that direction.

To accomplish these goals, we—Snell, Smith, Emerson, and two graduate student assistants—conducted in-depth, face to face interviews with 26 Christian church pastors and 51 church parishioners (five of whom were interviewed as couples) in Indiana, Ohio, North Carolina, Texas, Kansas, Colorado, and California. The interview respondents came from many Christian denominations representing different kinds of conservative Protestant, mainline Protestant, black Protestant, and Catholic churches. In many cases, we interviewed pastors and church members from the same congregations, enabling us to compare the accounts of clergy and members in the same churches. Most of our interviews were about 90 minutes in length, although they ranged from between 20 minutes to nearly two hours long. We audio recorded, transcribed, and collectively analyzed the interviews and transcripts. We tell the stories that emerged from them in this chapter.

Two initial words of caution are in order. First, the interview data analyzed here are not randomly sampled nor nationally representative. Therefore, we do not claim that our findings are descriptive or representative of all American Christians, of any particular denomination or tradition, or of any congregation. Because we sampled many of our interview subjects through church networks, because participation in our interviews was voluntary, and because interview subjects knew beforehand that the subject of discussion was to be financial giving, we suspect that our sample of parishioners is biased toward those who are more regularly involved in church and who are more faithful and generous financial givers. It seemed to us that some of the potential respondents we sought to interview who we had reason to believe were only somewhat involved in their churches and gave away less money were more reluctant to be interviewed or more difficult to contact through church networks. If anything, then, we think our sample represents more committed and generous Christians. Further research with random, representative samples of interview subjects is needed to determine whether our findings here are also true of Christians generally at the national level and of subtypes of American Christians specifically. In the meantime, we can with our data begin to explore some of the themes, stories, experiences, ideas, emotions, and meanings expressed by the believers with whom we spoke. We do think that our findings begin to shed light on the experience of financial giving of at least some American Christians. We believe what we learned reveals some of the cultural, cognitive, and organizational mechanisms that are likely at work in shaping the financial giving of many American Christians. And we think that our findings here suggest some important lines of inquiry for future studies of religious financial giving. Still, our analysis below should be interpreted and applied with caution.

Second, we found in our interviews what is common in much of this kind of research, namely, that our interview respondents were often rather inconsistent, ambivalent, and even sometimes contradictory in their statements and stories. Few people operate with clear, simple, and consistent frameworks of thought and explanation, and those we interviewed were no exception. Many of our interviews highlighted for us the intricate, complex, and sometimes confusing ways that social issues can be expressed in the lives of people shaped by varied ideas and experiences drawn from family, church, work, the media, and many other institutions and contexts. Despite their efforts to be reasonable and consistent, people do not always make clear sense to themselves or to others, nor do their behaviors always perfectly match their beliefs and attitudes. Even so, in the midst of such complexity and inconsistencies, certain patterns emerged as we studied our interviews. Particular stories repeated and themes surfaced across individuals and churches. We recount those stories and themes in the following pages.

Good Intentions

Talking with American Christians about the issue of financial giving can leave one with the initial impression that all is well, the key issues are settled, that Christians know what to give and why. Early in such conversations, American Christians often speak fairly clearly about why they give. Almost always, their motivations express moral commitments to be faithful to God and to care for others. Most often, Christians focused their explanations for giving as a good and right response to God. They said things such as, "God asks it," "Everything we have belongs to God," "God wants us to share," and "It's part of what you do as a Christian." One explained, "I mean, that's why you're here, is to give away the gifts you have and to share with other people." A number of Christian parishioners also said that they give because God has blessed them, professing that "I know what God has done for me" and "God has tremendously blessed me." One told us that giving is "my obligation for having been blessed." Others reversed that causal direction, stating that they believe God will bless or has blessed them as a result of their faithful giving: "I truly believe that if you give then you will be blessed" and "God blesses those who give."

A second theme about Christians' motivations for financial giving concerned their awareness of pressing needs existing in the world. Most described themselves as "very aware of the needs" and "acutely aware." One parishioner stated her motivation for giving as "just my own volunteerism, being exposed to different people." A number of the parishioners cited trips to developing countries as responsible for their broader awareness. Many of them also said that they think most Americans are aware, or becoming more aware, of the existence of needs in the world. "People in the last 50 years have become more aware too," stated one. "I think people are more aware today," agreed another. Presupposed by this explanation is the belief that people or Christians have a moral obligation to try to help others in need. Many of the parishioners directly connected this to their Christian faith. Others seem to believe helping others in need was an obligation of all humans, regardless of faith. One explained, "You know, if you can't do a little something in the world you live in, then you're just a crabby old scrooge." Another noted that "Nobody's any better than anybody, but some people are just more fortunate." And another stated, "There's really no reason that I should have more by virtue of the fact that I was born white, and in the U.S." For all of these, awareness of needs itself generated the moral obligation to give money generously to help meet those needs.

An overwhelming majority of the American Christians whom we interviewed also told us that they give money away because that is simply what they were raised to do. "I learned because that's how I was taught," said one, quite typically. These people often described experiences early in their childhoods in which they witnessed their parents giving into the church offering plate and specifically teaching them that giving was something they ought to do.[1] Even so, while the mechanism by which they learned to give was familial, the motivation behind it was always still clearly moral and theological, in that they said their parents believed that giving to church was a baseline moral responsibility. As one said, "That teaching has come by my parents, by way of the church."

At one level of analysis, then, many American Christians seem to be on a good track when it comes to understanding and practicing generous financial giving. Initial readings looked positive. However, our ongoing conversations with Christian pastors and parishioners began to make it clear that the matter is more complicated, unsettled, and difficult than it looks upon first glance. What follows in this chapter begins to explore some of those difficulties as we heard them.

An Unsettled Topic

Our interviews, once we got into some depth with the people we spoke with, made it evident that the question of financial giving actually turns out to be an unsettled issue to most American Christians, both pastors and parishioners. There were some consistently happy, positive stories in our interviews about generous financial giving. But, beyond those, only a small number of those we spoke with turned out to convey a real sense of comfort, security, and confidence around the issue. The majority in various ways proved to be at least somewhat troubled by the question and uncomfortable with their own dealings with the matter. In short, we came to see as our conversations unfolded that all in fact does not seem well with American Christians when it comes to the matter of financial giving.

PASTORS

Most of the pastors we interviewed expressed varying degrees of discomfort and frustration with the issue of financial giving. Most did try to put a good face on the issue, particularly early in our interviews, conveying confidence and satisfaction on the matter. But very often as our interviews unfolded, pastors also began to express various feelings of helplessness, annoyance, and aversion to the issue. To be sure, some pastors were confident and comfortable with financial giving. But most were not. Such uneasy feelings manifested themselves first when pastors spoke directly about their personal approaches to the issue in their churches. Some said, "Money is probably one of the most divisive issues in the churches" and "it's an enormous pressure." Another remarked, "I hate it. All it takes is one comment and it sets me off. I hate it, I absolutely hate it." Pastors related to us how sensitive the issue of money is for many of their parishioners and how uncomfortable that makes them talking about it. One related, "You know, I think when you deal with people's money, it's like touching a live wire. Tension. Some people are just gonna react very negatively." Another stated, "You get people that are, you know, ouchy about it. And so pastors kind of struggle with actually saying [anything about] it out loud." Yet another confessed that, "I wish we could be more open about it, but people are touchy." Others seemed uncomfortable because they viewed finances as "unspiritual," as this pastor said, "Probably the most troubling experience to me—and [yet] I know it probably needs to be handled—is that every board meeting I've had here, the majority of the time and attention is given to the budget, which seems unspiritual." Some pastors told us that talking about money with their congregations is one of the biggest challenges in their entire vocations, something they have to work very hard to address. "It's a hard topic," said one. "We tend not to try to be afraid of it, you know. We say we're gonna talk about it, and we do talk about it. But it's hard." Another pastor said about the money issue, "I, you know, we all have our challenges in our given vocations. Everything's not supposed to be peaches and crème and red roses. There're some things about our vocation, no matter what it is, that are going to consistently stretch us and cause us to grow."

Pastors also spoke frequently and unhappily about the pressure they feel from their congregations not to talk too much about money. Many pastors seem anxious that their parishioners have the perception that "all this church ever talks about is money." An overwhelming majority of the pastors specifically mentioned this fear, stating that they had either personally heard it from their own congregations or were trying to prevent that perception from forming. Some pastors said things like, "I don't know how many times I heard, 'That pastor is always talking about money, money, money,'" and "Some people will just tune you right out, 'Oh, he's talking about money again,' and 'We're not coming back here, all they do is talk about money here.'" Other pastors viewed this as a more general problem of which they needed to steer clear. One noted that "I don't want the reputation of always asking and talking about money. Now that's not true." Furthermore, some pastors told us that their parishioners, for their part, will also not discuss money. One said, "You know, people and money, I mean they'll talk about everything else. They'll talk about the economy, their sex life, but they won't talk about money. It's the last taboo in the church." Furthermore, many of the black Protestant pastors we talked with highlighted an acute concern relating to their congregations about money, stemming from what they believed were past church leaders who created an unhelpful role of "the flamboyant pastor." One even talked about a perception he feels that "preachers are pimps." Many of the black Protestant pastors we talked with described feeling the "need to look the part as a leader." As one explained, "There is a pressure, there is a level of prosperity that seeps into even that context. What you drive or what you wear is communicated as a badge of success or a badge of blessing." For many pastors, then, negotiating the various demands swirling around these issues of money in church is stressful.

Furthermore, many pastors of all sorts mentioned getting negative vibes about money from other pastors. They have heard other pastors complain about having to talk about money, remembered them sharing their own negative experiences around parishioner giving, and recalled them voicing their encounters with parishioners' complaints that "all they ever talk about is money." The majority also stated that they feel fairly isolated from other pastors on the matter. As one pastor explained, "I'm fairly isolated from a lot of my fellow clergy." Many said that they simply do not talk to other pastors about giving, that there is "not enough honesty and true collegiality" on the issue, as one remarked. Others said that, when pastors ever do talk about money, the discussions are brief. Some suggested that certain pastors with whom they talk focus primarily on their positive fundraising experiences, as if they were avoiding or covering up the more difficult issues around money with which nearly all of them struggle. Consequently, when it comes to money, many pastors seem to feel at least somewhat unhappily alone and uncomfortable in dealing with it.

The struggle that some pastors have with money in their churches is complicated by their uneasiness around their own personal handling of money. As one pastor explained, "You cannot lead when you haven't followed." One Catholic priest mentioned some difficulty in priests' talking about giving money with their parishioners because they themselves do not need to worry about their own finances:

> I've never had a time where I was responsible for a mortgage personally, or for rent, or car insurance, or, or anything. So there is a way in which I know I am a step away from any of the kind of financial things that touch many families. How do you meaningfully engage and challenge folks who on a daily basis live from paycheck to paycheck or maybe even less than? That makes one a little bit intimidated.

Many pastors also stated that they are personally uncomfortable talking with parishioners about giving money because of the direct implications for their own income. Pastors fear that they will be perceived as acting on self-interest. "Since my own livelihood is connected directly with how much people give," one told us, "there are real tensions there that are awkward. It is like I am raising my own salary." Another said that he shies away from directly addressing the matter: "I just let the topic of money come up as it does, which it has and does quite often, and then just kind of allow that to speak to people. And really that kind of removes me, and I wouldn't see that my people necessarily see me this way, but they could potentially see me as a pastor, as a person, with self-interest." The same Catholic priest quoted just above also mentioned the situation within some Catholic orders, where priests are supported by the dioceses rather than being paid directly from a congregational budget salary, that can cause discomfort. He also described the uneasiness he sometimes feels when shopping for groceries, for instance, because he thinks that people watch him to make sure he is not purchasing luxury items with his dioceses-paid income. Additional difficulties mentioned by pastors included writing single sermons that effectively speak to the entire spectrum of low to high givers in a single church, struggling with difficulties leading parishioners toward serious discipleship and stewardship, and troubles making requests for giving practical for parishioners. As one pastor stated, "For a lot of pastors, they can stand there and hold the Bible and blah, blah, blah to people, but they can't convert it to something that people can hang their hat on in their everyday living." And more generally, pastors stated that they simply do not like to address the matter of money. As one pastor explained, "In fact, I don't like to deal with money because I'm not very good with money myself." Another told us, "I think it used to be less comfortable for me to talk about money, but now I feel much more comfortable, partly because of a change in my own giving. I found that in order to deal with it with integrity, I needed to be clear about my own commitments in that area [and before I was not]." Similarly, another pastor explained that her approach to talking at church about financial giving changed as she personally began giving more:

> My thinking and behavior on all this changed when other individuals or programs have challenged me personally. When I first started getting involved in church and decided to go into ministry, the rector of my church sat me down for a sort of exit interview and said, "You realize that giving money to the church is an essential part of Christian faithfulness?" That sort of woke me up and I started to give more.

Thus, pastors with less than fully clean consciences themselves may not boldly teach generosity in their churches. Other pastors said they feel inhibited in dealing with money issues because of stories of corruption and scandals in the churches, which they worry have decreased their credibility. "We're now on the heels in America of tragic, deflating scandals, where a few have behaved in ways that make trust a real problem," one observed.

> A few have affected most. And you see a renowned television preacher or evangelists or respected and esteemed Catholic priests who have had, for one reason or another, a moral failure, a failure in leadership—the ripple effect brings disillusionment and disappointment. And people who are disillusioned and disappointed don't tend to give a lot.

Another pastor stated flat out that "preachers in the pulpit are the culprit" for the lack of generous giving by parishioners. The comments of many pastors on the question of money thus reflect a notable lack of confidence in their thinking and feeling.

Pastors also voiced discontent with their lack of training and denominational support for dealing with money issues. A number of them talked about having relatively little to no training or education about money in their pastoral preparation. When asked what training they had received, many said, "None!" and "none at all," sometimes laughing. One pastor explained, "It's not something you do in seminary, at least we didn't." It thus came across strongly to us that pastors often receive little to no denominational support through education, instruction, or pastoral networks on how to handle this difficult topic. In any case, many pastors seem to have made peace with the so-called "80/20" rule, namely, the apparent fact, treated as "gospel" by many pastors, that about 20 percent of any congregation gives about 80 percent of the dollars collected. That seems to many pastors simply to be a fact of life. But that does not mean they are happy about it.

The uncomfortable and distressed feelings we heard from pastors also came out when they addressed why they think so many Christians do not give money as generously as they might. One theme of frustration we heard, for instance, was the lack of training in families to give regularly and generously, parents who have not socialized their children well into financial faithfulness. One pastor observed, "I'm not sure that people are being raised in the church tradition the same way they have been in the past, with the same kind of model for giving that they might have been in the past. So partly, [the lack of giving] could be a family upbringing thing." Another explained how the lack of role modeling occurs when parents donate money in ways that their children cannot see, giving the example of one man in his congregation who gave one annual lump sum:

> So he'd come in with a check for $2,500, a pretty significant gift at the time, and he was just very proud and ready to give it. And I'd think, "Buddy, you're missing it. You are not being a model for your children. They see you pass the offering plate every Sunday. They don't see you giving that big check." They don't ever see that he is a contributor to the church. So he's missed the opportunity to be a good role model in that way.

The same pastor wondered at another point in his interview, "Giving is a learned thing. It's just amazing to me how so many people will give the same thing or the same amount year after year. It doesn't matter what appeals you make [it's always the same, because] that's what they learned." Other pastors told us they think American Christians do not give more money because of some personal deficit, such as a lack of trust in God, a lack of faith, or a lack of commitment. One pastor described this by saying, "You know, you can be a Christian and not trust God. You can be a Christian, and not pursue him, seek him." Other pastors mentioned the lack of generosity as resulting from parishioners' being personally overwhelmed with fears that prevent them from acting. One pastor stated, "I think people are afraid, people feel overwhelmed. Most church people are very good people, who want to be faithful. But they're overwhelmed by what they see happening, or they don't know what to do about it, or they think they can't make a difference."

Not all pastors were critical of and frustrated with their parishioners about money. Some spoke in quite sympathetic terms, explaining how societal pressures make generous giving difficult. They explained how low giving levels are due to lack of awareness of need, to Christians being inundated with too many good causes, and to a generational tightness with money due to uncertainties, such as the Great Depression and World War II, that some people have experienced in their lifetimes. Many others cited a lack of education as another obstacle. "Some people have grown up giving in the church," one noted, "and generosity has been a part of their practice, as they've been taught that by their parents. But I think those numbers are getting fewer. And so, unless the church or congregations can teach that generosity, or help people experience giving to others outside of themselves, I think the church is going to struggle with receiving [low] contributions." And another simply stated, "My people perish for a lack of knowledge." Other pastors pointed to low incomes and debt with which parishioners struggle. One explained, "Dollars are disappearing because funds have been tighter for people." Another stated, "Economic times have had an effect on my thinking around giving. . . . as ebbs and flows go, the national economy climate. I would hope that when the tide rises, all ships will rise, and we'll be one of those ships that rise right along with our members, if things get better with the economic picture for our country." One pastor stated that Americans are "in debt up to our eyeballs," and thus Christians, despite their good incomes, do not have the money to contribute to churches and charities as they would like. Nevertheless, despite expressions of such sympathetic views, the majority of pastors we interviewed clearly expressed significant amounts of discomfort, anxiety, or frustration when it came to financial giving in their churches.

PARISHIONERS

Pastors were not the only ones in our interviews expressing uneasiness with the financial giving question. Many parishioners reflected similar thoughts and sentiments, though from different angles of vision. Most non-clergy Christians we interviewed clearly felt concerned about the question of good uses of money. Very few had the matter settled in a definite, secure way. Many appeared to be living with unresolved ideas and feelings with which they struggled. Others were simply not sure whether their actions were good or right enough. Some expressed definite feelings of guilt about their lack of generosity. Nearly all of the ordinary Christians we spoke with said they believe that they should be giving at least some of their money to religious or charitable causes. They differed in the amounts they thought they should give and the degree to which they see this as an essential aspect of their spiritual lives. But they all talked about the issue of financial giving as at least one element of their Christian responsibility. Many of the parishioners we interviewed acknowledged the biblical call to giving money, stating that it was at least in part an "obligation" or "responsibility," something that "God wants us to do." Despite describing it this way, however, they also often seemed quite confused in their understandings around financial giving. They appeared to struggle with how to think about it well, as reflected in this remark: "I think it's our personal duty, or not duty. I guess that's not the right word. I think it's our responsibility." They also seemed to struggle with figuring out exactly how much and to whom to give. One, for example, asked, "Do you give 10 percent to the church? And only more than that do you give to anything else? Or do you just divide 10 percent up however you want? Or, I don't know." Some also seem conflicted generally with the obligations and merits of giving: "I don't know if I think charity should be demanded of you, but obviously it raises a lot of money, which I think in the end is a good thing."

Trying to make sense of their different views left many parishioners with mixed emotions. To be sure, a number of them said that they were confident in their giving. "I'm doing what I'm supposed to be doing," one insisted, "That's what I'm supposed to be doing." Another said, "I feel pretty confident, otherwise I would change it," and yet another, "I'd say I'm confident. I don't know if there's really any reasonable reason to feel guilt over it." However, the vast majority said that they both felt confident and yet also felt some guilt or uneasiness about their level of giving. "I guess it's an uneasy feeling," one confessed, "like you don't really know if you're doing the right thing." Many said they "could give more," and one parishioner recounted, "I threw a dollar in both collections, and I knew that I should have given more." For some, they explained that they do give regularly and maybe even generously, yet they said they felt uneasy about the fact that they know they could give even more than what they already give. One, for instance, said, "I always feel like I wish I could give more, and I feel bad if I don't." Another stated, "I don't think I'll ever feel good about the amount of money that I give. If I were at 10 percent, I would feel fairly righteous about it, but I would still wonder if I could give a little more what difference it could make." Still another parishioner related that, "I'm confident in my knowledge that I should give, and that I want to give. But I'm uneasy that I don't feel like I'm giving enough right now." One similarly reflected on a previous time when he was not giving as generously, recalling: "Well, I'm confident. It's easy now. [But] there were times when it wasn't so easy and I had to make some choices. And I think looking back that they weren't the right choices because I think that I could have given more, and I tried to rationalize it then and say I couldn't." Thus, many confessed that for the most part they knew that they were not living up to what they are able to give and expressing some discomfort about that.

Yet some of the same parishioners also stated in other parts of their interviews to the contrary that they did not feel guilt or felt they only had a small amount of guilt about that dissonance. One, for example, said, "Well, I suppose that I could really, you know, cut down my own needs to have more money to give, but I don't feel guilty about that." Another said, "Well, I never feel like we give as much as we could, or should. But I never feel guilty." Others admitted a bit more guilt: "Confident, you know, the only, yeah, there might be a slight amount of guilt, 'cause like I said, you can always give more. But that wouldn't keep me up at night." And another parishioner said she is "pretty confident. Every once in a while I feel maybe a twinge of guilt that we could give more." Another tried to explain, "I feel relatively confident about it. I don't loose sleep about it. I don't feel much guilt about it. I do have some guilt about it though." Yet another stated, "It's not really uncomfortable. It's just, 'Darn, I wish I could give more. I wish I could.'" One parishioner simply took both sides: "I'm comfortable, but then I'm not comfortable." Another parishioner told us that he addressed his conflicted feelings by simply no longer giving to the church at all, explaining, "And so stopping giving is the only thing I've done, and that's freed me, you know, to not be in a dilemma about what they're saying they need it for."

We were struck, then, by what seemed to us in many American Christians as a kind of "comfortable guilt"—that is, living with an awareness and feeling of culpability for not giving money more generously, but maintaining that at a low enough level of discomfort that it was not too disturbing or motivating enough to actually increase giving. Many Christians did not have clean consciences about money. But neither did they seem prepared to change their financial dealings in ways that would eliminate their modest levels of guilt. If anything, for at least some Christians, guilt appeared to be one acknowledged motivation for however much money they did actually give. Some described their giving as a result of the guilt and embarrassment that they have by nature of being born into a wealthy country and having so much more than others. "Well, you know, my overall feeling as a North American, as a wealthy, middle-class North American, is that it's outrageous how we live," one told us. "I don't particularly enjoy being an American who is sitting in this country of wealth while people are dying and starving." Another said, "Instead of being proud of my [financial] achievement, I'm sort of embarrassed by it. And if I didn't have the opportunity to turn around and give that out, I would feel like I shouldn't exist." Others stated that they give money because of the uneasiness that they feel in holding on to money they have and spending it on themselves. "I just wouldn't feel comfortable holding on to it," one said, just as another related, "I'm uneasy when I spend a lot of money on myself." But most who spoke along these lines said they would feel guilt if they did not give money because they know God wants them to give: "I would feel guilt. I don't know if I can say anything other than that. There's sort of something just entrenched. I couldn't, I just couldn't do that, I don't think. And nobody has ever, I don't think, set out to put a guilt trip intentionally on me like that. But I think I would feel like I'm failing in my duty." One parishioner stated, "I would have trouble with cutting God out of the pie," and another, "I see it as a promise, and it would be like breaking a promise." So, the potential guilt many parishioners said they would or do feel stemmed from their perceived obligation to God. As one related: "I see it as a giving to God, so it would make me sad that I couldn't or wouldn't do it, for whatever reason. I don't think God would condemn me or anything, [God] would understand, but I personally would be sad that I couldn't do it."

Given all this uneasiness about financial giving, one might suppose that parishioners seek out conversations with others "in the same boat" in order to work out how to make sense of their unsettled thoughts and feelings. However, our interviews suggested that this is not the case. Few Christians ever talk with anyone, except perhaps their spouses and maybe closest friends, about financial giving. Even so, such conversations seem to focus solely on whether or not and how much money they gave. One parishioner explained that he talks about giving "just with my wife, but I would say we probably spend very little time if any talking about it." Another parishioner said that she and her husband talk about giving, but mostly to argue, because he does not think that they should give as much as she would like them to. Some of the couples we interviewed together described points of tension between them in deciding on the amount of money to give. But for the overwhelming majority with whom we spoke, giving was not something they ever talked with anyone about other than as a part of their family budget. One explained, "It's something that I don't think people like to talk about. I mean, I don't like to talk about it either." Another stated, "We'd rather talk about our sex life than how much we give to church." And so it appears that most American Christians are generally uncommunicative when it comes to financial giving issues.

Lack of Clarity

In addition to many kinds and layers of uneasiness with the question of financial giving, we also noticed a general lack of clarity, especially among the parishioners we interviewed, about a number of related matters. There was on this question of financial generosity a good bit of muddle, or at least lack of consensus or consistency, that seemed to disorder the entire issue as it presents itself in churches.

VOCABULARY

One of the ways this lack of clarity and concurrence was manifest was in the disagreements that appear to exist around the standard language Christians often use to talk about giving. Pastors described a number of ways in which they talk with their congregations about giving to the church or other good causes. Most seemed to use the language of "tithes and offerings" or "stewardship." Some pastors talked only of tithes and offerings, some only of stewardship, and others a mixture of the two. The majority of the parishioners we interviewed described their churches as addressing the topic of giving fairly regularly. A significant minority, however, suggested that the topic was addressed not so frequently, ranging downward from "recurrently," as an integral part of their worship, to infrequent or "spotty." One parishioner described, "It's not really talked about much beyond the fact that it exists, and at some level the parish supports that activity." Another said, "The basket's always there." A few parishioners said that communication about giving occurs mainly through the church bulletin or newsletters. And a small minority said that the parishioners are primarily left to decide about giving on their own. One parishioner explained that there is "more of an assumption that people are doing it, and that they're seeking God to find out where God wants them to plug their money. That's probably what it is, each person for themselves deciding what God wants them to do, or where He wants it to go."

But what about the actual meanings of the vocabularies used? We asked parishioners how they think and feel about the words "tithing," "steward-ship," "charity," and "financial generosity," among other concepts. Many reacted positively to these terms, but many also gave us neutral to negative reactions. For instance, some parishioners said they thought "stewardship" was "something bigger than you," "sharing," "being wise with what you do," "a way of life," "balance," and "all encompassing." But others said, "it's lost any punch that it once had, and so it means a million things to a million different people." Yet others simply don't know what the word means, don't feel any emotional connection to it, or merely said, "Time, treasure, talent folks—the little blurb on the bulletin." One parishioner told us the word stewardship is "over-used and under-lived." Parishioners had a similarly scattered reaction to the word "tithing." Some said that "it's the right thing," "a partnership," and a "deep involvement in one's church." Others remarked that the word was "neutral," "a little negative," "too rigid," and "old-fashioned." One explained, "I struggle with that one. And I've never really heard anybody on either side that has really convinced me one way or the other." The word "charity" evoked by far the most mixed reactions, even from the same parishioners. People described it as "community," "giving to those who have less," "really giving," and "more of a virtue." But they also said, "It's more of a negative connotation" and "I don't like that word as much. I'm not sure why." Some described it as having both "negative and positive connotations." Others explained that "charity is a good thing, but it can be abused." For many, the word brought up the idea of organizations, "charities" as an institutional noun rather than a characteristic of love and generosity. For these, the word seemed to evoke concerns about whether donated money is being spent well or not. Finally, "financial generosity" consistently made those we interviewed think of other people, not themselves, specifically often extremely wealthy donors such as Bill Gates and Oprah Winfrey. Overall, we sensed a lack of any strong personal connection to any of the descriptive words. Some described them as feeling "made up," "a cold term," or "forced." So in approaching the matter of financial giving by Christians, the entire field of discussion appears to lack a common vocabulary with shared meanings and emotional connotations with which to carry on a meaningful discussion. So it was not clear from our interviews what word choices would be the best language for churches to employ when addressing the matter. It was obvious, however, that, whichever vocabulary churches do use, it cannot be assumed that parishioners have a clear understanding of what they mean or experience common emotional resonance with various words and meanings.

METHODS OF GIVING

Another way that the lack of common understanding or practices around financial giving was evident in our interviews concerned the means churches used to collect gifts, tithes, offerings, or whatever else financial donations might be called. Regardless of the specific language used to discuss it, pastors talked a great deal about the various strategies they employ to encourage giving within their congregations. The most common of these is the weekly collection through the passing of offering plates during worship services. However, though the vast majority of the pastors mentioned collecting money this way, a few said that they intentionally do not employ this method and instead offer boxes at the back of the church into which parishioners can drop money as they exit. One pastor explained, "We don't give through the passing of a plate, because we just told people that, 'If you want to give, there's boxes here.' So we don't have a time in the service, we just mention it as they leave." Another popular method for collecting money was through giving envelopes into which people put cash or checks to give during services or take to send their checks with through the mail from home. More than half of the pastors we interviewed mentioned using envelopes; some also mentioned that they print their envelopes with categories by which parishioners can earmark their monies for specific purposes and programs within the church. Many pastors described this method as practical and even necessary for tax reporting. Some pastors also said that they use envelopes to track specific parishioner giving and, within Catholic churches, attendance. One Catholic priest told us, "The only way that I know that you are coming to mass on a regular basis is the presence of your envelope." Despite this common use of giving envelopes, a few pastors mentioned that they purposefully do not utilize envelopes, because no one in their churches used them. "Very few people mail[ed] them in when we provided envelopes, and when we stopped using envelopes, those people still mailed them in [in their own envelopes]. The convenience of the [provided] envelope didn't matter." Much of this also appears to be in flux as at least some churches are experimenting with, for example, setting up automatic electronic withdrawal systems for regular giving, which serves a similar purpose as envelopes and so may be replacing them. One pastor of a church that has had success using automatic withdrawals stated, "I think checks will disappear in ten years, and you know less people are carrying cash. People use debit cards at the 7-11 now. So that was when I started thinking, we need to provide a way for people [to give] who pay all their bills online."

Another usual strategy that pastors mentioned is an annual campaign drive. This can involve a range of practices, from preaching one sermon on giving to a five week fund-raising drive. Sometimes the campaign is also accompanied by an annual banquet, dinner, or other type of event. One element of these annual campaigns that many pastors described as effective was employing member testimonies. "The most powerful means, in fact, during stewardship season, is the individual members' testimonies," said one pastor. "When people testify about it, talk about it, how they came to the place where they are in their giving, it's powerful stuff." Along with annual campaigns, churches typically ask parishioners to make an annual pledge; some do this through a preprinted pledge card. Many pastors also mentioned tracking systems their churches employ to measure giving to compare to pledges, and sometimes the use of reporting systems to tell parishioners whether they are meeting their pledge goals. One parishioner attending a church with a pledge card system said, "We pledge everything, the gas company, we pledge to the bank on our car loan. We are doing these pledges all the time, and the church is asking to be one of those priorities." However, many of the pastors who discussed this strategy also mentioned some resistance to it from their members. One explained:

> Now there are times when, you know, some people will balk a little bit about making a pledge. [They'll say:] "Well, I just choose to give as much as I can on a weekly basis. I really don't want to give a pledge." And then we'll talk about that a little bit more and I'll say, "Now you do make pledges to other things. You make a pledge to pay your credit card bill."

In response to such resistance or a sense of diminishing results, some pastors we interviewed have decided to stop using the pledge system. Others have decided to revise it in some way, such as calling them "Intention to Give" forms or adding an accompanying "Service Pledge" form to highlight the importance of other ways parishioners can give to the church. A few of the pastors have also decided to steer away from tracking giving on pledges altogether. "I've been here for 16 years, and ever since I've been here, there has been no pledge system or tracking of giving. The only tracking that takes place is just what the government needs."

Capital campaigns are another strategy churches employ to collect money. Pastors generally expressed the most success with this strategy. "It is much easier to raise money for capital or building campaigns than for regular annual church budgets," some said. However, capital campaigns are a limited strategy usually employed during a specific time for a particular project, such as renovating the church or building a new facility. Once the particular need is met, however, the strategy is no longer applicable. Therefore pastors did not suggest this as a viable means for long-term giving efforts.

Additional strategies that a smaller number of pastors mentioned were the making of telephone calls from either the pastor or other members of the church, home visits from members, giving to the church through wills, and targeted fundraisers for specific projects. However, such methods had apparently produced mixed results. Most pastors said that they intentionally do not employ fundraisers as a strategy. One pastor viewed fundraisers as counterproductive to regular giving to the church, arguing that fundraisers "end up undermining the ministries financially because the people develop the mindset that 'I don't have to follow the scriptures' [in not always giving regularly]." Pastors also mentioned a variety of prepackaged giving strategies, most of which came from their denominations or other churches, which also met with mixed results, as one pastor noted: "A canned campaign is exactly that." The only packaged campaign that some pastors mentioned as being successful was with an educational program called Financial Peace University, which teaches parishioners how to be more financially responsible throughout their daily lives and thereby have greater means from which to give.

Another "strategy" that some pastors mentioned was their choice to not be personally involved in their church finances at all. A number of pastors described this as removing them from the challenge of being perceived as "all about the money" or self-serving in raising their own salary. One explained, "I don't get involved with individual stewardship. I don't know who gives and who gives what. I don't want to know." Another said, "Boy, I keep not only a veil, but a steel curtain, a steel wall. I don't want any idea how much people give." This approach varied from a choice to simply not connect giving levels with specific people, so as not to bias their pastoral duties, to a definitive separation of themselves from all financial matters of the church entirely. This seemed to be largely driven by the fear of being perceived as a pastor or church who always talks about money. Ironically, almost none of the parishioners we interviewed mentioned holding or hearing of such a perception. This could be partly the result of the fact that we believe we sampled parishioners who are more heavily involved in their churches and likely to be at least somewhat more generous givers than the average churchgoer. Still, we think it is worth noting that the parishioners we talked with hardly ever mentioned money-fixated pastors as a concern. Only one parishioner mentioned it and merely stated, "You know it's the money speech, which I guess turns everybody off a little, but how it turns me off I really can't describe it, because I know it's necessary." A few other parishioners mentioned that they have heard other parishioners say such comments, although they also always added that they did not share this perspective. For example, one said, "I've been to other Christian churches that there are a lot of sermons about, 'We gotta have more money. We gotta have more money.' But not in the particular parish that I go to, it's not ever put that way." Another said, "There're always people who want to grumble about, 'Here they go again.' But at the same time, it's like 'This is how they raise their money.'" Another told us, "I know that one of the reasons that people don't want to go to church, or a typical reason is, 'Oh, they're always begging for money all the time.' That's just not been my reaction or experience." In fact, some parishioners specifically said that pastors talking about money is a good and necessary reminder to them. Many made comments along the line of, "No, it's not overdone."

Another way that American Christians do not share a common outlook on methods of giving and getting money concerns who does the asking for the money. Some parishioners we interviewed stated that pastors' asking for money in general terms is ineffective. They said things like, "That whole thing of the priest asking, or I guess just that whole thing of who the messenger is, bothers me." This concern was sometimes described as related to the fact that the pastor's salary is connected to the money given. Along these lines, many of the Catholic parishioners described their annual Bishop's Appeal as being particularly ineffective, perhaps because as one parishioner said, "The higher the money is going to go, like to the Pope, the less likely I am to give." These parishioners tended instead to want to hear member testimonies related to giving. As one parishioner explained, "So, a lot of it is just a commitment because of active belief in what they're doing, not just because somebody tells you 10 percent, but because you can see the real faces, and you know, picture the causes that the money is going to." Another stated: "I like the approach they take, yeah, as far as what the laity says. They don't preach from the pulpit, as far as pastors getting up there and saying, 'Blah, blah, blah, we need money.' I think it should come from the laity, people that have been at the church for a long time."

Parishioners said that they like this because it made the message "come alive for people." Another approach along these lines that they thought was effective was when past recipients of giving speak to the congregation. One parishioner said, "I think having a person speak before the church as recipient of, you know, past giving, and testifying to what that money has done to improve their lives would be good." However, a number of other parishioners offered contradictory messages, saying that they felt that asking by the pastor was appropriate and effective. "I think you have to ask," they said. This difference may be due in part to how comfortable the person who is asking for the money is with the topic. As one explained, "I think people who feel uncomfortable about asking for money don't necessarily do a good job of it, and it comes off a little awkwardly and becomes an embarrassment for everybody." In any case, it turns out that different churchgoers have different views of who best should ask for money.

Furthermore, American Christians differ on whether to give all of their money through church or not. One way that some of the parishioners we interviewed like to give is through the church as a "screen" of sorts. Perhaps in reaction to what they described as feeling inundated by information about charitable organizations and having a lack of knowledge about which causes to support, many of the parishioners said that they have moved to an approach of giving all of their money to the church in the hopes that the church will adequately screen the causes and organizations that it will then support. One parishioner said, "I mean at least that's where it filters through. And it's a great, you know, way to have it filtered through." Others said, "I feel like they're doing a good job of searching out needy charities and good causes to sponsor and support" and "Rather than figure out where the money's going, if I know that I am giving it to my church, I know that it will be used well." Another stated, "So when our church would get money together to send some place, that was the best way to do it because I figure they've already done their homework on it." Many parishioners described the responsibility of giving as being primarily about finding the church that they want to support and then trusting the church to investigate and support worthy causes. As one parishioner described, "I do have a responsibility in deciding where to put that money, in carefully choosing which church and which organizations to support, but then it's up to them to spend that money wisely." At the same time, other parishioners wanted to maintain their ability to give some of their money to church and some of it to non-church organizations and causes, stating, "I don't think generosity has to be religiously associated" or "at the end of the year, I try to give to some cause that is needed in our community," highlighting the specific non-church organizations that they give money to.

Thus, in sum, it was obvious from our interviews that, across pastors, churches, and denominations, there is no clear, consistent strategy that clergy employ or that particularly appeals to parishioners. As many pastors spoke in support of each of the strategies mentioned as against, and many described having had mixed results with any or all of them in their own congregations. Some swear by envelopes; others do not want or need them. Many churches set their calendar year around their annual campaigns; others find that ineffective. Tracking toward pledges appears to work for some and is shunned by others. Some like their pastors to ask for money straightforwardly and others do not. Some want to give all of their money through the church while others want to be in charge of choosing each destination for their giving. In short, there does not appear, at least from our interviews, to be any predetermined prescription or "best practices" on which pastors can rely in order to successfully encourage giving from their parishioners. Instead, churches seem to operate somewhat experimentally from a mixed bag of "this, that, the other, or none of the above." One could argue that a pragmatic, "different strokes for different folks" approach should be most effective in America's decentralized, congregational-based church system. But much of what pastors and parishioners told us suggested that the status quo was not in fact working especially effectively. Most churches are at least getting by. But, again, there appear to be more than a little uneasy, discontented, uncomfortable, and frustrated feelings about the entire matter, process, and results of Christian financial giving in churches. Our own sense from the interviews is that the sum total of the assortment of methods employed by different churches to facilitate financial giving by members does not reflect so much a positive diversity of highly functional differences appropriate for specific contexts; rather, it seems to reflect more of a somewhat unimaginative settling for familiar routines—that are themselves significantly oriented toward avoiding problems and upsets—accompanied sometimes by tentative groping toward experimental alternatives, which usually produce mixed results. Hence, in our view, an overall lack of clarity was evident too in the multiplicity of the methods.

"DISCRETIONARY OBLIGATION"

We noticed one other theme in parishioners' interviews that seemed to us to also reflect one facet of the larger lack of clarity around the general matter of Christian financial giving. That theme grew out of the insistence by many parishioners on what seemed to be incompatible claims about who owned money and how obliged owners were to give some of it away. On the one hand, many parishioners affirmed that all of their money was a gift or blessing from God, of which perhaps they were simply stewards, from which God rightfully asked them to give generously. On the other hand, many of the very same people insisted that the money they owned was *their* money, that it was their right and responsibility to decide what to do with it, and that nobody other than themselves had any say-so in how it ought to be spent. In the end, the position described seemed to be something like "autonomous obedience" or "discretionary obligation" or "individualistic servanthood." Of course we know that life and people are complex. Nobody puts all the pieces together perfectly consistently. Most research interviews on any subject involve a lot of complexity, paradox, inconsistencies, and sometimes outright contradictions. But we were struck here with what seemed to be a structured and widespread paradoxical cultural category that seemed to create problems for Christians in approaching the issue of generous financial giving. Many American Christians simply seem to have a hard time putting together two discordant ideas. On the one side, many seem to genuinely believe in the biblical notions of stewardship and discipleship, which are profoundly challenging to the autonomous individualistic self. But at the same time, most of them are also deeply committed to American autonomous individualism and accompanying notions of self-determination, absolute private property rights, and consumer sovereignty. Most appear to "resolve" the tension by simply insisting on both and avoiding facing the contradictions. When we asked parishioners if they saw financial giving as more voluntary or as something required of them by God, nearly all of them said "both." This apparent incongruity played out in interview after interview, as parishioners made such statements as, "I don't think that giving is mandatory. I feel that everyone *should* give in one way or another." Another explained: "I think God requires it, but you know, he also tells us that he doesn't want us to give if we don't want to. He wants us to be cheerful about it. So then it becomes voluntary. You know, it's a requirement, but it's also an honor. It's a way of honoring him. So, you know, it's both."

Parishioner individualism also surfaced in their responses to a pair of hypothetical questions we posed, asking them how they would think and feel about churches mandating a requirement of 10 percent giving for membership in good standing (the same questions we investigated with our survey, reported on in the next chapter). Across the board, parishioners opposed such a requirement. Some parishioners said they personally would not be that bothered by it because they are already at that level or more but struggled with such a requirement being imposed on others. Several parishioners said they would disagree with the requirement because of its exclusionary nature, noting that Jesus would not want to exclude people who could not pay such an amount from the church. But many parishioners rejected the requirement simply as a reaction to the idea of requirement itself. They said, "Nobody has a right to tell you," "I don't need someone to mandate what I can do," and "That's between me and God." People said such were "personal" matters that the church has no right to speak to. Many conveyed the distinct sense that "It's my money" and "I earned it." Parishioners reacted with statements like, "If you're going to tell me I have to do it, then you better believe I'm not going to do it," and "The whole thing of getting up in front of the church and saying, 'This is what you have to do,' maybe it works somewhere, for some people, but not for me." So, many parishioners seem to feel that giving is, at least in part, a requirement from God, but they do not believe the church has the authority to invoke the recognition of such a requirement. They often said that they believed their money came from God and was never theirs to begin with, but when presented with a scenario in which God's church specified a level of giving (which many believe is biblical) as a baseline for faithfulness, they reversed these statements by insisting that their money was their own.

Our point is not that ordinary American Christians are dishonest or dumb or shifty. Our point is that the available cultural tools with which Christians work out their thinking and feeling involve tensions and contradictions that people have a hard time managing with consistency. Lack of clarity manifests itself in Christians' affirming seemingly incompatible values and commitments. These positions of what we might think of as "autonomous obedience," "discretionary obligation," and "individualistic servanthood," it seems to us, create confusions around the nature of financial faithfulness as well as opportunities for giving to slip to levels lower than what the better side of many Christians would ideally like to offer. We think that understanding the riddle of ungenerous Christian giving will require paying attention to the complexities of such paradoxical and perhaps contradictory cultural assumptions and outlooks.

Obstacles to Giving

Nearly all the parishioners we interviewed said that they in fact could give more than they do and believe that they should give more. They differed in their emotions around this disparity, varying from sustaining confidence to feeling some confusion to feeling guilty. Yet most, as we noted above, also expressed their readiness to live with the confusion or guilt, to remain adequately comfortable with the disparity between ideal and real. Most felt that they could live with the dissonance in their lives without needing to change their behavior to be more consistent with their beliefs and ideals. Part of the explanation for this is the many reasons that Christians cite for the lack of their own and others' more generous financial giving. In our interviews, parishioners dedicated a great deal of time to discussing the reasons that they personally, or others more generally, do not give away more money. While the reasons Christians gave for why they should give money were brief—which typically focused on often not well-developed or expressed theological and moral convictions—the reasons they provided for why Christians do not give more money were long, well developed, and somewhat complex.

One explanation that a few of the parishioners offered for why other Christians do not give more money is a lack of faith. Perhaps as a result of seeing their giving as due to their own faith, they stated that other Christians do not have an adequate faith foundation to support the giving that a well-supported faith would motivate. These parishioners said that not giving is "very un-Christian," and not giving is "just a lack in their religion altogether." One parishioner stated such a person has "not understood Jesus' mission and God's purpose in sending Jesus." In other words, people would give if they were really strong Christians, so their lack of giving is evidence of their lack of faith. The church's best response to this problem, then, would be to better teach the foundation of Christianity. As one parishioner explained, "My experience is that there's not a real effort to convey what it really means to be a Christian, which is to be not of this world, and to be concerned about those who have the least." In that sense, then, the church is also at fault. A few parishioners also cited a lack of awareness of needs as explaining low Christian giving. The presumption is that Christians believe they should give to address needs and would give if they were able; the conclusion is that Christians' not giving means they must not know about the needs that do exist in the world. Only one parishioner we interviewed offered this as a reason that they themselves do not give more money, saying, "Because I don't know what a person's needs are who's out there." A few others did suggest that this is why other Christians do not give more, saying, "They're really oblivious to the fact that the whole world doesn't live the way we live." One noted a general lack of awareness as the result of living in a wealthy society: "I think that, you know, the extrapolation of a society that's been blessed with so much wealth is that we don't even see it. We don't get it [real needs]. It's just not there." However, the vast majority did not mention this as an explanation, and some specifically rejected such a claim. "I'm very aware [of needs], and I think that people who say that they aren't must not look at the newspaper, or magazines, or watch the news." Another said, "I think you would have to be born under a rock, I mean seriously, not to know that organizations need money." And again, "I don't see how they can, how anybody cannot know about the [needy] condition [of the world]. I mean, there's no way that they don't know."

Despite this general agreement that lack of awareness of needs alone was not a cause of low giving levels, some thought that though Christians may be aware of needs generally, they may not know what specifically to do about those needs. One explained, "I'm aware of lots of needs around the world. I'm not always as aware of where the Christian organizations are that are involved." Others noted the many organizations available yet felt some confusion over how to pick one to which to give. "Well, there's too many organizations," said one, "and it's difficult to know whether the information you're getting is really honest." Many other parishioners, however, explained that they know both that needs exist and that organizations are available to meet those needs. In fact, many parishioners described themselves as being inundated with information about good causes and talked extensively about the names and functions of various charities and the mailings they receive from them soliciting money. But many of them also said that they do not know which organizations *best* meet these needs. "We get quite a lot of mailings," one remarked, "We're very aware. If there's anything that we're not aware of is how effective the resource is used by that organization." This explanation is directly related to another reason mentioned to explain low levels of financial giving: administrative distrust. Numerous parishioners mentioned concern about how funds are used as a reason inhibiting their personal giving and perhaps giving by other Christians. Some expressed muted concerns, like, "I'm a little careful about who I give to" and "It's not clear how it would be used." One couple described their inaction in the face of a natural disaster by saying, "We didn't do anything because we didn't know who to trust." The parishioners mentioned various scandals that they have heard of locally and in the news, and cited as general knowledge that many organizations spend too much of the money on their own overhead and not enough on the need or cause itself. They sometimes described people or organizations as "misusing the funds." And they were concerned about being taken advantage of as a result of the fact that, "some people will try to take advantage of you." Some were also concerned about their money being used by individuals for purposes other than what they intend it for: "Sometimes," one said, "you give money to 'em, and sometimes people will go behind your back and give money to somebody else. That's how people are, you know."

Another reason for a lack of Christian giving, according to some of the people we interviewed, was lack of ability to give. These parishioners seemed to think that Christians believe they should give and may be aware of needs, and rather simply lack the monetary ability to follow through on their convictions. A handful of the parishioners cited bills and debt as a hurtle to their own giving ability, saying, "Bills come first" and "I got all the bills, and my children, you know here at home, and trying to do this and that." Some others also thought the lack of money could be a problem for other Christians, suggesting that "It could be other bills that they got" and "People do not have a surplus of money. The common man doesn't have it, and a lot of people go from pay check to pay check." One parishioner who thought that bills and debt might inhibit generous giving related that to the reason many parishioners feel guilty about their lack of giving: "In a sense, a lot of people's guilt comes from what is being said [to encourage giving], in response to people's lack of ability to give." Yet another concern, whether other people give their fair share, was another reason some parishioners said inhibited their own willingness to give. From this perspective, even when people have money to give, have the faith to motivate giving, are aware of needs, understand that giving can meet needs, know and trust organizations to use their money appropriately and effectively, they still may not give out of a sense that other people do not carry their fair share of the giving burden. One parishioner complained, "I mean, some of these people aren't contributing their part. It just sort of drags down, and you're shaking your head, 'no.'" Another said, "I think you always think that if you quit giving then it's not going to really make that much of an impact on anything." But he then went on to say, "But, if everybody felt like that, then I think that there would be just a lot of social problems needing the support and wouldn't be able to function."

The foregoing was expressed by some Christians in some interviews. But nearly all of the parishioners said that other American Christians do not give because of selfishness or greed. From this perspective, the problem is clearly not that people do not have the ability to give—they just don't want to. One said, "I would like to say that it's because they don't have the resources, but I know that that's not true." Parishioners described this as "nothing but pure greed" and "just pure selfishness." One stated, "I think that another thing is greed. People want to keep more for themselves, thinking that, you know, that that's going to help." These parishioners think that selfishness results in others ranking the giving of money to churches and charitable causes low on their priority lists, ranking themselves and their personal self-interest at the top instead. "The desire for wealth and things," said one, "has replaced core values." Note that the selfishness and greed explanation was used by nearly all to explain everyone else. But few owned up to selfishness and greed themselves. This implies that either the explanation is generally erroneous or everyone is blaming others without taking responsibility for the same problem themselves.

Potentially related is another problem some of the parishioners identified: financial fear and insecurity. The idea is that even though American Christians are generally wealthy and do have the ability to give money generously, they also have a fear of losing their money, which causes them to hold on to it tightly. One parishioner described this "one dollar more" mentality as driving his own hesitancy to give, admitting, "So I developed an over-sensitivity, I would say, about financial matters. I think I carry some of [my mother's] fear around, you know, about running out of money, getting into insecure situations. I think that's the root of it." In reply, we asked, "So that's in competition with your generosity?" to which he answered, "Totally, fiercely, fiercely in competition with generosity." Others stated, "I really feel that it seems so easy to get caught up in a fear of financial insecurity" and "There's that greed element that we're holding onto the money because we fear the future, or we fear at the end that we're not going to have enough." One described financial insecurity as the direct result of having wealth: "I think that people who have less are dependent on an outside force, and so when you have more, you're more dependent on yourself." From this perspective, people who have less money may be more willing to give it away because they have learned to trust and have less to lose, while people who have greater wealth fear losing it and are more used to relying on their own ability to keep what they have.

Thus, American Christians have a lot of ideas about obstacles to generous financial giving. Some explanations, such as bills and debt, take a "realistic" and accommodating posture toward the issue. Many others, however—such as lack of faith, ignorance of needs, selfishness, and greed—are more critical, implicitly suggesting or explicitly stating reasons for ungenerous giving that our interviewees judged as unacceptable. While these ideas are, in one sense, simply some people's perceptions, they also represent the insights of "insiders" based on their own lived experiences. Some of these explanations—as we will note below—appear to corroborate our conclusions about some of the hypotheses examined in chapter 3. The evidence here is not definitive. But we think the input from this different angle adds to our assessment of and explanation for the riddle of ungenerous Christian financial giving.

A Consensus on Consumerism

We have noted above the lack of clarity among the various explanations offered by American Christians concerning low levels of financial giving in their communities. On many points, pastors and parishioners held divergent perspectives or expressed a variety of explanations on the matter. However, nearly all of the people we interviewed did converge in agreement on one major explanation for inadequate financial giving by American Christians. The number one reason that both pastors and parishioners cited as the major barrier to Christian generosity is the individualistic, consumerist nature of American society.

Pastors said that the individualism in American society, including within the church, undermines the priority of financial giving. "We have a very selfish, I-focused church," they said. "It's a lack of inner-transformation," others judged. "We're selfish. The theology of scarcity, that 'I need to hoard everything I have and need to be investing for my own security,'" they said was a big problem. Very many pastors explicitly named consumerism as a major culprit in discouraging generous financial giving, which they explained as a confusing of needs with wants and a consequent reluctance to give money away. "It's about me, what I'm getting," they said. "People living beyond their means," others described, "and churches living beyond their means." One pastor summed up the consumerist mindset by saying, "We're holding our wallets, check books, and purse up, and we say, 'Okay, Jesus, we dedicate ourselves to you, but we're gonna hold these back.'" Many pastors described this as the "challenge of prosperity." One said: "We are the most affluent, richest society ever, and yet our giving to missions is probably the most pathetic. We have missions going in this direction, but not in that one. Why is that? I just really think that we give, but we give minimally. I think it's also, again, driven back to who we are." Another stated, "When the standard of living goes up, the level of practice and service goes down." This Methodist pastor opined: "The best way to kill the church is to make every Methodist a millionaire." Another claimed, "I find that the more people have, the more tightly they hold on to things." Yet another noted, "Typically speaking, giving is down, and typically speaking, the lower income the family has, the greater percentage of giving of their income is to charity." Along these lines, some of the pastors also mentioned the problem of consumerism in the church, "the attitude that the church is a business instead of a ministry." One pastor claimed that mega churches are pushing a consumerist mentality of the church. Another said that, because of this, parishioners "come to expect services from the church." These pastors think that churches' services have come to be viewed as a "product" available for people's consumption. One pastor summed the consequential dilemma as, "I think our people are hungry, hungrier than they've ever been before. The problem is just that the church isn't feeding 'em."

The parishioners we interviewed also overwhelmingly named consumerism as the fundamental cause of low Christian giving. Many stated that Christians do not give because they are spending their money on the latest consumer products. One explained:

> Probably because the world we live in, people want to keep up with the Joneses. They have that mentality. And to do that you have to have money. And because we have so much stuff, I mean basically there's all kinds of crap out there to buy. And a lot of people get in trouble with that. And you can't be a good steward with your money if you're spending it on your own. You have to use some of it to help others.

Another agreed: "I think a lot of times people have become slaves to a standard of life that, you know, really nobody needs." Yet another said, "We live in an extremely consumeristic culture, and the pressure to live a particular kind of lifestyle is tremendous." From this perspective, then, Christians may have a faith-based conviction to give, but the larger consumer-oriented society and culture tempt people to desire to purchase ever increasing goods for themselves, so that giving generously becomes impossible. One parishioner told us, "It's a test of your faith. There's thises and thats, and then there's the material world which causes people to think that they need this and that and the next thing. And all that yells really loud at people." Another explained similarly, "Christians are too shaped by the world. We have slipped into not reflecting on the radical nature of the calling of the countercultural Christianity that seems apparent in things like the Sermon on the Mount." All of this creates real tensions and challenges, according to many we interviewed. As one parishioner explained, "They're very conflicting messages. It's hard to go from Sunday worship and feeling great about what you hear to then going out into the world where everyone has the latest [consumer products]. So it's conflicting."

Throughout this explanation of consumerism as a major culprit in impairing generous Christian giving, the voices struck us as genuine and often personal. The people we talked with were not simply blaming others for failures or bad faith. Many were also confessing personally how difficult it is to live a generous life in America's high-pressure, mass-consumerist culture. It was clear to us that, if interviews can tell us anything, consumerism presents many Christians with a real challenge that appears to be an important piece of the puzzle explaining the riddle of this book.

Two Contrasting Congregational Cultures

Some studies of differential financial giving focus on the demographics of more and less generous givers. Others focus on the theologies underlying the asking for money or the organizational methods used to collect money. These approaches certainly shed helpful light on the differences between generous and less generous givers and congregations. Our interviews for this project, however, suggested the crucial importance of another factor: the different kinds of congregational cultures that leaders foster in their churches and that church members sustain.[2] One theme that emerged from our interviews with pastors and parishioners was the starkly divergent general approaches to money and giving that different congregations seem to cultivate in their members, discourse, practices, and styles. In analyzing our interviews, we came to see two "ideal types" of congregational cultures and discourse that dominate the field on this matter. (By "ideal types," we do not mean preferred or recommended systems; rather we mean descriptively pure versions of some models of church culture at the extremes that help us to see real differences in the world.) Some of our interviews represented one ideal type, some the other, and some fell in the middle. We think it will be helpful to lay out these ideal type positions and describe how they feel and seem to operate. The first of these we have come to call the "Pay the Bills" mentality or culture. The second we call the "Live the Vision" mentality or culture. Although we do not have the data to verify this, we strongly suspect that these two cultures produce very different levels of giving in congregations of the same size and tradition. And these cultural differences strike us as potentially very important in shaping levels of Christian financial giving at a national scale.

PAY THE BILLS

A number of pastors described an approach to talking with their churches about giving that seemed primarily driven by a narrow focus on the literal budgetary needs of their churches. We call this a "Pay the Bills" church culture, which we found in every major Christian tradition in which we interviewed, but perhaps especially in Catholic churches. Clergy who operated with this conceptual framework described money as something they discuss with their congregations because "it is necessary." They appealed to their parishioners with pleas like, "The church needs you. The church needs your time, your talent, and your treasure. We need you to contribute," and "We cannot neglect the nitty-gritty, everyday necessities of life." This fundamentally practical approach led pastors to seek to help their parishioners understand that the use of their church facilities and services creates bills that need to be paid, which members should see themselves as responsible to pay. Pay-the-Bills pastors described their approach by saying things like, "We try to emphasize here, that if you're coming, and you're utilizing the people, utilizing the programs, and what we have to offer, then you really do need to support it financially. It's just part of the, you know, the expectation." Along similar lines, another said, "So I say, 'If you're worshiping here, and you're enjoying the heat and the air conditioning of what this place has to offer, then you should feed [money] into it.'"

Parishioners in Pay-the-Bills oriented churches reported that their pastor addressed giving by explaining, "We have a lot of bills to pay," and "This is how much money we need." One stated, "Yeah, the priest talks about it, just like if they have needs, I'm trying to think about if it was the boiler or something, they needed a huge amount of money to repair. They also needed to redo the parking lot. So I mean there is talk about people needing to give more money." Another reported that her church says, "We do have an electric bill, a gas bill, and building maintenance, and if you want to gather here, we need to financially keep this place going." Still another described this culture by saying, "Of course they always [have the] take-home [message] that, you know, running a church isn't free, and that they have minimal things to pay for, like the electric bill, and keeping things clean, and keeping the maintenance up on the buildings. Just stuff like that."

Pastors who seemed to be operating within this general approach described the means to success as clearly communicating the needs of the church. One explained: "You'll see in our bulletin every week exactly what the collection is, and whether we are where we need [to be]. Are we at what we need to meet our budget? Or are we behind? And on our debt. We show our debt [in the bulletin]." These pastors tend to see the parishioners as fellow contributors to the long-term viability of the church facilities and organization. "I think one of the great things in churches," explained one, "is when there is a need, the roof got broken off or your furnace broke or something, and the parishioners are there with you." From this perspective, the pastor's key job is to articulate the practical need, to which the parishioners should respond accordingly. "Tell people what the need is," one recommended, "and why it's worthy of their support and then let them give." Thus, Pay-the-Bills churches talk about money when they have specific, clear, and present needs. As one pastor explained, "Otherwise, I kind of wait until I'm reminded, not intentionally, but that's just the way it works out; there's either a need, or we sense that, you know, this would be helpful, then I'll remember to put it in [the sermon]."

Many of the pastors who see financial giving within this Pay-the-Bills culture view their talking about money as an obligation. From their perspective, the church would collapse organizationally and physically without that conversation, and therefore they must address it. Their sermons about money are driven by the fact that the boiler needs replacing, or the heating bill has increased, or it is time to hire a new youth pastor. So pastors taking this approach often think of the discussion as a requirement, which they often see as a "struggle," "a challenge," or "drudgery." One pastor stated, "At its best it's about keeping our feet on the ground and keeping us real. Otherwise, we can be lost in ideals, and [talking about financial needs] helps connect them, I think. Other times, it's just a pain in the derriere, you know?" Some of the Pay-the-Bills pastors observed that, in their view, "most people don't want to give." Therefore, these pastors want to "downplay" and avoid talk about money. Many of these pastors said that they take a "low key" approach and try to "soft-peddle" and "soft sell" the issues. Some said they would "never do it in a homily." One pastor said that a church member once told him, as feedback, that they thought he was "almost apologizing" when asking for money. Another said he tells his congregation: "We've got the way to do what we need to do. That's the good news. The bad news is it's in your pocket."

Because of the perceived tension between the needs of the church and the desire of congregation members to hold on to their money, Pay-the-Bills pastors often described their appeals for giving to the congregation as highlighting the self-serving advantages of contributing. "So we are trying to let people know, you know," explained one, " 'It's really worth your while; look, it's beneficial to you.' " Another pastor said he would specifically make an appeal at the end of the year to let parishioners know that it was the "last opportunity if you want to get any tax write-offs," thereby identifying the needs of the church with the financial self-interest of the members. Another point these pastors commonly mentioned was that the financial needs of the church continue whether the members are present in church services or not. As one said, he frequently reminds his members during the summer months that, "if you're gonna be traveling, leave your money home."

The conceptual framework of the Pay-the-Bills culture seems to cause pastors to have a tendency to see talking about money and giving as "unspiritual," and thereby beyond the realm of their true vocational calling. The giving money issue is something they "have to deal with" rather than something they feel called to engage as intrinsically or spiritually important, saying things like, "That's not what I was ordained for." As one pastor stated, "Our training is much more about celebrating the sacraments, about preaching, about pastoral counseling. So it's funny how much of our time and consciousness [money] can take up." As a result, as we saw above, many of the pastors operating within this approach expressed discomfort in talking about money, ranging from being moderately uncomfortable to holding strong aversions to the topic. Recall, for instance, the pastor above who said he simply "hated" the issue of money. These pastors described numerous challenges which they generally detest, including conflicts with their congregations or boards, committees, and dioceses about the building, their salary, staff cuts, and other budgetary matters. They also described financially disgruntled church members, the "all they talk about here is money" accusation, and experiences of people leaving the church as a result of money issues and giving appeals. Referring to a particular fundraising strategy called a "flash call," in which he recorded a giving appeal that was sent out via phone to all the church members, one pastor explained the struggle with this approach by saying:

> One lady who had lost her husband in the previous year really took it hard. It's like, you know, "You didn't call me to see how I was doing when my husband died." You know, yes, I didn't know that. And she was very offended. And I called back personally and apologized and said, "You know I didn't like doing [the recorded calling campaign]

either, and I wouldn't do it again." That was probably the worst campaign for me. I don't like hurting people.

Other Pay-the-Bills pastors, however, did not describe such struggles because they simply did not get involved at such levels. They said that people's giving was between them and God. "Many people respond," said one, "Other people, they're not going to do it, and then that's between them and God. That's not my problem." Other pastors said, "What am I going to do about it?" and "I can't shoot 'em."

Despite apparent struggles and frequent uncomfortable-to-negative experiences, the Pay-the-Bills approach was not entirely unsuccessful for some churches. Many of these pastors described their positive experiences with successful fundraisers, times when congregation members gave significant one-time gifts, and experiences when people "came through" in times of real need. "When people see something is needed, they'll give," some happily observed. "We're in debt," another explained, "Improvements to the capital center required a lot of repair. But I'm not worried about it because people will come through like they always have." Such positive experiences were usually framed as the specific budgetary needs of the church being met. "Again, just to see that provision being met," pastors said. "We meet our goal," others declared, or it all "went well enough to make the necessary repairs." Additionally, success for some Pay-the-Bills pastors was defined as an ability to separate themselves from the financial matters of the church, allowing them to focus on the spiritual aspects of the church to which they feel called. "Somebody can run the books for you," one told us, "and keep an eye on all of that, [they] can give you the analysis of those books, of the finances, and handle the HR kinds of things. And if you've got somebody that can do that, then the priest can really focus on what we were trained and called to do." Success for these pastors also involved an ability to balance the need to talk about financial giving with the other, more important aspects of their vocation. "I have every confidence that God has not put us here to struggle with this one issue," explained one pastor, "without giving us also the joys of the other things that happen in the full life and work of the church." One gets to eat one's dessert in addition to having to eat one's vegetables, it would seem.

LIVE THE VISION

The Pay-the-Bills approach stands in stark contrast to another ideal type conceptual framework that was also clearly reflected in our conversations with other pastors. In distinction from the first perspective, some of the pastors with whom we spoke[3] held the view of money and giving as an essential part of faithful, daily Christian living that must be addressed confidently by the church in a natural, holistic manner. "It's a part of life," they said. Pastors in this "Live the Vision" approach saw talking about financial giving as merely another one of the many aspects of Christian life that they are called to address. As one explained: "And so, yes, if we talk about marriage, then we talk about marriage, then it comes up. If it's children, then we talk about children. If it's the tithe, then we talk about the tithe. Whatever comes up." "So we include money and financial resources as a part of that whole package," said another, who continued: "Obviously money is something we are dealing with all day long. We are constantly thinking about it when we buy things. It's a part of us, of our lives. Therefore, money has power. And it is something we really need to deal with, the money issue in life." One pastor put it this way:

> It's a big deal in people's lives. Jesus talked about it in various ways, recognizing it would be a big deal to people. And to avoid talking about it just because it makes people uncomfortable sends the message that, "Well, this part of your life really isn't spiritual. We can talk about prayer, and we can talk about good works, but money is off limits." And that's not helpful, spiritually or institutionally.

Rather than being driven by the necessities of the budget, this approach was primarily driven by a view of generous financial giving as a fundamental part of the Christian worship experience and life of faith. One pastor put it this way: "I think that giving money is a part of building the kingdom of God, and the role of us Christians is to help build his kingdom. And so, when you put that into perspective, what is our role? Then giving is just a piece of it. It's just a piece of the praise. It's a piece of the worship."

Giving was described by Live-the-Vision pastors as a means of truly honoring God, of allowing God to be present in all aspects of one's life, including one's use of money. "Giving money is allowing God to be God over all of your life," said one, "and not part of your life, but all of your life." Another agreed: "You look at your check book and see how you're using your money, and that's a reflection of your spiritual life." As opposed to talking to their congregation about giving primarily in order to pay the debts and bills of the church, these pastors described giving as a "conviction from the heart," saying things like, "Give till it feels good" and giving is a "joyous celebration" or an "adventure." Thus, financial giving was cast as an important opportunity to live fully, to grow, to become who one truly is. Money was framed not as a necessary resource for organizational upkeep but as a crucial means of shaping one's values, vision, purpose, identity, and life direction. Thus, the personal, spiritual, and moral significance of money and giving were radically expanded.

Pastors with the Live-the-Vision approach saw their role not as providing information about budgetary needs but as challenging and "cultivating" their parishioners' "faith journeys." One said, "We don't expect people to be able to give a lot right off the bat"; but he was fine with that, because he viewed his job as forming people in long-term change toward greater faithfulness to a larger, ongoing vision. Another explained that he is "helping people grow in their faith." "Stewardship is primarily a faith issue," said another, "not primarily a money issue. And so, it's a step forward in faith because that's just what it is." Another said that when people enter church, they "come in as baby Christians." But because their job is conceptualized as forming an ongoing growth process, these pastors were clear in saying things like, "We want to cultivate people's giving, so they can grow behind it, but we don't want to force them to give it either," and "I understand that sometimes it will take a while for people to get the concept." For these pastors, giving is the secondary outcome or result of a vibrant spiritual connection to God, and so the pastor needs to work to increase giving by helping people first grow in their faith. Talking about giving is one of the ways in which they try to move their parishioners toward a greater life conviction. Thus, preaching generosity may be more about building faith than securing money. "You need to let that be your conviction," stated one. "You know, I teach the word of God. You listen to it, you look at it, you decipher it yourself. And then you let God put that conviction in your heart." One pastor explained that a mentor told him early in his career:

> "Don't try to get $10 out of a person with $5 faith." He said, "You won't get it, and you'll just make them mad." He said, "Your goal as a pastor is to grow, to help people grow spiritually so they have $10 faith. Then they will give it. Not only will they give it, but they will give it joyfully. And they'll say, 'You know, I am a part of something really important, and I want to give my best to what God's doing in the world.'"

From the parishioner's perspective, this often looks and feels a lot like building relationships in community as more important than raising money. As one said, "I think [church leaders] need to really become involved and individualized with the members of their church, and allow that relationship to be, you know, the most important thing, rather than their adherence to or giving of money."

This Live-the-Vision viewpoint is driven primarily from a sense that the church, and the pastors as the leaders of the church, need to provide parishioners with a clear vision of truth and goodness and value. Rather than seeing money as outside of the Christian vision or mission, as removed from the calling of pastor, these pastors see financial giving as an integral aspect of the whole life approach by which pastors "invite people to participate in that larger vision." This "business unusual," as one said, is creating the church as a "conduit to help people." "Stewardship is not just what people give to the churches," said another, "but what the churches are doing in the community." Giving is also seen "as a call and a commitment, and as a covenant with God," not simply a taking care of the necessities of life. From this perspective, giving money "is about the mission, and one of the resources is the offering plate that helps fund the mission." The work of this type of church, said one pastor, is "to continue as best we can to struggle and plan, pray, and dream about where is God calling us in the future, and how can we lay the groundwork for the people who follow us." Instead of talking about money out of a sense of obligation because the building needs heat and the mortgage is due, talking about giving is conceptualized as providing people with an opportunity to be a part of something larger and more important than themselves. One pastor stated, "When you give people the chance to step up to the highest purpose under heaven, and you invite them to join you in the most important purpose of the universe, it's a moment of joy, and you bring meaning." In other words, Live-the-Vision culture tries to sacralize money for believers within Christian terms.[4]

Parishioners we interviewed who are members of Live-the-Vision led churches made comments such as, "Faith is not a switch that you turn on and you've got it. It's a life-long growth." Another said, "I think it's just part of growth. As you grow in your Christian faith, your philosophy changes, and I think that is part of the responsibility of a church, is to grow, and to reach people that you wouldn't normally reach." Yet another stated, "We're intended to be part of a larger body, and if we aren't then we don't flourish." And another said:

> Now they [in church] do talk about giving, and tithing, and how important that is. But they also talk about other issues that are pressing for many people, young and old, about budgets, trying to make ends meet, and trying to save for retirement. So the message is not just about "You should give to the church." It's about, "These are stressors in our life [that we need to deal with]."

Regarding the purpose of the church, another parishioner said, "The reason the church exists is not for us, but for mission. And the way in which mission takes place is by giving."

Thus, a key aspect of the Live-the-Vision approach is thinking about giving as a way to respond to a world with many needs. Maintaining a church building and congregation is only one part of a much larger vision for love, mission, engagement, and transformation. And what we found in most of our parishioner interviews is that those are the causes that best motivate Christian givers. We specifically asked parishioners what works and does not work in terms of motivating them to give money. They overwhelmingly named raising money to address community needs as a very effective motivator. They mostly said they like to support giving to "cultivate a sense of community and connectedness." To be sure, a handful of parishioners did say they would like their money to support causes internal to the church, saying "just basically the upkeep" and "The most that I like is the money to actually go towards the church, not towards any other events or whatever in the community." Another told us, "Well, because I know that it takes money to run a church, of course, churches have to pay for the light bill, and for electricity, and for gas, and everything like that." However, this was clearly the minority. The vast majority of the parishioners we spoke with said that they would most like their giving to support causes external to the church. They said they would most like to see their giving "help the poor," "combat racism," and "provide shelter to those less fortunate." Many of the parishioners mentioned that they like to support the missionary work of the church, and one parishioner explained, "I would want my giving to go into funds that would help bring [outside] people to Christianity." The majority of the parishioners stated that they are more willing to give money to the church when they know that at least some of the money will be used external to the church. As one said, "So that's sort of the mission focus. That's where I want to give my money to because that's something that I'm more passionate about. I know that the church needs money too, but those are the things that I'm more passionate about giving my money to." One parishioner called giving for causes internal to the church as "building castles for ourselves." And another explained, "I feel less comfortable when it feels like the money I give comes right back to benefit me most of all. I feel much more comfortable when I see my money, when the money that is given goes specifically to benefit others, needy people, things outside of the church." Because, as one parishioner explained, "people don't like to give to things like the building ... people just can't get excited about contributing to the general budget." A few of the parishioners also said that when the church is collecting money for its own purposes, such as in building campaigns, they appreciate when as part of that the church gives money to external causes as a proportion of the money collected. "When you can actually see that, yeah, you know, we are doing something outside ourselves," one said. "It's not just about us, here, in this nice comfortable building."

Live-the-Vision pastors described their own positive experiences with financial giving not in terms of big donations some of their parishioners had made but rather primarily about times when they observed their congregation members growing in faith and spiritual life. They talked about periods of "radical spiritual growth" and instances of their members finding joy in being a part of the vision. They told us happily of experiences with outcomes such as, "And then he found himself totally overjoyed about being a part of something bigger than himself." One pastor told this story of a new member to the church:

> She joined a church, and she said, "Pastor, I wanna tell you something." She say, "My lifestyle has been, I haven't been in church. And so, I've been saving up all my money, and saving enough to go back to work." And say, "I can't, I can't pay tithes. I just, I can't pay tithes." And I looked at her, and I said, "Let me tell you this," I say, "do you really want to pay tithes?" And she said, "Yes, I want to pay tithes, but there's no way." I say, "I tell you what," I say, "pay what you can and allow the Lord to give you the rest." I say, "But when he go and give it to you, then you need to pay it, you know." And she says, "Ok." Two weeks later, she came through the door, and she said, "Pastor, I need to tell you something. This is my check. This is my tithe check."

Another pastor recounted his experience by saying, "I've been pastoring for 14 years, and I can't really think of a bad experience that we've had as far as our financial affairs and telling people. And I really believe that the reason why is because we don't pressure people to do it. I think that's the key, that when a person does it, they do it because that's their conviction."

Note that it is not that the challenges for pastors around money described above no longer exist. These pastors still acknowledge money as a difficult topic that is "not all rosy." But as one Live-the-Vision pastor said, "That's not going to stop me from talking about it because I think there is a tremendous blessing in giving financially, and being a steward. So why would I not talk about it? Because that would be cheating people out of their lives, and what God is doing." Another stated: "It's your dream. It's your passion. It's the purpose for your being. Don't rob people of the privilege of supporting the work of God. Don't shrink back from asking. Don't shrink back from talking about finances." The pastors with this perspective were much more likely to describe talking about money with others as comfortable. One explained: "Talking about money is easy. If you deal with, here's the thing, if you deal with the issues that make or break life, they literally, if you get a stranglehold in your life on your relationships, your passions, and your money, you get those things doing [well], just, clicking, everything else just tends to fall in place." Such pastors said that they were comfortable talking about money because people like to be involved with the vision of the church. As one explained, "Especially if you gonna beautify something, build something bigger, build something that's going to touch the community, people want to be involved with stuff like that." Another said, "To see hungry people fed, and lost people found, and hurt people healed, and relationships restored, I mean to be a part of that is the greatest thing that I can imagine." Yet another noted simply, referencing a biblical proverb, "Without a vision, people perish." And because of this conceptualization as calling people toward a greater purpose through their giving, these pastors seemed more at ease with the difficulties surrounding money. One stated, "Even though it occasionally makes people squirm or can occasionally make people feel a little awkward, it's been important for us to remember that we are presenting people an opportunity, and not to be embarrassed or ashamed of doing that." And so it's about

> having the nerve to go ahead and speak about it, knowing that people will use it even as a defense, saying, "Oh, preachers, that's all they ever talk about is money." That's probably one of the biggest challenges. And to keep in mind that you're called upon to help these people, to help them with a lot of stuff, and among that is financial indebtedness that will ruin their marriage, and so go ahead and address it.

Pastors in this approach said it was very important not to avoid talking about money and viewed the challenges as part of the larger difficulty of helping people grow in their spiritual lives. "So we talk here about the most important issues of life, and how we handle the resources that God gives us is one of those topics," said one. "It's one of the most important topics of life, so I am perfectly comfortable. In fact, I feel honored to help people with this."

Again, these pastors talked about their approach specifically as not being driven by the need to pay the bills. One said, "I don't think it's ever been, 'We need you to dig deeper. We need you to give more. We depend on your money, you know, don't forget.'" Another stated:

> A lot of people tend to give to pay the bills, to pay for the overall budget, as kind of a fundraising thing. And churches are real tempted

to go that route and say, "Here's how much money we need, and we don't have this much, so we need more money." And you have to do that sometimes to raise the money, but it's not what the Christian faith teaches about why to give. I let people know that we need money. But when we do our pledge cards, the emphasis is on being thankful for what God has blessed you with.

This difference in approach seems to be fundamentally about what is driving the discussion. Rather than being need-based, giving is described as a means of showing gratitude. Another pastor explained:

So one thing we don't do here is we don't talk about "the church needs money." Our motivation is not that the church needs money. Our motivation is God blesses our lives. He gives us our whole life, and our giving is a response to that, and we invest ourselves in what God's doing. So we're partners with God in the world.

The same pastor continued: "Most churches are grumbling about how we don't have enough money to pay the bills [laughs]. Well that's not, that's not a dynamic, passionate community, if they're worrying about paying bills. They should be worrying about taking care of people's lives, and changing the world, rather than just getting the light bill paid." Parishioners in Live-the-Vision churches also described their experience there as in direct contrast to the Pay-the-Bills approach. One explained, "The homilies are never specifically geared to say, 'We don't have enough money. We want you to give more money.' They talk about a Christian spirit of being generous."

MIXED CULTURES

To be sure, pastoral approaches did not always clearly fall entirely into one ideal-type framework or another. Some pastors explained their perspectives on financial giving as driven entirely from a need to pay the bills. Others pastors always referred to giving as a natural component of their larger drive to grow the faith of their parishioners so they can live into God's vision. But there were also a number of pastors who made comments suggesting that they combine elements of both perspectives. Pastors talking and thinking about giving in their churches did not always represent a unified message. Most of these mixed-cultures pastors seemed to come from a Live-the-Vision mentality on a theological or conceptual level but also explained how they ended up talking to their parishioners primarily in terms of the Pay-the-Bills approach as a practical matter. They made comments such as:

Theologically what we're doing, what we try to do, is tie it into the whole concept of purpose. You know, why do we exist? And if we exist to accomplish a goal then the only way you operate is in this economy, in this system, it's financial. But because we have a spiritual goal, and because of the way everything functions we have to pay for things. We do need finances.

Another pastor stated, "It's a matter of convincing people the truth of it, and that takes a long time." But then when asked about the greatest challenge to Christian giving, he went on to say, "Paying the bills. Helping people understand the needs. You know, people need to understand the needs." And another pastor also expressed a mixed message by saying first that giving is "an offering to God, in response to God's grace, shown to us in Christ and in all of the great wonderful things that we have," but then going on to say, "We've gotta pay the budget. We've got to pay the light bill. We've got a $25,000 heating bill in this church every year and we make biblical reference to things, but then it gets down to the nitty-gritty." Later the same pastor also returned to the first theme: "When it's the ministry, or some kind of mission, people can get behind that, so we try to sell that rather than the budget." So, some of the pastors we interviewed appear to fall into a middle ground between the two ideal type frameworks or cultures. Most of these, however, seemed to mainly be struggling to make sense of how to implement their theological orientation of Live the Vision while addressing what they see as the practical Pay- the-Bills need to talk about the requirements of the budget. In theory they want to be the former, but in practice the logic of the latter often seems to take over.

It is worth noting, too, that certain principles seem to operate in both Pay-the-Bills and Live-the-Vision church cultures. One is the importance of churches being concrete about what money is being used for. Within the former approach, it is important to know not simply that the general fund is not in the red, but that the elevator was fixed or a youth minister was hired. Within the latter approach, it is important to hear that a certain number of children in Africa are being vaccinated or a specific missionary is working in a specific place, rather than simply that the church is supporting a lot of good ministries. Thus, many parishioners said they like the church to be specific about what the money is being requested for, that it works when the church says, "this is our goal, and this is what we have to have." As one explained, "People need to know what's being done with their money, and I think that most of us are reluctant to give blindly in the face of that." "If there was a specific reason that someone asked me," another told us, "like I said before,

I would be much more inclined to give than just to a general idea." Yet another said, "I appreciated the fact that they put it out there totally up front, that they weren't being vague about what the money could be used for." Many of the parishioners said that it is particularly effective when they receive some sort of report from the church or organization about how the money has been spent: "It's always great to get reports back from the charities that I give to, that tell me how much has been done with the money that we've all given." And another stated, "I think it would probably be most effective if they said, 'Here are things we want to do.' ... However small the goal is in mind, and people can see, 'This is where I'm helping,' instead of 'I give money so that the church can make more bulletins.'" Concrete needs work better than conceptual abstractions at generating generous giving.

Moreover, guilt trips and "pounding" the message do not seem to work well at any kind of church. Nearly all of the parishioners highlighted guilt trips as a method to avoid in talking about giving in churches, saying such comments as "the church should never guilt trip their parishioners into giving." Interestingly, none of the parishioners mentioned that they specifically had ever experienced guilt trips within their own church. They normally referred to other churches as laying on the guilt. As one parishioner said, "Some churches, not ours, but some churches go on the guilt trip. I think they should lay off that because that's not very effective." A closely related method that the parishioners rejected is what they called "pounding" parishioners on the head with talk of giving. These somewhat violent descriptions came in comments such as, "Don't hit 'em on the head with it every time" and "I don't believe that we have to pound, and pound, and pound on people to get it done." One way some felt that churches do this is by asking for multiple offerings. A parishioner, describing the method that her childhood church employed, explained this method as actually decreasing initial giving:

> We would always have two or three offerings through mass, so, you'd better not empty out your pockets during the first one, because there might be more. So it was just like a game you played with your money, and even as a kid, because it was embarrassing if a third collection came along, and you didn't have anything else. So it was always like holding back just in case, and that never seemed very faith-filled to me.

POSSIBLE IMPLICATIONS

Many parishioners we interviewed described their own approach to financial giving as informed by a Pay-the-Bills culture. "You know," said one, "to continue [as a church], the pastor needs a salary, we need light, we need heat, we need a building, we need all of that. So it's giving to provide for that." Another explained, "Somebody has to pay the heating bill, and sweep the floor after you leave. And you have an obligation, or a responsibility, if you can, to support that." However, many of these parishioners were people who also described themselves as having been raised to give faithfully from an early age. We suspect that they are likely already people who are committed to the broader purposes and importance of the church. If so, from their perspective it is obvious that they need to faithfully provide money to keep the doors open. But, we have reason to believe, there are also many churchgoing parishioners who are not already convinced that giving liberally to the church is a necessary or good practice, because they were not raised that way. We suspect that these are the people who react negatively to Pay-the-Bills messages, who say things like, "I think it turns people off if they constantly talk about, you know, the fund" and "I don't want to say that I am uncomfortable when you have to pay your bills. You have to. I am uncomfortable when it feels like all of the money is going there." As one parishioner explained, "The church needs this and the church needs that . . . and a lot of people don't see a responsibility toward the church. I think they are just tired of the church asking for money." For such parishioners, churches asking for money to pay the bills often created a disapproving response. They made comments such as, "I tend to have a negative reaction . . . I don't know, you know, if personally, I don't know if I respond [well] to that kind of plea" and "But sometimes on the paying the light bill stuff, that just doesn't have a lot of flare; and if I feel like I'm being scolded, you know, you kind of vote with your pocket book." Another parishioner described his worst experience of giving this way: "When you hear for five or six weeks straight that 'the church needs money, the church needs money, the church needs money, the church needs money,' and you're like, 'Fine, whatever, the church needs money, but you're not gonna get my money because you're not asking the right way.'"

In other words, we suspect that the Pay-the-Bills culture depends for success upon a constituency that has been raised in the church and long taught the importance of faithfully supporting the church financially. We also have good reason to believe that many churches cannot afford to assume that such a constituency will come in steady supply into the future. Long-term demographic and church attendance trends suggest that churches will simply not be continually repopulated with life-long churchgoers who are well educated in the faith. If so, it appears that a Pay-the-Bills approach will increasingly produce poor results. Less committed and less well-formed parishioners may need to be brought into their faith and the vision of the church much more solidly before they are willing to share their dollars generously. One parishioner, for instance, compared his previous experience in what sounded like a Pay-the-Bills church in this way: "Interestingly, when I felt that way, I didn't give on a regular basis, and looking back, I certainly didn't give anything near tithing level, or really anything substantial compared to what I could have." But now, in a Live-the-Vision type of church, he gives much more generously. Another parishioner said that the church needs to do some " 'inreach' before they can outreach." Yet another told us:

> I think there could be more people who, if you touch their hearts in any kind of way, they're more willing to open their wallets. If you keep hassling them and keep telling them, "You have to; it's your responsibility. You need to, and you need to come to the church, and this is how it's done," [those] people are going to close their wallets and put them back in their pockets and not share what they have.

Still another parishioner explained, "And as long as you're focused on yourself, the church does not thrive, just like that's true of the family. If you're focused on yourself, then regardless you cannot thrive. And so a church that is focused on a mission all of a sudden will find that they have more money." Others agreed: "I think you just need to feel like it's more of a purpose than paying somebody else's bill" and "I would say that we should be working on creating the kind of church where people want to give, not [simply] saying that they should give."

Conclusion

What have we learned? Getting beyond people's simple survey responses, we find in interviews that the issue of financial giving is one that seems to matter to American Christians, yet about which they are not clear and settled but rather uneasy if not uncomfortable. Many American Christians—at least the ones we interviewed—are less than fully contented with the practice and amount of their voluntary financial giving. But most also seem content to live with whatever underlying guilt, confusion, or uncertainty they feel about it. Meanwhile, it appears that many American Christian pastors struggle with varying degrees of discomfort and frustration over the issue of giving in their churches. For many pastors the whole topic seems distracting, annoying, and maybe frustrating. For few of the people we interviewed does financial giving seem to be a clear, smooth, confident, happy matter. Rather, our interviews suggest, the entire issue seems to be one that could use some airing, clarity, and informing direction.

Our interviews also lend some weight to some of the hypotheses we considered in the previous chapter trying to explain the lack of American Christian financial giving. For instance, while many we interviewed know that they should give more money than they do, many also seemed to us to be less than entirely clear about the high expectations in the teachings of their faith traditions about tithing, generosity, and stewardship as essential aspects of Christian spiritual life (hypothesis 4). At least some appeared able to perhaps rationalize a lack of giving by a sense of confusion and uncertainty around expectations. We also found a lot of evidence in our interviews that these unclear expectations are partly the result of pastors as leaders somewhat fudging the topic because they feel uneasy themselves about money and about asking their parishioners to give it generously. Very many of the pastors we interviewed say that they were poorly trained to deal with church money issues, are under pressure to not appear to their parishioners as money-hungry, and feel isolated from their colleagues when it comes to squarely addressing money issues in their churches. Some also believe the giving of money is simply not a spiritual matter and so not an essential part of their vocation. A few are even uneasy about their own personal faithfulness in handling money with integrity and generosity and seem therefore less than fully confident in addressing the matter with their churches. For these and other reasons, it seems to us that pastoral leadership in many churches may be lowering expectations around financial giving in their churches (hypothesis 6). We also sensed in some of those we interviewed some distrust of the causes and organizations to whom they do or might give money—especially those not directly involving their own congregations, which they generally seem more to trust (hypothesis 5). For some this may serve as a mere post hoc rationalization for money that they would not give anyway. But our sense is that a significant increase in the public transparency, accountability, and institutionalized credibility of the many religious and charitable causes and organizations to which American Christians might consider giving money would have the real effect over time of considerably increasing the amount of money they give. Our interviews also seem to lend support for the hypothesis that the radical privatization of the matter of voluntary financial giving creates an atmosphere among American Christians of isolation and autonomy that leads to lack of communication and accountability (hypothesis 8). We suspect that if it were somehow possible for American Christians to increase their communication in an open and healthy way with one another about their beliefs, feelings, intentions, confusions, and struggles around the issue of financial giving, that would create an atmosphere conducive to greater generosity. Furthermore, our interviews also seemed to validate the idea that many American Christians do not give money more generously because of the non-routine nature of their giving practices, which are often only occasional and situational rather than consistent, structured, and routine (hypothesis 9). Many who we interviewed are deliberate and planning in their financial giving, but many are not. For the latter, the unstructured giving practices seemed to make it all too easy to get by with giving a little bit here, a little bit there, the sum total of which may not add to a lot.

What about the other hypotheses? We did not find much support in our interviews for hypotheses 3 (unperceived needs) or 7 (collective-action shirking). Very few of the Christians with whom we talked conveyed any lack of awareness of legitimate needs in the world that some of their money might help to meet. Most people appear to know that the world is full of needs and money can help to address them. Likewise, few of the Christians we interviewed seemed to us that they were not giving as generously as they might because they were worried that other Christians were also not giving generously. If anything, the strong individualism of nearly all American Christians prevents them from linking their own financial giving behaviors to anything anyone else is doing. Most of those we interviewed appear to believe sincerely that they are only responsible for their own actions and that they are going to make their own choices regardless of what anyone else does. Our sense, therefore, is that the riddle of ungenerous American Christian giving is not going to be much explained as a collective action problem solved primarily by requiring coordination across givers.

That leaves us with the first two hypotheses yet to consider: objective and subjective resource constraints. What do our interviews suggest about those? The key to evaluating the issues of resource constraints, we believe, is understanding the mass consumerism that many Christians tell us dominates their daily lives. We have every reason to believe that most American Christians *objectively* do have enough income to give generously to others and still have enough left over to lead perfectly healthy, happy lives. If they were committed to generous financial giving and prepared to plan their lifestyles and budgets from adult life's "starting line," they could increase their giving dramatically. But the mass consumer economy and culture and the advertising industry that helps to drive them powerfully shape many Christians' perceptions and decisions in ways that end up constraining their willingness and ability to give money generously. For one thing, consumerism focuses people's attention not on the blessings and abundance in their lives but on all that they do *not* possess, on the myriad products and experiences that are just out of reach. In the process, regardless of their absolute abundance, many or most Christians come to feel a relative deprivation, a sense that they do not have all that they could, want, or should possess and experience. The system and culture are set up, in other words, to create permanent discontent. And so when people of all different social classes, including the quite wealthy, consider giving their money to religious and charitable causes, they actually find themselves—as absurd as it may seem—feeling pretty poor. It feels to them that they simply do not have the money to give. This perception is reinforced by the fact that many of the most important consumer purchases that households make are large and long term. For many families with money, a mere two buying decisions—the purchases of home and cars—are enough to lock household budgets into tight budgetary situations for decades. The mortgage and automobile loan payments alone, which are often maxed to the upper limit of affordability, are enough to make people feel that they can barely pay their bills. Add to those the countless smaller purchases of life—for recreation, cable television, eating out, vacations, and so on—and little money is left over to give away for religious and charitable purposes.

Thus, the subjective resource constraint hypothesis significantly helps to explain the lack of generous financial giving among many if not most American Christians. After all the ways that consumerism shapes their lives, people genuinely think that they do not have much money to give away. And, when taking into account the budgetary consequences of the major financial commitments made by many Christians in the prior purchasing of homes, automobiles, and other large consumer items, many in fact do not have a lot of money left in their bank accounts to give away after their bills have been paid. It is not that they do not actually have the annual incomes to give generously. It is rather that they have already made and continue to make long-term household and consumer purchase decisions that commit most of their money to be spent in ways that leave little left over to give away.

And so here we return to the themes of planning, deliberation, prioritizing, and routine. American Christians objectively do have money enough to be very generous financial givers. If they were to prioritize giving and structure their financial dealings and decisions in ways that enabled generosity, we believe they could in fact give away the kind of money that we estimated is available in chapter 1. But in very many cases, American Christians allow the influences of the mass consumer economy and culture to structure their priorities and decisions for them, locking them into long-term financial commitments and patterns that consume most of their resources. So, not much money is left over to give. Thus, a number of the church members we spoke with said their approach to giving is "I give what I can" or said they give "when the opportunity presents itself" or "if I have it left over." One stated, "If I don't have the money, I don't give it. I don't know that I really have a lot of rhyme or reason to it per se." Another told us, "As things come up, you know, [I give] whatever I feel like I can afford on my own, so that I feel good." Yet another stated, "I don't pay that much attention to it. I don't have a budget, so I don't pay attention or watch it that closely." Other parishioners similarly explained that "I don't really have much of a system" and "It really is looked at how much I can afford." Some described their approach as "someday" giving, viewing it as something they see themselves doing in the future when they are more financially able. "I hope to become like that with time," said one, and "if I won the lottery," offered another. More realistically, one parishioner observed of this mentality, "The richest men in the world have said, 'Just one dollar more would be enough.' But they never think one more dollar is enough." So the end result is the kind of "comfortable guilt" we noted earlier in this chapter: very many American Christians are aware that they should and theoretically would like to give more money for good purposes but, all things considered, they are not motivated enough to make the kind of changes it would take over time to actually do so. And so the patterns of American Christian giving end up looking like those that we observed in chapter 2.

Another way to state what we think we learned from our interviews with Christian pastors and parishioners is this: that despite many good intentions, when it comes to generous financial giving, "slippage happens." American Christians may start with an ideal of financial generosity and good works. But between those good intentions and their actual behaviors, a host of cultural, societal, organizational, and social-psychological factors cause a lot of slippage away from the ideal. Many Christians tell themselves, and in many cases we believe honestly so, that they are uncertain or confused about the dollar amounts of and best targets of financial giving. Then, as they consider the issue of giving money, different theological terms seem to mean many different things to different believers and are used inconsistently across churches. Furthermore, few Christians find that the issue is one about which they can talk comfortably with anyone else, so they are typically left to work the issue out in the privacy of their own heads. Then, many uncomfortable pastors all too often seem to avoid or soft-peddle the call of most of their own traditions for Christians to give generously of the money with which God has blessed them and made them stewards. And many pastors who do forthrightly encourage giving tend to frame the motivation and meaning in terms of the practical need to pay the church's payroll and electric bills—which we suspect inspires only the most well-socialized and committed, life-long church-goers. In many cases, the use of money seems disconnected from any strong vision of a thriving spiritual, human life. On top of that, at least some Christians appear to worry about the trustworthiness of the organizations to which they might give money, which connects in their minds to the problem of good stewardship. Moreover, very many do not set up a routinized system for giving, but rather give in situational, spontaneous ways. Then, up against all of these attenuating dynamics drive the powerful forces of mass consumerism, which by contrast are highly effective at firmly structuring people's long-term financial obligations through mortgages, car loan payments, and credit card purchases. In the end, for many, the seductions of mass-consumer advertising and the glut of products in stores prove more compelling than most sermons about blessings and sacrifice and church budgets. Consequently, before most American Christians of whatever income brackets know it, they are feeling weighted down with monthly bills, behind in the new consumer products market, and financially strapped. By that point, a lot of slippage has happened. At this point, many people feel justified in putting only modest amounts of money into the church offering plates, if any at all—even as they also know somewhere in the backs of their minds that they ought to give and wish they could be giving more.

To close this chapter, we must reiterate that we cannot assume that the Christian pastors and parishioners we interviewed are representative of all of their Christian counterparts around the country and in their denominations. Our interview respondents comprise a convenience-based, quota sample that we cannot with confidence generalize to American Christianity as a whole. If anything, we suspect that we oversampled among all Christians the more committed and financially generous ones, meaning that a truly representative sample would have revealed even more confusion, hesitation, discomfort, and lack of financial generosity. Yet if those we interviewed are even only roughly representative of American Christians more broadly, and if our interpretations of our interviews are mostly valid, then it seems that the answer to the riddle of ungenerous American Christian giving that we have posed in this book is going to be complicated and difficult. If so, then any possible effective response to that problem is likely also going to have to be multidimensional and challenging to implement. More sermons and better stewardship programs alone, it appears, will not do. From our perspective, more comprehensive responses will be needed that adequately account for the texture of congregational cultures, organizational processes, accountability and transparency, stronger leadership, and, ultimately, a coming to terms with the power of the American mass consumer economy and culture as they impinge on practical Christian faithfulness.

CHAPTER 5	A Mental Experiment in Raised Expectations

IN CHAPTER 3, we referred several times to the Tithing Experiment
Survey we conducted in the summer of 2006. In this chapter, we examine
the findings of that survey in greater depth to try to better understand the
meanings and motives behind the financial giving of U.S. Christians. Our
goal is still to help explain the riddle of ungenerous Christian giving in
the United States. Instead of investigating empirical evidence about actual
giving, however, we focus here rather on how American Christians think
about what might be and how they would respond. This chapter examines
the results of a focused mental experiment in which we asked a nationally
representative sample of U.S. Christians to ponder their response to the idea
of their churches raising expectations on the financial giving of Christians.
Our idea in doing this is that by having ordinary Christians all over the
United States run this mental experiment in their heads, we may be provided yet another angle on understanding how Christians think and feel
about the issue of religious and charitable financial giving. Note that we are
not necessarily advocating the actions proposed in the mental experiments
described below, but we do think they are worth for theoretical reasons having people consider and examining people's answers. We think the results
are interesting.

In 2006, we fielded a module of survey questions about religious giving
on a national survey of adult Christian Americans, the methodology for which
is described in the endnotes of the introduction. Our module was linked to
demographic information from other survey questions already asked of the

sample, which aid in the analysis below. Non-Christians were not included in this sample. The central question in our survey module was this:

> Suppose your church made a new requirement for church membership: members must give 10 percent of their after-tax income to the church or other good causes. Those giving less than 10 percent could still attend church, but would not be considered members in good standing. How would you personally most likely respond to this requirement?
> 1. I would start giving 10 percent of my income
> 2. I would attend church, but give less than 10 percent of my income
> 3. I would move to a different church that does not ask its members to give 10 percent
> 4. I would drop out of church life altogether
> 5. I already give 10 percent of my income

We intentionally wrote this question with the strong language of "requirement," "must," and "not considered members" in order to raise the stakes high enough to see where people would stand on a demanding proposition. We also specifically wrote it to include "other good causes" so that givers could choose to donate to a wide range of causes beyond their own churches. And we intentionally specified "after-tax income" to make all respondents clear on the magnitude of the requirement and to make it less costly than 10 percent of gross income.

Table 5.1 reports the percent of church-attending Christian respondents of various types who answered each of the answer options. We limited this analysis to only those American Christians who attend church at least some, since the question would not make sense to Christians who never attend. In table 5.1 we see, in the top row of numbers, that 16 percent of our sample claim to already give 10 percent of their after-tax income. Based on the findings of survey data reported in chapter 2, we have reason to think that some social desirability bias is operating here, that some proportion of this 16 percent is being overly generous with their estimation of their own giving. It may be that all of the answers reported in this chapter reflect a somewhat positive bias, a possibility worth keeping in mind. In any case, of the church-attending Christians we sampled, only 7 percent said that they do not give 10 percent of their after-tax income now but would begin to if their churches made doing so a new requirement for membership. Thus, only a very small minority of church-attending American Christians would respond positively to such a new requirement. The vast majority, it turns out, would not cooperate. Twenty-five percent of respondents said that they would continue attending

TABLE 5.1 Answers to the survey question about raised tithing expecations* (in %).

Religion variables	I already give 10% of my income	I would start giving 10% of my income	I would attend church, but give less than 10% of my income	I would move to a different church that does not ask its members to give 10%	I would drop out of church life altogether
Attending Christians	16	7	25	35	16
Protestant	23	9	17	38	13
Baptist	26	15	12	38	9
Catholic	7	5	40	26	22
Other Christian	16	5	16	46	17
Church attendance					
Regular	25	9	28	31	7
Irregular	6	5	22	39	27
% income churches expect to give					
0	4	10	13	38	35
1–4	1	8	41	28	22
5–9	5	3	47	32	12
10+	25	7	20	36	11

*The exact questions is: "Suppose your church made a new requirement for church membership: Members must give 10 percent of their after-tax income to the church or other good causes. Those giving less than 10 percent could still attend church, but would not be considered members in good standing. How would you personally most likely respond to this requirement?"

Source: Tithing Experiment Survey, 2006.

church but give less than 10 percent of their income. Thirty-five percent reported that they would move to a different church that did not ask for 10 percent. And 16 percent of the sample—more than twice the size of the 7 percent who would start giving 10 percent—said they would drop out of church life altogether. Right off the bat, then, we observe a strong resistance by a majority of church-attending Christians in the United States to the idea of being required to tithe.

Table 5.1 also reports on variations in these answers by types of Christians, levels of church attendance, and respondents' perceived existing expectations of financial giving on their church congregations. Our sample of respondents is broken into Protestants—with Baptists as a subcategory of Protestant—Catholic, and Other Christian who do not self-identify as either Protestant or Catholic. We see that Protestants, particularly Baptists, are the most likely to claim that they currently tithe. Baptists are also the most likely to say they would begin tithing if required by their churches. Catholics are by far the most likely to say they would continue to attend but not give 10 percent and to say that they would simply drop out of church life altogether. Furthermore, as expected, regular church attendees (those who attend church once a month or more often) are more likely to say they currently tithe or that they would begin tithing if required by their churches. Nonregular attendees (those who attend church but less than once a month) are more likely to say they would find a new church that did not require tithing or drop out of church life altogether. Finally, we observe a correlation—already mentioned in the prior chapter—between readiness to tithe and belonging to a church with higher perceived expectations of financial giving. Tithers are much more likely to belong to churches that teach tithing than those that do not. At the far side, currently church-attending Christians who attend churches that they perceive as having low expectations for financial giving are also the most likely to say they would drop out of church life altogether if their churches started requiring tithing as a condition of membership. This may be because churches with higher expectations form their members to be more generous. It may be because more generous Christians select themselves into congregations that have higher expectations. It may be some other reason. But the association between church expectations of giving and parishioner readiness to give is evident.

For those church-attending Christian survey respondents who reported that they do not now already tithe and that they would not begin tithing if their churches required it, we then asked the following question to try to draw out their thoughts, feelings, and motives for resisting tithing:

What would be your *most important reasons* for *not* giving 10 percent of your after-tax income if your church required it for membership in good standing? (click 1–2 of your most important reasons):

1. I could not afford to give 10 percent of my income
2. I have the money but do not want to give that much money away
3. As a matter of principle, the church has no right to ask its members to give specific amounts of money
4. I doubt that other church members would give 10 percent of their income and I would not want to give 10 percent of mine unless I knew everyone was doing so
5. I do not trust those to whom I would give money to spend it wisely; there would be too much waste and abuse of donations
6. Government taxes and spending are already taking care of most of the needs that my giving would go toward
7. There are not enough legitimate needs in the world to require so many people giving 10 percent of their income in order to meet
8. I would rather spend that money myself on things that I enjoy
9. I don't know, no reason in particular
10. Other (specify):

Respondents could choose up to two answers as their most important. The nine answer categories presented were randomized by computer program, so that no bias would be introduced by answer ordering. Table 5.2 reports these respondents' answers to the question above, some of which we alluded to in the previous chapter. We cannot know if these are respondents' "real" reasons and "true" motivations, but still they indicate the categories of thought and feeling that respondents most likely resort to for explaining their unwillingness to give money more generously.

In table 5.2 we see that the vast majority of respondents unwilling to tithe cluster into only a few of the answer categories. The most popular answer, chosen by 59 percent, was that "As a matter of principle, the church has no right to ask its members to give specific amounts of money." The second most popular answer, at 52 percent, was, "I could not afford to give 10 percent of my income." Nine percent said that "I do not trust those to whom I would give money to spend it wisely; there would be too much waste and abuse of donations." Beyond those three answers, only a few percent chose any of the other answer categories; and 7 percent simply said that they did not know why they would not give 10 percent, that there is no particular reason. Only 3 percent (combined), for instance, said bluntly that "I have the money but

TABLE 5.2 Reasons for not being willing to give a required 10% of income by religion variables, church attending Christians (%).

	As a principle, the church has no right to ask members to give specific amounts of money	Could not afford to give 10%	Do not trust those to whom I would give to spend it wisely, too much waste and abuse	Government taxes and spending already taking care of most of the needs	Have the money but do not want to give that much away; would rather spend the money on things that I enjoy	Not enough legitimate needs in the world to require so many giving	Doubt other church members would give 10% of their income, would not want to give 10% unless knew everyone was giving	Don't know, no particular reason
Attending Christians	59	52	9	4	3	2	1	7
Protestant	57	55	7	3	2	1	~	8
Baptist	53	58	8	3	~	2	~	11
Catholic	59	54	10	6	5	4	1	8
Other Christian	66	37	10	3	2	~	1	3

Church attendance								
Regular	56	51	8	4	2	3	~	10
Irregular	62	53	10	4	4	1	1	5
% income churches expect to give								
0	52	41	15	3	5	5	~	7
1–4	60	53	9	9	6	2	2	9
5–9	59	54	9	9	7	1	~	5
10+	60	55	7	2	1	2	1	8

Source: Tithing Experiment Survey, 2006.

do not want to give that much away" or that "I would rather spend that money myself on things that I enjoy." In short, nearly all church-attending American Christians who resist the idea of their churches making tithing a condition of membership appear to do so on the grounds that (1) they cannot afford to give that much and (2) in principle the church has no right to ask members in good standing to tithe. Smaller numbers, nearly one in ten, seem to resist the idea out of distrust of the potential recipients of the money.

Table 5.2 also breaks out these answers by types of Christian, levels of church attendance, and respondents' perceived existing expectations of financial giving on their church congregations. There we see no major variations between Protestants and Catholics, other than Catholics are perhaps a bit more likely to express distrust as a reason for not tithing. We also observe no major differences between those who attend church regularly versus irregularly. Finally, few significant differences revealing meaningful patterns emerge across variations in perceptions of church expectations of giving. Below, however, in table 5.6, we will examine results from multivariate regression analyses that attempt to isolate the most important independent factors associated with different reasons for resisting a potential church requirement to tithe.

In our Tithing Experiment Survey module, we also asked all respondents a question about how much they would support or oppose the hypothetical 10 percent giving requirement. Here was our exact question wording:

> How much for or against the giving requirement (10 percent of after-tax income for church membership in good standing) would you personally be if it were proposed by your church leaders? Would you:
> 1. Strongly support it
> 2. Somewhat support it
> 3. Feel neutral
> 4. Somewhat oppose it
> 5. Strongly oppose it

Table 5.3 presents the results of respondents' answers to this question. There we see, in the top row, that the vast majority, two-thirds, of church-attending U.S. Christians would oppose a tithing requirement for church membership in good standing. Fourty-four percent would strongly oppose and 22 percent would somewhat oppose such a requirement. Another 20 percent of church-attending respondents report feeling neutral about the requirement. Only 9 percent say they would strongly support and 5 percent say they would somewhat support a tithing requirement. In the lower part of table 5.3, we see support for a tithing requirement somewhat associated with being Protestant compared to Catholic, with regular church attendance, and with belonging

TABLE 5.3 How much for or against the giving requirement—of 10% of after-tax income for church membership in good standing—respondents would personally be if it were proposed by their church leaders, by religion variables, church-attending Christians (%).

Religion variables	Strongly support	Somewhat support	Neutral	Somewhat oppose	Strongly oppose
Attending Christians	9	5	20	22	44
Protestant	11	5	21	23	40
Baptist	13	6	28	21	32
Catholic	5	4	18	22	51
Other Christian	13	2	24	19	42
Church attendance					
Regular	13	5	23	23	36
Irregular	5	4	17	21	54
% income churches expect to give					
0	3	2	22	9	64
1–4	7	5	25	17	46
5–9	5	4	20	31	40
10+	12	5	19	24	40

Source: Tithing Experiment Survey, 2006.

to churches perceived as holding higher expectations for financial giving. But those differences are small.

We know, however, that American Christians' answers to the three questions above may be influenced by factors other than types of Christian, levels of church attendance, and respondents' perceived existing expectations of financial giving on their church congregations. To further explore the social locations of people with different responses to the prospect of a church tithing requirement for membership in good standing, we examined differences in answers to our survey questions by other demographic variables—specifically by income, education, gender, marital status, race, urban residence, regional location, and age. First we analyzed these factors in bivariate cross-tabulations (tables 5.4, 5.5, and 5.6). Then we used multiple regression statistical techniques to isolate the most important of these variables that

TABLE 5.4 Answers to the survey question on raised tithing expecatation* by demographic variables (in %).

Demographics	I already give 10% of my income	I would start giving 10% of my income	I would attend church, but give less than 10% of my income	I would move to a different church that does not ask its members to give 10%	I would drop out of church life altogether
Attending Christians	16	7	25	35	16
Income					
<$25,000	18	12	23	33	14
$25,000–$49,000	16	9	24	36	15
$50,000–$84,999	17	3	29	32	19
$85,000+	13	1	25	42	19
Education					
H.S. or less	17	8	27	29	18
Some college	17	8	22	42	11
B.A. degree or more	15	5	24	36	19
Female	14	8	27	38	13
Married	17	4	25	36	17
Race					
White	15	4	27	38	16
Black	27	28	14	23	8
Hispanic	16	3	30	23	28
Urban	16	7	25	35	17

Region					
Northeast	11	4	38	25	22
South	24	10	17	37	11
Midwest	14	6	31	34	14
West	10	8	20	41	22
Age					
18–24	18	11	15	42	13
25–44	15	6	19	41	20
45–64	16	8	29	18	16
65–97	18	6	34	31	11

*"Suppose your church made a new requirement for church membership: Members must give 10 percent of their after-tax income to the church or other good causes. Those giving less than 10 percent could still attend church, but would not be considered members in good standing. How would you personally most likely respond to this requirement?"

Source: Tithing Experiment Survey, 2006.

independently associate with different answers to our financial giving questions (tables 5.7 and 5.8).

In table 5.4, we see first that earning a higher income is *negatively* associated with already tithing and being willing to start tithing if churches required it. Churchgoing American Christians who earn higher incomes, in other words, appear less likely and willing than lower income earners to give 10 percent of their after-tax income. Race effects also stand out in table 5.4. Black Christians appear much more willing to tithe than white and Hispanic Christians. The same seems true for church-attending Christians who live in the South compared to other regions. Education, gender, marital status, urban residence, and age, however, do not appear correlated with differences in readiness financially to give more generously.

What about general supportiveness of or opposition to our hypothetical church policy requiring tithing as a condition of membership in good standing? Table 5.5 explores differences in the same demographic factors examined in table 5.4 on the question of support for or opposition to the proposed tithing requirement. There we see, again, a noticeable correlation between higher income and greater opposition to the hypothetical tithing policy. Earning greater income makes churchgoing Christians not more but less supportive of churches requiring members to give away 10 percent of their income. Education level also appears correlated with support for required tithing—the least educated seem the most supportive and the highest educated the least supportive. Again, black Christians seem more supportive of the tithing policy than Christians of other races. None of the other factors, however, stand out as revealing prominent differences in support for the hypothetical 10 percent giving requirement.

It is not always easy in a format such as tables 5.4 and 5.5 to sort through differences in these many variables individually, or to guess their effects on giving outcomes independent of each other. To help do this, therefore, we conducted multiple regression statistical analyses of the association of our demographic and religion variables on the giving variables. Multiple regression is a statistical technique that enables us to identify the specific, independent strength of association of each individual variable with the outcome variable by removing the possible overlapping influence of other variables. The significance of each variable is thus examined "net of" or "controlling for" the possible influence of all of the other variables. This enables us to isolate which of all the examined variables stand out as most important in strongly correlating with the financial giving outcome variables.

Table 5.6 shows the results of multiple regression analyses for churchgoing Christians of the relationship between all of the variables we have examined so

TABLE 5.5 How much for or against the giving requirement—of 10% of after-tax income for church membership in good standing—respondents would personally be if it were proposed by their church leaders, by demographic variables, church-attending Christians (%).

Demographics	Strongly support	Somewhat support	Neutral	Somewhat oppose	Strongly oppose
Attending Christians	9	5	20	22	44
Income					
<$25,000	14	7	22	19	38
$25,000–$49,000	9	4	26	21	40
$50,000–$84,999	4	4	18	25	48
$85,000+	5	2	7	26	59
Education					
H.S. or less	10	3	26	24	37
Some college	8	8	18	22	45
B.A. degree or more	9	4	13	19	56
Female	8	5	23	23	42
Married	7	4	20	19	50
Race					
White	6	4	18	24	47
Black	28	3	26	23	20
Hispanic	11	8	19	12	50
Urban	9	4	20	22	44

(continued)

TABLE 5.5 (Continued)

Demographics	Strongly support	Somewhat support	Neutral	Somewhat oppose	Strongly oppose
Region					
Northeast	9	6	18	24	44
South	11	6	22	22	39
Midwest	9	1	20	23	47
West	5	4	19	19	53
Age					
19–29	8	1	25	34	32
30–45	6	5	20	18	51
46–64	13	6	13	21	47
65–97	8	4	29	22	37

Source: Tithing Experiment Survey, 2006.

far and the financial giving questions analyzed in tables 5.4 and 5.5. Rather than providing the actual numeric statistical coefficients and results of the probability significance tests, here we simply state whether the variable exerts a significant positive or negative association with the dependent variables. Only significant variables are stated in table 5.6.

We see there that, when controlling for all of the variables together, a few of the factors stand out as statistically significant in a multivariate analysis. Racial differences, for example, clearly matter. Controlling statistically for all of the other variables, white, Hispanic, and other race Christians are significantly less likely than black Christians (the reference or comparison category) to support and cooperate with a tithing requirement for church membership. Income also stands out as a significant factor. Again, net of the other variables, higher income earning churchgoing Christians would be less likely to support and cooperate with a tithing requirement for church membership. That income effect is independent of household size—meaning, in most cases, having more children to support—which is itself significantly associated with a greater readiness to tithe. Table 5.6 also reveals spotty differences between residence in the South (the reference category) and in the Northeast and West. Net of the other factors, Pentecostal Christians also appear more positive than Catholics (the reference category) toward the hypothetical tithing requirement. More frequent church attendance is positively associated with readiness to tithe, as is belonging to a church perceived to hold higher expectations of giving. Gender, age, marital status, education, urban residence, and Internet access are not statistically significantly associated as independent variables with readiness to tithe. We see, then, that certain key variables—particularly income, race, and church attendance—consistently associate with readiness to give 10 percent of income to church and other good causes.

Finally, we examine more closely demographic associations with the reasons churchgoing Christians report, who do not and would not give 10 percent of their incomes if required by their churches, for their unwillingness or inability to do so. In table 5.7, we see that higher income earning Christians—while rightly less likely to say they could not afford to give away 10 percent of their income—are more likely than lower earners to say both that the church has no right to ask for tithes and that they do not trust those to whom they would give their money. We also see that black Christians who do and would not tithe are observably more likely than Christians of other races to say that churches in principle have no right to ask members to tithe. They are also slightly more likely to say that they could not afford to tithe. Hispanic Christians, by comparison, are more likely to say that they would

TABLE 5.6 Summary of OLS, ordered logit, and logistic regression results for religious giving variables, church-attending Christians.

	Perceived income % churches expect members to give	Would be supportive of a church 10% giving requirement	Response to 10% giving requirement			
			Would start giving 10% of income	Would attend but give less than 10%	Would move to church not asking 10%	Would drop out of church life altogether
Female						Negative
Older age					Negative	
Married					Positive	
White	Negative	Negative	Negative	Positive	Positive	
Hispanic		Negative	Negative	Positive	Positive	
Other race			Negative		Positive	
Black (ref)						
Education						
Higher income		Negative	Negative	Positive		
HH size			Positive	Negative		
Urban						
Northeast	Negative			Positive		Positive
Midwest	Negative					
West		Negative				
South (ref)						

	(1)	(2)	(3)	(4)	(5)
On Internet	**Positive**			Negative	
Catholic (ref)					
Baptist					
Pentecostal	Positive	Positive	Negative	Positive	
Other Protestant			Negative		
Other Christian	Positive		Negative	Positive	
Higher church attendance	**Positive**	Positive			**Negative**
Church expects higher giving	n.a.				Negative

Note: Bold means significant at the p<.05, not bold means significance at the p<.10.

Source: Tithing Experiment Survey, 2006.

TABLE 5.7 Reasons for not being willing to give a required 10% of income by demographic variables, church-attending Christians (%).

Demographics	As a principle, the church has no right to ask members to give specific amounts of money	Could not afford to give 10%	Do not trust those to whom I would give to spend it wisely, too much waste and abuse	Government taxes and spending already taking care of most of the needs	Have the money but do not want to give that much away; plus, would rather spend the money on things that I enjoy	Not enough legitimate needs in the world to require so many giving	Doubt other church members would give 10% of their income, would not want to give 10% unless knew everyone was giving	Don't know, no particular reason
Attending Christians	59	52	9	4	3	2	1	7
Income								
<$25,000	50	56	7	5	2	1	~	13
$25,000–$49,000	60	54	9	3	1	3	1	4
$50,000–$89,999	60	56	7	4	4	4	1	7
$90,000+	70	35	14	4	6	1	1	5
Education								
H.S. or less	53	57	7	3	2	3	1	10
Some college	61	54	8	5	2	1	1	6

B.A. degree or more	66	42	12	5	5	1	1	5
Female	61	55	6	4	2	3	1	5
Married	60	51	9	4	3	3	1	6
Race								
White	59	53	7	5	3	1	1	7
Black	72	59	8	1	~	~	~	5
Hispanic	55	50	17	3	2	6	~	9
Urban	58	52	9	4	3	3	1	7
Region								
Northeast	58	65	6	4	3	1	1	6
South	63	43	9	3	2	1	~	8
Midwest	57	55	7	6	3	4	1	6
West	55	50	12	5	4	3	1	9
Age								
19–29	60	46	10	5	3	~	~	13
30–45	58	52	8	4	2	3	~	5
46–64	62	55	10	5	4	1	1	6
65–97	55	51	8	4	2	3	2	10

Source: Tithing Experiment Survey, 2006.

TABLE 5.8 Summary of logistic regression results for religious giving variables, church-attending Christians.

	Reasons cited for not giving 10%				
	As a principle, the church has no right to ask members to give specific amounts of money	Could not afford to give 10%	Do not trust recipients to spend wisely, waste and abuse	Have money but do not want to give 10%; would rather spend money on things that I enjoy	Government taxes and spending taking care of most needs
Female			Disagree		Disagree
Older age					
Married					
White	**Disagree**				
Hispanic	Disagree				
Other race	**Disagree**				
Black (ref)					
Education					
More income	Agree	Disagree	Agree		
HH size					
Urban	Disagree	Agree		Agree	
Northeast					
Midwest					
West					

On Internet		Agree			Agree
Catholic (ref)					
Baptist					
Pentecostal			Agree		
Other Protestant					
Other Christian	Agree				
Higher church attendance				Disagree	
Church higher giving expectations				Disagree	Disagree

Note: Bold means significant at the p<.05, not bold means significance at the p<.10.

Source: Tithing Experiment Survey, 2006.

not tithe because they do not trust those to whom they would give. Few other of these demographic variables stand out as revealing significant differences.

In order to sort through the independent effects of our demographic and religion variables on offering various reasons for not tithing, we again used multiple regression analyses to identify statistically significant associations. The results—all of which, again, concern churchgoing U.S. Christians who say they do not and would not give 10 percent of after-tax income even if their churches required it for membership in good standing—are reported in table 5.8. There we see that the race and income associations noticed in table 5.7 remain significant in a multivariate analysis. Compared to other races, black Christians who will not tithe are more likely than Christians of other races to explain that by saying churches have no right as a matter of principle to require 10 percent (in the table, Christians of other races are more likely than blacks to disagree with that statement). And higher income earning Christians are more likely than lower income earners to say both that churches have no right to ask for tithing and that they do not trust those to whom they would give money. Higher earners are also less likely than lower earners to justify their unwillingness to tithe as the result of an inability to afford to give. Other variables reveal sporadic significant effects, none of which, however, we think are theoretically important.

What Does It Mean?

What, then, are we to make of these survey findings? What have we learned? To begin, we must remind ourselves that our results in this chapter refer not to actual situations faced in real life, but rather to hypothetical scenarios posed in abstract survey questions. It could well be that real churchgoing Christians would respond differently to actual requests by their churches for members to give 10 percent of after-tax income. We do not know how real people would react to such an actual situation. We never will unless and until some churches try implementing that policy. Meanwhile, what we have to rely on are answers to survey questions about hypothetical scenarios. We nevertheless think that even answers to survey questions about abstract scenarios do tell us interesting and revealing things.

First, the findings of our 2006 Tithing Experiment Survey questions suggest that few American Christians, even churchgoing Christians, stand ready and waiting to give 10 percent of their after-tax income if only their churches were to firmly ask them to do so. Only 7 percent of churchgoing Christians who do not already tithe yet said they would begin tithing if their churches required them to tithe. Seventy-six percent of churchgoing Christians said flatly that they simply would not tithe. They would either ignore the requirement, find a different church, or drop out of church life altogether.

Of course, it may be that, in real life, if people's actual churches did a good job of beginning to institute a tithing policy, more church members would respond more positively than they reported they would here. Then again, they might respond even more negatively. We do not know. It may also be, in fact is likely, that people's answers would change in a positive direction if the idea "required for membership" were removed from the policy. We asked a strong version to see what people would say. What is clear is that most American Christians do not like or want to be *required* to do anything specific when it comes to their money, at least by their churches. But American Christians might respond more positively if their churches significantly raised giving expectations in a more encouraging, voluntary, flexible way. Then again, they might not.

Second, the findings of our 2006 Tithing Experiment Survey presented in this chapter suggest that American Christians tend to explain their not giving more money than they do by appeal to two reasons. The first we just mentioned: they do not want to be *required* by organizations, including churches, to do anything with their money. In this American Christianity reflects American individualism. It apparently is up to each individual or family, whether alone or before God, to decide what they will do with their money. No institution has the right to interfere with that individual decision. What we see here, then, is that "God" and "the church" are radically decoupled, such that the former has authority to ask for money while the latter does not—meanwhile, since God apparently has no "official" representative in society, God's call to give money generously gets lost as a theological abstraction.[1] The second most common reason American Christians offer for not giving more money than they do is that they cannot afford it. They report that they do not have the resources to give 10 percent of after-tax income. Whether or not this is objectively true—for few U.S. Christians do we think it is, as we argued in the previous chapter—it certainly seems to operate as a subjectively important factor. Even if "I can't afford it" is a post-hoc rationalization, it is still revealing that more than one-half of churchgoing Christians resort to that category as a way to explain their lack of tithing. A lot of American Christians appear to be living in a subjective world of scarcity, not abundance, gratitude, and generosity.

Third, income plays a fascinating role in all of this. Counter to what one might expect, but consistent with what we found in chapter 2, earning higher incomes does not make American Christians more generous with their money. It actually appears to make them more stingy, protective, and distrustful. It is lower, not higher, income earning Christians who tithe more, would be more likely to start tithing if asked, would be more supportive of a tithing requirement for membership, and who trust the churches and good causes to which they give money. This is despite higher income earners knowing that they have more money to give.

This may be because higher income earners feel a stronger general sense of social power and entitlement and so are unwilling to have "outsiders" intrude on their financial matters. It may be because they believe they have worked harder for their money and so are more entitled to controlling its use. It may be that higher income earners tend more, because of their greater disposable resources, to be able realistically to consider other consumer expenditures and financial investments that compete with financial charitable giving than lower income earners do or can. It may be that less generous people make life choices and behave in ways that end up earning them higher incomes over time. Or it may simply be that the more money one has the generally harder it is to let it go. More research would be needed to ferret out such possibilities. In any case, the point here sufficiently reinforces one we observed in chapter 2: the relative generosity of American Christians has very little to do with financial capacity to give. If anything, overall, those with more objective capacity to give more money tend to give less.

Fourth, racial differences among American Christians influence the matter of raising expectations of financial giving. After controlling statistically for differences in income, churchgoing black Christians compared to churchgoing white and Hispanic Christians appear more supportive of a required tithing membership policy, more prepared to start tithing if such a policy were implemented, and less likely to try to skirt such a policy by not giving or by moving to a different church. In an interesting twist, however, among churchgoing Christians who do not and would not give 10 percent of their after-tax income if their churches required it, blacks are statistically significantly more likely to say they would not do so because as a principle churches have no right to ask members to give a specific amount of money. Black American Christians may therefore be more polarized than others on the issue of the church's authority to ask for generous financial giving. However we explain that, it nevertheless seems apparent that research seeking better to understand the relative financial giving of U.S. Christians needs to take racial differences, particularly between blacks and others, into account.

Finally, not surprisingly, greater church participation associates with greater openness by American Christians to increasing their financial giving. Among U.S. Christians who report attending church more often than never, those who attend more frequently are significantly more likely to support a potential tithing membership requirement and to pay a tithe if required. They are also significantly less likely if they were required to tithe to move to a different church or drop out of church life altogether. And, among Christians who do not and would not tithe, they are significantly less likely then lower-frequency attendees to say they have the money but do not want to give 10 percent, that they would rather spend it on things they enjoy. None of this is unexpected. It all makes sense. More frequently attending American Christians are almost by definition more invested in their churches and probably their faith. They have more to lose by compromising their membership status through stinginess. They as a group are also closer to already giving 10 percent of their income, so closing the gap would likely be less difficult. But more frequently attending Christians are also more subject to the theological and moral teaching influences of churches. All other things being equal, when their churches begin to press out Christian teachings about and raise the stakes on financial giving, more frequent church attendees are more likely than irregular attendees to be shaped and influenced by such teachings. We might surmise, therefore, that one means of increasing the financial giving of American Christians specifically would be to increase their church participation more generally.

Conclusion

Our purpose in this chapter is not to propose that all American Christian churches implement a policy requiring all members in good standing to give 10 percent of their post-tax income to their churches and other good causes. At least according to the teachings of their own faith traditions (see appendix A), it seems to us that most Christians should in fact be doing something like that. But our purpose here is not to advocate such a policy. Our purpose rather is simply to try to get another angle of vision on the assumptions, perceptions, meanings, and motives concerning the financial giving or lack thereof of American Christians. We fully realize the hypothetical nature of the survey questions we have examined here. We are aware that people might behave quite differently than they say they would if faced with real-life situations in their actual churches. Still, we think we have learned some important things in this exercise about the potential generosity of American Christians, their attitudes about compulsion and free choice, their perceptions of scarcity and abundance, and the influence of greater income in financial giving. These insights, we hope, will contribute to the larger challenge of better understanding the ungenerous giving of most American Christians.

W E BEGAN THIS book by noting a sharp and puzzling contrast. On the one hand we reckoned that American Christians enjoy an immense potential to use their vast wealth to accomplish amazing things in the world that would be of great value to them. On the other hand we noted that the majority of American Christians are actually quite ungenerous financial givers, relative to the normative teachings of their own faith traditions and to their potential for bountiful giving. As a result, many of the causes and accomplishments that American Christians profess to value turn out in fact to get underfunded or not funded at all. That contrast created for us a riddle to try to explain: how and why it is that the wealthiest national body of Christian believers at any time in all of church history end up spending most of their money on themselves rather than generously sharing it with other people and for other needs, or what they consider good causes, including strengthening the ministries of their own churches. Our attempts to solve this book's riddle have often necessarily been tentative, uneven, and less than fully definitive, especially given the limited and scattered nature of the available empirical relevant data. Still, we believe that we have made some progress toward better understanding the causes of ungenerous American Christian financial giving. We summarize the picture that the previous chapters have developed in the following review.

Explaining Ungenerous Giving

First, everything involved in the matter of voluntary Christian financial giving takes place within the larger context of a massive economy, powerful culture, and ubiquitous advertising and media industries that are driven by and dedicated to the promotion of mass consumption. Contemporary American life in the spheres of production, consumption, household living, recreation, entertainment, and mass communication is dominated by the ethos and practices of mass consumerism. Materialistic consumption has become a nearly inescapable way of life in the United States. In fact, American religion itself seems to be increasingly drawn into this consumerist mentality.[1] Therefore, every Christian impulse to generously give money away inevitably runs up against potent counter-impulses driven by mass consumerism to instead perpetually spend, borrow, acquire, consume, discard, and then spend more on oneself and family. Such forces are not merely matters of personal "values" but are structured into deep-rooted institutions of employment, transportation, media, home ownership, entertainment, and the distribution and selling of masses of discretionary purchases and material luxuries. Indeed, given the structure of the American economy, if Americans did not continually consume massive amounts of material goods, then the economy would slow down and eventually collapse. Mass consumer capitalism must grow or die. Whatever the relative larger merits of such an economy and society, one thing seems clear to us and also to nearly all of the American Christians whom we interviewed for this project: the dominance of mass consumerism works powerfully and in many ways against American Christians freely and liberally giving away significant proportions of their incomes to people, ministries, needs, and good causes, as most of their own religious traditions call them to do. The first and perhaps most formidable rival to generous voluntary financial giving of American Christians, then, aiding and abetting any of their natural human tendencies toward selfishness and stinginess, is America's institutionalized mass consumerism.

Second, a lot of Christian church pastors appear to be quite uncomfortable with the issue of money in their churches, uneasy about the best ways to approach the issue with their parishioners, and often frustrated with the lack of faithful generosity evident in many of their church members. A lot of pastors appear to have been ill prepared to successfully address money matters in their churches, and many seem to feel isolated from their clergy colleagues as they struggle with the issue. Many are also afraid of being branded by the money-grubbing stereotype. They can also hate the fact that by asking their parishioners to give money generously they are easily seen as trying to boost their own salaries. At least some pastors are also individually uncomfortable with their own personal perhaps less-than-entirely-faithful handling of money in their own lives. As a consequence, more than a few pastors seem hesitant when it comes to engaging the financial giving of their parishioners, sometimes actively avoiding boldly teaching their churches about faithful Christian stewardship and generous financial giving. For some pastors, simply being able to pay the church's bills, end the fiscal year in the black, and keep up with essential building maintenance and upkeep over time has come to seem satisfactory. Even then, many pastors appear to feel like they are walking a tightrope in their churches simply to avoid upsetting their parishioners by calling too much for more money, on the one hand, and avoiding running into organizational financial woes by not calling enough for money, on the other hand. The net result seems to us to be a lot of pastors out there who have made peace with low expectations, tolerance for chronic paltry giving by many of their members, and the use of money collection procedures oriented as much to minimize problems and conflict as to effectively build their churches and the spiritual faithfulness of their members.

Third, more than a few American Christians seem to be at least somewhat uninformed or confused about the meanings, expectations, and purposes of faithful Christian financial giving. American Christians we spoke with lack a common vocabulary that evokes shared connotations and emotions. They attend congregations that employ a variety of different methods of collecting tithes, offerings, and gifts, which are themselves based on divergent and sometimes contradictory theological and organizational justifications. Many American Christians also seem caught between their biblical belief in the ultimate divine ownership of all of their possessions and call to faithful stewardship and generosity, and their individualistic beliefs[2] in their private ownership of their own wealth, their autonomous control over its disposition, and their absolute rights to personal property and consumer sovereignty. Not being sure how to fit these two together, many simply assert both and live with the tensions and contradictions. We have seen, however, that, when push comes to shove, in many cases, the individualistic beliefs typically leading to consumerist acquisition tend to win out over the biblical beliefs leading to confident generosity. Part of the answer to the riddle of ungenerous Christian giving thus seems to us to involve a lack of clarity among American Christians about the expectations for giving by their faith traditions and church leaders.

Fourth, at least some American Christians who might otherwise give money more open-handedly seem to harbor some mistrust for some of the organizations to which they would give money, which appears to cause them to hesitate. Americans can in many ways be very generous people. But many are also suspicious of being taken advantage of by scams, malfeasance, and scandals. The news is filled with enough stories of abuse, embezzlement, falls from grace, misused funds, con artist scams, poor management of non-profit organizations, nepotism, and other forms of unprofessional conduct and scandals in both nonreligious and religious organizations that one can understand why potential financial givers have reason to doubt whether the money they might give will be used honestly and well. Such mistrust and suspicion breeds a lack of generosity, logically justified by the legitimate purpose of being the good steward of money by making sure it is not misused. The good of financial responsibility, when tainted by distrust, thus comes to serve the bad of miserly giving.

Fifth, complicating all of these matters is the fact that nearly no American Christian seems to talk with anyone else about the question of voluntary financial giving. Money and income are sacred in America. And generous financial giving is popularly associated with a strong social-desirability bias, meaning that most people think that others admire liberal givers. Yet most American Christians, we have seen, do not give away as much money as they think they should and perhaps wish they did. As a result, the issues of the motives, amounts, and purposes of voluntary financial giving are not only touchy but have been radically privatized. What anyone gives and why is defined as entirely their own affair, at best a private matter entirely between them and God. Few Christians appear to talk openly even with their spouses about the matter. Fewer talk with other family members, friends, or pastors. The topic is nearly taboo. Consequently, few American Christians approach the question of faithful financial giving within any social context encouraging role model learning, relational support, information sharing, or accountability. The de facto practice is: every person for themselves. And that, we have reason to believe, does little to facilitate generous financial giving.

Sixth, further complicating matters, many American Christians appear to want to avoid adopting systematic, routinized methods for carrying out their financial giving. Instead, they seem to want to give whatever money they do give away in an unplanned, situational, almost impulsive manner. For many American Christians, the idea of employing premeditated, designed systems for deciding how much money to give and how it should be routinized, in order to ensure that they will actually give fully that amount of money for an extended period of time, seems off-putting. Structured systems, such as making annual giving pledge commitments, using weekly giving envelopes, not to mention setting up an automatic banking payment system, seem to strike many American Christians as rigid, impersonal, legalistic, and even unspiritual, insofar as they are thought to not rely on the inner promptings of the Holy Spirit at specific points in time to generate freewill giving. Furthermore, for many Christians, the idea of first by design taking a certain percent of one's income "off the top" as "first fruits" to give away before any money is spent on anything else is a foreign, improbable, or difficult idea. They would rather give as they feel able, respond as the spirit moves, spontaneously put in the offering plate what strikes them as right in the moment, write the check for the good cause when they feel inspired, or put in the offering plate whatever cash they happen to have in their pockets at the time. We know, however, that such unplanned, situational approaches to nearly anything produce spotty results. In the case of financial giving, they almost always end up producing less money than planned, routinized giving.

Put these factors all together and we may conclude it is a wonder that American Christians give away as much money as they do. As best as we can tell, numerous powerful cultural, organizational, interpersonal, and institutional influences work together against generous financial giving. In the face of these dynamics, it would seem to require the truly highly committed, deeply involved, well-taught, very organized, culturally critical, and confidently led Christian to faithfully give away, say, 10 percent of his or her income. Such Christians do exist in American churches. But they are a distinct minority. And so the actual financial giving of American Christians as a whole turns out to be something like the ungenerous levels we observed in chapter 2. What anyone might do, in practical terms, to try to respond to this situation in order to increase levels of giving, we attempt to address next. Following that, we return to more sociological themes.

Possible Practical Implications

We did not write this to be a practical "how-to" book for increasing the voluntary financial giving of American Christians or others. Nevertheless, we are aware that some of our readers will come to this book with the practical concern and perhaps responsibility for encouraging financial giving in their congregations, denominations, ministries, schools, programs, or other non-profit causes or organizations. We think it worthwhile, then, to try to draw out in this conclusion some of the possible practical implications of our research findings that might help move people to become more generous financial givers to such organizations. What follows is not a scientifically validated systematic plan or program for enhancing voluntary financial giving. Rather here we simply offer a set of informed conjectures based on the findings of the previous chapters about changes that leaders concerned about generous financial giving might consider implementing in ways appropriate to their situations. Some are general ideas, others are more specific.

- The first practical implication of our findings above is that pastors and church leadership will be more effective in encouraging generous financial giving among American Christians if they foster a "Live the Vision" culture in their churches instead of a "Pay the Bills" culture, as we sketched them in chapter 4. Organizational transformation at the cultural level is not easy and there is no ready, step-by-step program to implement in order to move from one to the other. But our interviews suggest that knowing where one wants to go can help a great deal. For instance, in forming local church cultures, church leaders can focus primarily on nurturing members' Christian spiritual lives, not on budgets per se; on serving the world, not on organizational maintenance; on the virtually unlimited opportunities for faith-guided change, not parochial budgetary demands; on the congregation as a home-base for widespread Christian faithfulness and ministry, not as an end in itself; on pastors as enablers and equippers of others, not "full service providers" of local spiritual goods; on Christian discipleship as a transformation of the self, not on people getting their felt needs met. This may be easier said than done. But without such guiding visionary signposts and goals, churches will all too often simply muddle along in an introspective, pragmatic mode that fails to challenge its members to stretch and grow. We do not claim to have thoroughly understood what we are calling the Live-the-Vision pastoral leadership style of church cultural development. Further research and discussion could no doubt shed more light on other social forces associated with that culture, including its language, practices, texture, and strategies. But we think the distinction between the two ideal type cultures is significant, financially important, and warrants further exploration.
- Any pastors or other church leaders who harbor any element of uneasy conscience about their own personal financial dealings should, it seems, make whatever changes are necessary to "get their own houses in order" so that they are in a position to address their churches on money matters without hesitation or discomfort. One way to indirectly encourage financial giving in others is simply to openly tell about one's own practices, not to boast but simply to be transparent about an important matter for which there is a lack of open role models. Pastors and church leaders can only do this, however, when they are first confident and assured about their own financial dealings. It seems necessary to us for pastors to first "walk the talk" and begin tithing 10 percent of their own income (which may also require churches ensuring that pastors are

paid well enough to afford this). Such active and open leadership and modeling, if communicated well, could prove important in fostering a healthy congregational culture around financial giving.

- As part of shifting church cultures from Pay the Bills to Live the Vision, many pastors and church leaders could be more bold, forthright, and positive about the centrality of the right relation to money in Christian life and the teachings of their own faith traditions about stewardship and generous financial giving. Such preaching and teaching, we think, is best done throughout the year as a natural part of the overall faith formation of the congregation on many fronts, not merely as a predictable thematic topic during "Pledge Week" or "Stewardship Month." It seems to us that there should be ways to communicate all of this in a matter-of-fact, confident, enthusiastic manner that does not play into pastors' fears of being seen as money-grubbing. If some American Christians do not give more money because they are less than fully clear about biblical and denominational teachings about stewardship and financial giving, then pastors and church leaders can remove that impediment, or excuse, from the table. The goal could be pedagogically and informationally simply to ensure that all church participants are well educated on the larger topic of money, wealth, stewardship, and giving. Pastors may discover that they overestimate the knowledge on this topic that their church members have heard and internalized. Lack of information and understanding on the subject might be eliminated as a possible factor depressing financial giving. If Christians then still decide not to give generously, it will not be because they do not know any better.

- We immediately want to say, however, that we believe that lay church leaders, and not pastors, should take the lead in communicating specific financial information and calls for giving to church members. The conflict for pastors having to ask for money that directly pays their own salaries is understandably too uncomfortable, and there is no good reason that pastors should have to play that role. It seems to us, based on our research here, that church leaders should employ a division of labor on the topic. Clergy and other ministers who are supported by their congregations should regularly preach and teach biblical and theological principles about money in order to form a larger vision and culture in and among their church members. Then lay church leaders and members should take the lead in making specific announcements and calls about needs and opportunities, possible ministries to fund, pledge cards to complete, budget reports to offer, and so on. This keeps pastors placed in their rightful positions of preaching, teaching, and community formation. It also demonstrates to the congregations a solidarity of clergy and lay leadership in taking a constructive, visionary approach to financial giving from different angles. Overall, the issue of financial giving can become one that is raised and pressed by the entire official and informal leadership of a congregation and not simply the head pastor.

- The more that churches call upon regular members recurrently to talk to their peers in front of their congregations and Sunday school classes about their own learning and growing in financial giving, their own motivations and inspirations for generosity, and the ministries and causes that they are excited to support, the more generous, we suspect, the other members of the congregation will become. Such "testimonies" and "sharing" by regular members help to break the ice of silence on the topic of financial giving, draw the spotlight of the money issue off of clergy, and help to foster a general atmosphere of interest in and enthusiasm about all of the ways that members are growing and the good things that their donated money is accomplishing.

- Church members might also well be challenged by church leaders to make financial giving a "first fruits" priority, by strongly suggesting that members deduct their decided-upon amount of giving money "off the top" as soon as the paycheck arrives. We know, for instance, of people who budget in 10 or 12 percent of their income as a fixed "cost" that is "paid out" automatically, like their mortgage or insurance payments. If such a challenge is successful, this will compel church members to step back and intentionally consider how much money they wish to give. It also should counteract the subsequent anti-generosity pressures of bills to pay and temptations of discretionary consumer purchases in ways that could have longer-term effects in revising the spending patterns. Having to "bite the bullet" and take giving money off the top right away is also a practice that can reshape people's understandings of financial priorities, commitments, and planning in crucial ways.

- Although we believe the issue of credit card debt is generally overplayed in the media, the fact is there are still a minority of Americans who do not know how to use credit cards well and are in serious debt under the burden of high interest rates. More generally, many Americans seem not to know how to budget their money well, make wise buying decisions, work within their financial constraints, and plan for their financial obligations and futures. We have seen churches that offer evening programs and classes in financial stewardship that seem very helpful for providing the kind of basic information, tools, and skills in smart financial dealings to people who are looking for help. Some are led by outside program representatives and consultants, others by financially knowledgeable lay leaders in congregations. At least some American Christians seem motivated to get their financial houses in order and simply need some direction, education, and encouragement. Providing practical, nuts-and-bolts help in such cases appears not only to improve people's economic situations but also often to strengthen their marriage relationships, enhance their overall outlooks on life, and dramatically alter their financial abilities to become generous financial stewards in their churches and beyond.

- Similarly, church leaders might consider creative methods to help routinize the giving of their members. We are not in a position to recommend specifics here. But on sociological grounds, at least, we know that annual pledges are better than weekly spontaneous giving decisions; the use of weekly giving envelopes is better than wallets and purses pulled open as the plate passes; systematic weekly checks pre-arranged from the bank are better than having to remember to bring the checkbook every Sunday morning. Overall, it would seem to be a good idea to discourage spontaneous giving, unless it is for money given as "freewill offerings" in addition to other money planned for routine giving. The more congregations can get their members to routinize their financial giving in what we might think of as "disciplines of practice and accountability"—just as they routinize most of the rest of their lives, from getting up to go to work to paying the mortgage—the more financially generous those members will prove to be over time.

- Our research for this book leads us to believe that the greater the proportion of a church's annual budget that goes to ministries outside of the church itself, the more church members will be enthusiastic about generous financial giving. Having the vast majority of a church budget spent within the church for internal church purposes tends to promote a Pay-the-Bills mentality, which we think leads in turn to unenthusiastic, ungenerous giving. But churches that can continually tell their members about all of the great ministries and services that they are providing beyond the walls of the church can boldly ask members to give generously without that being seen as a money grab. Pastors who are afraid that their members will view their calls for generous financial giving as self-interested attempts to pad their own ecclesial turf can readily undercut that (probably false in most cases anyway) perception by showing that in fact a good proportion of the church budget is going into community, regional, national, and global Christian ministries of evangelism, care for the poor, missions, emergency relief work, medical ministries, and so on. Our interviews suggest that many American Christians would be much more enthusiastic about giving more money if they knew, in specific dollar amounts, that a good bit of it was going outside the church. Devoting a significant chunk of a church budget to ministries beyond the church itself also removes the "cap" on the amount of money that is "needed," creating a situation of unlimited possibilities for good to be accomplished with money given. There are not only local payroll and electric bills to pay, there is an entire world of hurt and need that parishioners have an opportunity to engage.

• Churches might also consider baby steps toward the formation of discussion groups focused on financial faithfulness as one aspect of Christian life. Or they might encourage existing church-based small groups or accountability groups to openly engage the topic of financial giving. Church leaders may also encourage couples to talk more openly together about their values, priorities, and commitments when it comes to family budgets and religious and charitable giving. Given the touchiness of the topic, this is a potential mine-field. But, as a matter of principle, greater openness and communication, and perhaps even accountability, should have the effect of increasing financial faithfulness and generosity. Church leaders might ponder appropriate ways to develop their communities in those directions.

• Churches might also help to increase the generous financial giving of their members overall by providing them with reliable information about ministries and organizations beyond themselves to which they recommend members give money. If some church members are unsure about good places beyond their congregations to which to give their money, it might help for their churches to provide and draw attention to information about a variety of recommended giving options. This could range from seminaries and colleges, to missions organizations, to relief and poverty reduction organizations, to a host of other possibilities. Having some respectable authorities in churches who have taken the time to investigate a variety of giving opportunities, to verify their trustworthiness, and to publicize and recommend them to church members could increase members' giving by increasing the information flow, expanding giving options, and reducing possible uncertainty and mistrust. In this, of course, churches need not require that people give to these particular organizations or imply that there are not other equally worthy giving options. The idea would simply be to provide reliable information and guidance to those who might benefit from it. Providing such information should also have the positive effect of creating a local culture that says the church is not only raising money for itself but is interested in forming believers into people who care about the world broadly and give money wisely, widely, and generously. Denominations could consider offering similar recommendations on a Web site, for instance, providing a list of recommended organizations with contact information to which their members might give money.

- Churches would do well, we think, to spend as much time telling church members what their money has accomplished as they do asking for more money. It is our impression that many people who give money have the uneasy feeling that their money disappears into a black hole. There are often few or no information feedback loops that tell people in tangible terms what their donated money has accomplished. Theoretically they may believe that their money is being used by people they think they trust for purposes they think are good. But the actual, specific impact of their money often goes unknown. We think that communication efforts to "close the information loop" by providing specific feedback on how money is being spent to accomplish what goods will help to continually make the value of giving tangible and rewarding to the givers. This could involve oral reports, slide shows, videos, bulletin updates, or other communication mechanisms. If church money is being spent in a local ministry, members can go for a site visit, if not to volunteer themselves to see and hear about the work of the ministry firsthand. Likewise, it is probably worth spending a certain amount of money, as an investment in future giving, to enable givers to travel to more distant locations to see personally what good their money is doing in the world. However it is done, the point is to make the importance and value of financial giving real to the givers by regularly showing them what their money is accomplishing rather than leaving them in the dark and expecting them to keep giving.

- In keeping with the idea of fostering a congregational culture focused on faithful financial stewardship as a way of life, as a personal discipline integral to a flourishing human life before God, and not simply a necessary obligation to pay the bills, churches might consider recurrently offering lay or professionally led classes and seminars on budgeting, financial planning, getting and staying out of debt, savings, and giving. Many Americans simply have not learned such skills and information, either the larger conceptual ideas behind proactive money management or the nuts and bolts of sound financial dealings. Consequently, many are not adequately "on top of" their financial situations, are paying high interest rates on consumer loans, are not saving enough for needs such as retirement, and so are certainly not in positions to be responsible, generous givers of money to church and beyond. The point is not to turn churches into financial advisor institutions or self-help clubs. The point is, in the larger context of holistic Christian education, to provide members with the practical knowledge, skills, and tools for more faithful, responsible dealing with money—a matter of great spiritual importance—so they can better put into practice what the Bible and their faith traditions teach about money.

- Churches should strongly encourage parents to actively teach their children about financial giving. Many parents who do give money seem to assume that their children will learn faithful giving automatically by osmosis. So it does not appear that very many are entirely clear in talking with them about their own giving. But we have every reason to believe that parents' explicitly telling their children to what and whom they give and why is a crucial piece of their larger formation into people who will give generously when they themselves grow up. Parents' clearly teaching their children about intentional financial giving is a critical element of the broader work of Christian communities teaching faithful stewardship over the long run. Encouraging parents to teach their children about giving money has other benefits. For one thing, it shifts the focus of the one talking about money away from the pastor and onto regular church members. For another thing, it compels parents to have to think about their own practices, commitments, and values around money and generosity in order to be able to explain it without embarrassment to their children. For many reasons, then, the simple process of parents' taking the time explicitly to explain, even once, to their children about their financial giving practices should help to increase generosity in the short and long runs.
- In all of their dealings with money issues, churches, it seems to us, should work hard to approach them with positive, enthusiastic,

visionary frames of mind and language. We suspect that many, if not most, American Christians would be happy to be part of something larger that is visionary, moving, and exciting, even if it is demanding of them and requires sacrifice. What most people do not want to be part of is something that is standard, lackluster, and insular. So, stressing the size of the church deficit, hammering on the need to pay the bills, reminding people of the building repairs that are pressing, and other approaches that are easily heard as drudgerous "guilt trips" tend, we think, to be not very effective. By contrast, many people seem to us eager to be inspired and changed by a larger, demanding vision of a flourishing life and world transformation rooted in the gospel. Many people seem prepared to be motivated by all of the good that their money can achieve, all of the suffering and death they might help to reduce, all of the constructive ministry they might help to make happen. If, as we suspect, many American Christians are getting by on "comfortable guilt," churches will do well to think of opportunities to present to them, to constructively relieve their niggling guilt, by providing positive visions for accomplishing real good through greater generosity. The point of faithful Christian financial giving is of course not to feel good per se. But faithfulness may certainly be accompanied by a sense of self-affirmation, of having done the good and right thing. Helping people to see exciting, compelling, constructive uses for their money should have the effect of dissolving some of their impediments to more generous contributions, facilitating more open-handed giving behavior, and showing people how it is that they might *want* to give money generously instead of avoiding and resisting it.

- Anything churches can do to create critical distance between their church members and mass consumerism would seem to help in a larger process of increasing their financial generosity. Many Americans are concerned about materialism and aware of the pressures of mass consumerism. But many are also still powerfully drawn into it. If, as scripture seems to teach, the good use of money is a spiritual and not simply financial matter, then these are topics perfectly legitimate for churches to broach. Churches do not have to become ideologically anti-capitalist by any means. But helping people to see certain disconnections or tensions between their Christian faith and the world of advertising, incessant consumer spending, and trust for security and happiness in material goods ought to help position people mentally to become more generous givers. We cannot here offer a developed plan or program for accomplishing this. But it is not hard to imagine certain practices that could help. For instance, church members could regularly share with their congregational peers about how things like voluntary moderation or simplicity, watching less TV, cutting down on trips to the mall, learning skepticism about advertising, and so on can help to foster local cultures in which the questioning of mass consumerism is possible. These are difficult and delicate matters and must be engaged with great thought and care. But it seems to us that churches seeking to nurture good financial stewardship and generosity simply cannot afford to ignore the challenge of mass consumerism and hope simply to co-exist peacefully with it. The two are too much at odds to ignore. Ultimately, the issue here is not simply about a competition for dollars, but rather the basic narratives and worldviews that capture people's imaginations and commitments and thereby form their lives. Very many Christians seem to us to be keenly aware that mass consumerism presents a dangerous threat to Christian faith and growth—at least that of others, if not their own—especially when it comes to money. If so, it would seem that churches need to consider ways to confront that threat constructively and practically, as a simple matter of fostering Christian discipleship.

- On a larger, longer-term scale, it seems to us that seminaries, divinity schools, theology schools, Bible institutes, and denominations should consider more seriously how training for responsible leadership around money issues as an essential aspect of Christian formation and ministry should fit into their curricula and continuing education. Most pastors tell us they simply were not trained or prepared to deal with issues of money, budgets, financial giving, and working with parishioners on the topic. If Christian churches and denominations wish to do a better job at educating members in faithful stewardship and raising and handling money in effective ways, they are going to have to do a better job first in training and supporting their clergy and lay leadership who take the lead at the local level on these matters. Right now, entire generational cohorts of pastors are working at the grassroots who tell us that they simply have not been trained and prepared to deal well with money issues. In addition to revising the curriculum of ministerial training for future generations of pastors and priests, denominations and para-church ministries might consider developing new continuing education training seminars to assist and support pastors and lay leaders in their work in this area. In the course of researching this book, we have seen signs of some denominations investing resources in these ways. More and better of these efforts we think can work over time to increase the financial generosity of Christian believers.

- Even more broadly, the more that national-level Christian leaders and organizations can develop collaborative institutional systems for the financial auditing, accountability, transparency, and "seal-of-approval-giving" of Christian para-church ministries and organizations, in order to minimize the risk of financial malfeasance, scams, and scandals, the better. Trust is absolutely essential for generous financial giving. So anything that can be done to reduce people's often legitimate uncertainties and suspicions about possible misuse of funds should have the effect of increasing generosity. Some such financial accountability organizations already exist, such as the Evangelical Council for Financial Accountability (ECFA), Ministry Watch, and Wall Watchers.[3] The better such organizations can be developed, the more widespread can be their purview, the more effectively they can function, and the more that ordinary Christians are aware of their certifying work, the more they will be able to build and sustain the kind of trust that is needed for widespread, generous financial giving. Pastors and other church leaders should therefore encourage Christians to pay attention to the certification of such accountability organizations in deciding where to give their money.

- Finally, it seems clear to us that the effort to increase the faithfulness and generosity of Christians' financial giving will have to involve a readiness on the part of church leaders to lose some church members in the short run. Any change of any magnitude in any organization tends to make some people unhappy. That's just how people and organizations are. Churches simply cannot make significant changes and keep all of their people pleased. Not everyone is pleased now. Some American church-goers are sufficiently out of tune with hard Christian teachings that, when churches start to move in directions that better align their handling of money issues with Christian integrity, those people will become disgruntled and leave. Of course there is no need for churches to go out of their ways to alienate people. Far from it. The point, really, is to make substantial changes precisely in order to help people who are currently not living up to their own best self-expectations to begin to freely choose to do what they ought and finally do what they want to do. But churches that are afraid of upsetting or losing any member will be paralyzed in any attempts to move in these directions. Pandering to least-common-denominator standards, demands, and expectations will do little overall to help Christians become more generous with their money. Churches lacking in vision, standards, and expectations will tend to attract people lacking in vision, standards, and expectations. In response, we suggest that churches and denominations consider deciding what faithfulness entails and begin moving decisively in those directions, expecting to lose some members early on. Some may fall off the wagon in the short run. However, churches that make changes to become more visionary, outward looking, and world transforming will also eventually attract a larger number of people over time. Some of those alienated members who left at first may even find themselves assured, convinced, and attracted to return as members in churches that have become quite different.

We offer these hopefully practical suggestions with some hesitation, since we are not professional fund-raising consultants, church budget advisors, or even church workers at all. We realize that we may have missed some crucial ideas here, and may have suggested other ideas that prove in practice to be unhelpful. Knowing that we run that risk, here we still advance this set of ideas that occur to us from the findings of this book, viewed particularly from a sociological perspective, which we offer tentatively for consideration and discussion by churches and other Christian ministries and organizations. Future research on the subject may suggest additional practical ideas for encouraging financial generosity or revisions to some of the ideas above. For now, these strike us as at least worth consideration.

Sociological Lessons

One of the interests motivating us to research and write this book was to use the puzzle of ungenerous American Christian financial giving to better understand human persons, motives, interactions, and social-psychological and organizational practices generally from a sociological perspective. We wrote this book not simply to figure out practically why American Christians do not give away more money, so that Christian leaders can devise new approaches and initiatives to increase their giving. If our analysis helps to lead to such an outcome, we will be pleased, and we ourselves have just tried to offer some ideas in support of that effort. But as sociologists we are also interested in learning from specific social puzzles, cases, and problems as more general characteristics of human social life. Much of what we have discovered here validates fundamental sociological and social-psychological dynamics in human social life and will not be earth-shattering news to most social scientists. But we think it worthwhile nevertheless in this kind of analysis to step back at the end and reflect on broader observations about human persons and life that we might draw out from our study. Some of those insights might be useful particularly to nonacademic readers. What, then, have we learned in this book to help inform or remind us about the human condition and the social lives of people? Briefly, we think we have learned and confirmed the following.

First, as a specific point, it is interesting and helpful to see that financial giving is not primarily a financial matter but a cultural, interpersonal, and organizational matter. That is, the most important influences shaping financial giving have not so much to do with dollars, budgets, and bank accounts as with visions, norms, values, priorities, leadership, discourse, communication, social relations, social trust, and institutional processes.[4] American Christians, we have seen, do not give money according to their objective financial capacity in income. Other cultural and organizational factors are essential to bring in for understanding the riddle of stingy Christian financial giving. The larger sociological lesson here is that many specific domains of life are typically shot through with social, cultural, and organizational influences not normally associated with them. Most aspects of life in human society are interconnected together in complex and sometimes unexpected ways.

Along those same lines, we have seen from this book's research that it is not so easy to draw a hard and fast line between religious and spiritual versus social, cultural, cognitive, relational, and institutional realities. Many people of faith seem to us to want to segregate the religious and the spiritual into a distinct, "higher" realm of life, existence, or experience—disconnected from the everyday and "profane" worlds of organizations, relational networks, financial flows, cultural vocabularies, economics, consumerism, and so on. Certainly, from the perspective of the religious faiths themselves, there is something true about this, which we do not dispute. The Christian worldview, for instance, is simply incompatible with a naturalistic, materialistic philosophy—a real spiritual realm is also believed to exist in reality. Be that as it may, our point here is that the religious and spiritual are not disconnected from the social and historical life of humanity. Rather, the religious, social, spiritual, historical, sacred, profane, faith-based, and institutional link up and condition each other in many, complicated ways. Thus, to understand even matters of personal Christian faithfulness of belief and practice, for instance, may require inquiring into cognitive, cultural, organizational, historical, social-psychological, and interpersonal influences that shape them.

Another related sociological point from this study worthy of a reminder—about which many American Christians strike us as largely oblivious—is that people's behaviors, practices, and life outcomes are not merely matters of good intentions, ideas, and values. From our perspective, many people of faith in America operate as de facto philosophical idealists, supposing that if people could only get the right ideas in their heads, could simply hold the right worldview and values, could simply talk the right way, then their actions and experiences would follow in a straight line. Sociology helps us to see that things often do not work like that. It is not that worldviews and values and ideas do not matter. Far from it. But as embodied and social creatures, we humans are not simply beings who directly act out our ideas and values in straightforward fashion. Social facts—such as people's "social locations," institutional settings, available cultural vocabularies, economic contexts, and social role constraints—also often powerfully shape people's lives. As we have seen, for instance, the larger American economic mass-consumerist system of production, advertising, distribution, and consumption exerts—whether we admit it or not—powerful causal effects on the personal financial decisions and practices of American Christians. The economic shapes the moral and religious, the material influences the personal, the organizational forms the spiritual. Such a full-bodied understanding of the creaturely human condition, then, must jettison any de facto philosophical idealism and come to terms with the implications of the fact that we humans are profoundly constituted, formed, influenced, and governed by a variety of material, institutional, relational, and cultural factors and forces. This is simply part of what is entailed in being the social, relational, embodied creatures that we humans are.

In all of this it is also worth recognizing that cultural systems and social roles often involve various types and levels of ambiguities, inconsistencies, tensions, paradoxes, ambivalences, and contradictions. An old school of sociology and anthropology taught us that cultures are well bounded and highly integrated systems of symbols and meanings that govern the single "way of life" of the people of entire societies. But that kind of thinking has changed in recent years. We are now much clearer about the actual fuzziness, conflict, multivocality, and ambiguity inherent in all cultures, whether local or national or civilizational. People do not simply act out social roles that fit nicely into integrated cultural and institutional systems. Rather, people struggle to negotiate the tensions, conflicts, and inconsistencies between and within the many roles they play. Thus, individual Christians whose faith calls them to remarkable financial generosity toward others, but who also participate in an overwhelming system of mass consumerism and all of the temptations and imperatives that entails, must struggle through the tensions and conflicts involved in inhabiting those conflicting cultural and social systems. Likewise, it turns out that Christian pastors occupy a professional social role generating a strong internal tension between the imperative to be materially non-self-interested, on one side, and simultaneously the imperative to lead in a high-profile way in raising money for the very organization that pays their own salaries, on the other. In such ways, social and personal life is often replete with ambiguities, inconsistencies, and conflicts, the effects of which are well worth being aware of and appreciating if we hope to understand and somewhat guide our own life experiences and outcomes.

Another way to say much of this is simply to observe the fact that individuals do not constitute and govern their own lives autonomously from the people and institutions around them. American individualism is an illusion that obscures our understanding of what is true about the actual reality in which we live. All human lives are powerfully constituted, influenced, and controlled by the social relations and institutions in which they are embedded. Hence the financial giving of individuals is not simply determined by their own autonomous, personal values and decisions, impervious to the social world around them. Matters such as financial giving are rather powerfully affected by the structures of social trust, information flows, communication patterns, organizational processes, cultural framings, discursive structures, accountability systems, and so on that define human social life. It is also for this reason that institutionalized systems, routines, and habits matter in shaping outcomes such as the amount and targets of personal financial giving. Furthermore, deep and powerful human emotions, generated by the interaction of personal experience and shared culture, which are not entirely under the conscious control of self-governing human agents, also often powerfully shape people's actions and reactions to different situations—placing serious limits on their ability to behave entirely rationally and autonomously. So, people are misguided in thinking of themselves as fully autonomous, self-governing selves in charge of their own thoughts, behaviors, actions, and outcomes. We, rather, occupy a world of bodily, material, cognitive, emotional, relational, and organizational constraints that profoundly govern our thinking and doing. People have to take this fact seriously when it comes to matters in life that are important to them—including, presumably, faithful financial giving—and respond with an awareness of our human finitude and frailty, if they wish to accomplish what they want on those important matters. This may involve taking on what we called above "disciplines of practice and accountability" for ourselves and others, in order to make sure, given all of our human constraints and limits, to live the lives we think we ought to live as best as we are able.

Yet another sociological insight that we can deduce from the analysis of this book is that all social orders, even allegedly secular ones, are ultimately built on sacred objects of worship and reverence. The sacred element of human social life was a theme highlighted by an important, early twentieth-century French sociologist named Emile Durkheim.[5] Even today we can see that his theory is illuminating. No human society, it turns out, operates in, on, and with that which is purely mundane and profane. Somewhere in every society there are objects that are held to be sacred and so revered, defended, protected, worshiped, and honored by its members. In some societies, dead ancestors or emperors or ethnicity are sacred. In American society, we surmise from this book's study, it is money and individual autonomy that are sacred, perhaps even more sacred than even God, church, the gospel, and the Bible, for some American Christians. By virtue of being sacred in American culture, it is nearly impossible to question, to infringe upon money and individual autonomy. People react, as the pastors we interviewed told us. People, even good-hearted people, get "ouchy." This insight about the sacred in society generally, and about money and individualism in American society specifically, is worth recognizing and pondering. It both sheds light on and raises more questions about, among other important things, the puzzle of ungenerous Christian giving.

One final sociological observation fills out the lessons we think we have learned and confirmed in this study. We have emphasized in the previous paragraphs the power of macro social forces and cultural influences in shaping consciousness and action in human life. All of that is true. But that should not be emphasized to the exclusion of the individual agency of persons. People matter. People can make personal, cultural, and institutional change happen. Sociology affirms this point as well. Oftentimes the most powerful social changes are instigated, mobilized, and driven by small minorities of committed people who believe in and push for them. Furthermore, many of the social forces and influences that shape people's lives touch them on the local level. The big picture facts of American religious culture and organization do shape American Christians' lives. But so do local congregations, networks, ministries, and relationships. It would therefore be sociologically naïve to adopt a simplistic "society made us do it" mentality when trying to account for things like ungenerous financial giving. In fact, committed pastors and lay church leaders can shape local cultures in congregations in significantly new ways, which in turn over time influence the people in those congregations accordingly. The visionary leadership of individuals and small teams can exert tremendous influence on the people and organizations around them, even when there are countervailing cultural and institutional forces at work. Nobody can do and achieve exactly as they please. But neither is it the case that everyone is the helpless victim of social forces and circumstances. For the ultimate and most intriguing sociological insight about human social life is this: that the very same "social and cultural system" that we individuals experience as external to and often coercive of us is also simultaneously only the accumulated product of ongoing social interactions of individual human agents.[6] "Society" is the real, "emergent" result of the "structuring" that happens when people live their lives. It can therefore sometimes be changed by enough of the right people living their lives differently. This book we offer as one glimpse of knowledge on what we think is an important topic, which we hope informs many people as they go about choosing how best to live their lives.

APPENDIX A | Christian Church Teachings on Financial Giving

N EARLY EVERY CHRISTIAN denomination and tradition has official teachings about financial giving, wealth, and stewardship intended to guide members in faithful Christian practices concerning uses of income and wealth. This appendix provides a summary of many of those teachings in order to substantiate the point made in the introduction that American Christians have plenty of clear religious normative teachings instructing them to give generously of their means. The denominations and traditions here are reviewed in alphabetical order. Italics below are added to highlight particularly relevant passages.

African Methodist Episcopal Church (Zion)

The standard of faith for the A.M.E. Church is the Twenty-Five Articles of Religion, which John Wesley extracted from the Thirty-Nine Articles of the Church of England. The A.M.E.'s founder, Richard Allen, adopted the Twenty-Five Articles of Religion as sufficient for the African Methodist Episcopal Church. Article 24, on "Of Christian Men's Goods," reads: "The riches and goods of Christians are not common as touching the right, title and possession of the same, as some do falsely boast. Notwithstanding, *every man ought, of such things as he possesseth, liberally, to give alms to the poor, according to his ability*." The denomination describes its "Mission and Purpose" in this way:

> To minister to the spiritual, intellectual, physical, emotional, and envi-
> ronmental needs of all people by spreading Christ's liberating gospel

through word and deed. At every level...the African Methodist Episcopal Church shall engage in carrying out the spirit of the original Free African Society, out of which the A.M.E. Church evolved: that is, to seek out and save the lost, and serve the needy through a continuing program of: (1) preaching the gospel of Jesus Christ, (2) *feeding the hungry*, (3) *clothing the naked*, (4) *housing the homeless*, (5) *cheering the fallen*, (6) *providing jobs for the jobless*, (7) *administering to the needs of those in prisons, hospitals, nursing homes, asylums and mental institutions, senior citizens' homes; caring for the sick, the shut-in, the mentally and socially disturbed*, and (8) encouraging thrift and economic advancement.

American Baptist Churches U.S.A.

In June 1991, the General Board of the denomination adopted an "American Baptist Policy Statement on Encouraging the Tithe: Growing and Giving in Grace," an elaborate document, which includes the following selections:

American Baptists are living and worshiping in a time and a society obsessed with possessing. Many voices of our society urge decisions based on "acquiring," asserting that "personal worth" is determined by one's accumulation of money and possessions. We struggle to reconcile God's call to "give" with society's insistence to "get." As disciples of Jesus Christ, we are called to challenge the misappropriation of God's resources. In the struggle between "giving" and "getting," we look for guidance in *the practice of tithing as a biblical path to growing and giving in grace*. The tithe is, for Christians, not a legalistic obligation, but an opportunity for grateful response to God's grace. *Tithing, properly understood, provides a biblical, practical and timely guideline for giving*. It restores a sense of perspective about how to deal with our material goods. The tithe helps Christians reexamine their personal and congregational values and adjust their lifestyles to have more to share with others in a world of need....

Biblical stewardship teaches the recognition that all we have and all we are belongs to God. We are not the self-centered owners of anything. Rather, in light of the Gospels, we are to be responsible stewards of all we possess. The Bible calls for the grateful use of God's gifts and resources in light of God's purposes, through a personal lifestyle for which each is accountable to God. Such stewardship was a principal focus of Jesus' teaching. It is a central element of Christian discipleship....

As children of God and followers of Jesus, American Baptists have stewardship responsibilities in all areas of life...[including] carefully managing all financial resources God has entrusted to us, sharing them in the service of Christ's mission to all persons (Matthew 6:19–21, 2 Corinthians 9:6–7).... God has entrusted us with time, talents and resources—gifts we are expected to use wisely and generously. Trying to reflect God's image as "givers" in the midst of daily choices makes decisions concerning personal finances unavoidable. Though God does not declare money to be evil, God does warn us against worshiping money or becoming dependent on it. Jesus clearly taught about dangers inherent in accumulating wealth for its own sake. How we spend our money reveals our priorities and the depth of our commitment. Our stewardship addresses the reconciliation between financial and faith commitments....

Christians do not live by law, but by God's grace as revealed in Jesus Christ. If the tithe were demanded by the law, it is *inconceivable that we would consider giving less* under grace.... As affluent American Christians who are encircled by a consumer mentality where greed abounds, many of us no longer understand the meaning of words like "generosity" and "sacrifice." *We need a guide, a benchmark, a beginning point.* Clement of Alexandria called the tithe a formation for generosity. *We believe the tithe is the answer for American Baptists. Tithing allows us to express the new basis upon which we build our new lives....*

Talking about the tithe often raises questions, such as: Do we tithe net or gross income? Does what is given to charities "count" as tithe? Ultimately, each believer must decide the base amount upon which to tithe and the ministries to which it will go. However, the spirit of gratitude which the tithe represents can be destroyed when the spirit of these questions becomes legalistic and narrow. American Baptists should see tithing as an expression of Christian grace, not a legalistic way of earning grace. It is a response—not a requirement. The progression of stewardship toward and beyond the tithe can be a discipline that frees us to comprehend the fullness of the Gospel and the riches of God's grace. We believe American Baptists, under the guidance of the Holy Spirit, informed by the study of scripture and in the context of Christian community, will discern that *the discipline of tithing is a vital step in Christian discipleship....*

"How much is too much?" For some, 10% is a real sacrifice, perhaps too much to give. For many American Baptists, however, 10% does not begin to represent sacrificial giving. Because of this, *the tithe should be seen as a good beginning,* not the ultimate achievement, in the stewardship of acknowledging God as Owner and Giver of all. The tithe is a step in our pattern of discipleship, marking our practice of growing and giving in grace....

American Baptists are called to stewardship of all of life. The biblical record is clear: everything is from God and we are responsible to manage it according to God's priorities. In responding to the challenges of Christian stewardship in every area of life, we are called to shape decisions about our personal finances in light of God's claim on our lives.

Tithing, the giving of 10% of one's income to the work of God through the church, can provide a biblical, practical, timely giving guideline for Christian disciples.... Tithing...is a clear teaching within Old Testament law. This teaching is not abolished in the New Testament, but enriched and transformed by grace. Tithing, in light of the gospel, becomes a privilege under grace rather than an obligation under law. *Tithing may be seen as a minimum standard for Christians seeking a biblical base for financial stewardship....* We call upon each American Baptist to consider the biblical challenge of the tithe as an appropriate beginning response to God's grace. Where the tithe may be deemed not immediately possible, we encourage an intentional program of moving steadily toward the tithe in yearly increments. We call on American Baptists, who are willing and able, to accept the challenge of moving beyond the tithe. We call upon the laity in our churches to encourage and empower preaching and teaching on financial stewardship in general and the tithe in particular, and to share the testimony of tithing in their own lives.... *We call upon each person who reads and votes upon this policy statement to become a tither or move toward becoming one using an intentional program of percentage giving, with the biblical 10% as the tithing norm.*

Assemblies of God

This, the largest Pentecostal denomination in the United States, also instructs as a formal denominational position its followers to tithe 10 percent of income. According to the denomination, the following position, elaborated in its General Council Bylaws, Article IX, Section 7a, "reflects commonly held beliefs based on scripture which have been endorsed by the church's Commission on Doctrinal Purity and the Executive Presbytery":

Dear *Passing the Plate* reader:

The authors of *Passing the Plate* are developing a new, global research project to better understand the practice of generosity. If you would like to receive free information about that project when it is made public, please fill in the information below and mail this postcard to the address on the other side of this card. We will contact you with information when the project goes public. Thanks for your interest!

Christian Smith, Michael Emerson, Patricia Snell

Please send me free information about the Generosity Research Project at Notre Dame:

Name: _____

Address: _____

City/State/Zip: _____

Email (optional): _____

The Generosity Research Project at Notre Dame
Flanner 812
University of Notre Dame
Notre Dame, IN 46556

The Assemblies of God has *always been a proponent of tithing* (or giving one-tenth of one's personal income to support the work of God). We believe tithing is a recognition that everything we have comes from God. The practice checks our greed, promotes personal discipline and thrift, testifies to our faith, promotes God's work in the world, and alleviates human need. While we do not believe tithing to be a condition for salvation, we do believe it is a very important biblical model, one which should set the minimal standard for Christian giving for people in all income ranges. Though some people believe tithing was an Old Testament practice not intended for New Testament Christians, the Assemblies of God believes and teaches that *tithing is still God's design* for supporting the ministry and reaching the world with the gospel. Our bylaws state, *"We recognize the duty of tithing and urge all our people to pay tithes to God"* (Article IX, Section 7a.) It is true there is no direct commandment in the New Testament saying, "You must tithe to God one-tenth of your income"; but there is also no statement declaring the Old Testament plan as no longer valid.... Today's church still relies on the support of tithers. Christians can miss out on God's abundant blessing by looking on the tithe as the entire requirement for giving. The tithe is only one aspect of support for the church and its ministry of spreading the gospel. *The Bible also mentions voluntary offerings given by God's people over and above the required tithe....* The Assemblies of God is also concerned about people who withhold tithes when they do not like decisions and directions espoused by spiritual leaders. Christians should fellowship with a local body of believers and bring their whole tithes into that storehouse (Malachi 3:10). Though some of the Israelites may not have liked decisions made by Moses and his successors, they were given no alternatives. While we may designate some of our offerings (beyond the tithes) to ministries outside the local church, *the tithes rightfully belong in the church* with which the Christian identifies. And if one is not identifying with a local body of believers, he or she disregards God's instruction that we not forsake assembling together with believers (Hebrews 10:25). Some Christians do not tithe, claiming they cannot afford to give up 10 percent of their income. Simple arithmetic may suggest that 90 percent will not go as far as 100 percent in satisfying essential family needs. But God has built a multiplication factor into our giving of tithes and offerings. Malachi recorded God's words, "Bring the whole tithe into the storehouse... Test me in this...and see if I will not throw open the floodgates of heaven and pour out so much blessing that you will not have room enough for it" (Malachi 3:10). Though we do not give to God in order to get more back, as some suggest we should, God's promises are still true—if our giving is according to His instruction.

Baptist General Conference

"An Affluent Church in a Hungry World" is the seventh of thirty total BGC denominational standing resolutions, adopted by the BGC in 1979. In its entirety, it reads thus:

I. WHEREAS, we are living in a world that is crying out in its need as evidenced by the facts: A. One out of every seven people in the world is suffering from hunger and malnutrition, and B. Approximately 14,000 people die daily from starvation and related diseases; and WHEREAS, such statistics are beyond our comprehension, they nevertheless show a great and pressing need of our world. Now, as at no other time in the history of mankind, we are painfully aware of the great need of a hungry world, and in an affluent and informed society, we can no longer ignore the need of the world. No longer can we remain silent or uninvolved citizens of a country that can produce more food than it needs, but will not in order to control our own economy and maintain an affluent lifestyle for her citizens. Hunger, retardation, famine and death are the grim realities of much of the underdeveloped nations of our world. Even within our own communities, hunger is a reality to many poor, elderly and unemployed.

II. WHEREAS the Word of God is explicit in its instruction to Christians regarding their responsibility to the poor and hungry, as evidenced by: A. The Old Testament Scriptures Deuteronomy 15:10 promises: " ... the Lord will bless you in all your work and in all you undertake" when we care for the poor and do not begrudge the needy or harden our hearts and shut the hand against the poor. Proverbs 19:17 tells us: "He who is kind to the poor lends to the Lord, and He will repay him for his deeds." Ezekiel 16:49 tells us: "Behold this was the guilt of your sister Sodom; she and her daughters had pride, sur-feit of food, and prosperous ease, but did not aid the poor and needy." Isaiah 58:10, 11 promises rich blessings for those who care for the needy. B. The New Testament Scripture Mark 6:37 reminds us that our Savior not only fed the hungry, but instructed His disciples to do so. Galatians 2:10 shows it was the example of the early church to "remember the poor" and was the eager desire of the Apostle Paul. Matthew 25:40 shows Jesus' concern for the whole man, and that as we minister unto even the least of these His brethren, we have done it unto Him. 1 John 3:17, 18 exhorts us to love not only in word and speech, but in deed and in truth. If we see our brother in need, and close our hearts against him, we cannot say that God's love abides in us.

III. WHEREAS, the Baptist General Conference has been known down through its history as being concerned about the need of the whole man, as seen by our concern for children's and retirement homes, military and institutional chaplaincies and medical work abroad, we must confess that we have not done as much as we could, nor as much as we should. For example, as Conference churches, benevolent giving has averaged approximately 3/4 of 1% of our giving, and that primarily for local needs. Conference giving to world relief, until this past year, has been on a downward trend, and has been primarily in response to world emergencies. For example: 1974–75: $135,632, 1975–76: $117,950, 1976–77: $ 71,463, 1977–78: $ 86,690.

IV. WHEREAS, we are "An Affluent Church in a Hungry World," in obedience to God, we must respond to the cry of a hungry world, and seek to meet the need of the world around us and abroad. While there are no cheap, easy answers to solve a very complex social, economic, political and agricultural problem, *we must do what we can, while we can, and where we can.*

V. THEREFORE, BE IT RESOLVED: A. That as INDIVIDUALS, and members of the family of God, *we, the members of the Baptist General Conference, will seek to develop a lifestyle that will enable us to give an increasing flow of resources to help the poor, suffering, and afflicted in all the world, including our own communities, by:* 1) Becoming more informed on the need of the world through reading, listening, and discussing. 2) Praying for the needs and situations of which we are made aware, and asking the Lord to burden our hearts with the need of afflicted people. 3) Giving careful study to the Word of God on portions that pertain to Christian lifestyle, and that these studies be made privately, in our family and church studies. 4) *Making sacrificial downward adjustments in our annual expenditures for vacations, food, clothing, entertainment and recreation, and in the quality of our housing and transportation.* B. That as LOCAL CHURCHES, and members of the Body of Christ, we adopt a mission which includes in a biblically directed manner, the alleviation of the hunger needs of the world, by: 1) Encouraging our pastors to preach sermon series that deal with the subject of Christian lifestyle and caring for the poor. 2) *Encouraging the local churches to give a minimum of one percent of their total budget to world relief* through the Baptist General Conference. 3) *Continuing to show concern for local needs through expanded giving and service to minister to the whole person in our communities.* C. That the BAPTIST GENERAL CONFERENCE develop a method of operation which demonstrates to the world that we are concerned about the hunger and suffering of the world, by: 1) Endorsing through specific action, that Christian living calls for Christian caring, and that our dual citizenship obligates us to care for physical as well as spiritual deprivation, as stated in principle in the 1978 Resolution. As a Conference we should seek to *modify our concern and response from reacting to periodic disaster relief calls, and recognize hunger and starvation as a continuing world disaster.* 2) Directing the Board of Trustees to establish a line item in the UMC budget for World Relief in conjunction with local church giving to the Conference. 3) The Board of Trustees shall direct the World Relief Committee to annually study the need of world relief and submit a proposed budget. The World Relief Committee shall also be directed to seek creative ways to promote a greater awareness of world relief needs throughout our constituency.

The Catholic Church

Roman Catholic Church teachings are disseminated through a variety of forms. Among them, a long and coherent tradition of Catholic Social Doctrine has taught the universal purpose of earthly wealth, the rights of the poor to lives of participation and dignity, the obligation of rich nations to give generously for the development of poor nations, and the obligation of all lay Christians to work for the common good of society. Much could be written here about Catholic teachings that bear on the financial giving of believers. For present purposes, however, we focus attention on a readily accessible and authoritative source of teachings for U.S. believers, the 1992 *Catechism of the Catholic Church*. According to then Pope John Paul II, writing his approval and promulgation of the text, the *Catechism* is "a sure and authentic reference text for teaching Catholic doctrine," "a new, authoritative exposition of the one and perennial apostolic faith...[that] will serve...as a sure norm for teaching the faith," and a "genuine, systematic presentation of the faith and of Catholic doctrine in a totally reliable way." If lay Catholics were to want to know what the Church teaches about financial giving, the *Catechism* would be a definite place to turn. Selections in it relevant for instruction on the financial giving of Catholic believers include the following (from which original textual cross-reference notations and biblical citations have been removed here for ease of reading):

1351. From the very beginning Christians have brought, along with the bread and wine for the Eucharist, gifts to share with those in need. This custom of the collection, ever appropriate, is inspired by the example of Christ who became poor to make us rich.... Those who are well off, and who are also willing, give as each chooses. What is gathered is given to him who presides to assist orphans and widows, those whom illness or any other cause has deprived of resources, prisoners, immigrants and, in a word, all who are in need.

2401. The seventh commandment [You shall not steal] forbids unjustly taking or keeping the goods of one's neighbor and wronging him in any way with respect to his goods. It commands justice and charity in the care of earthly goods and the fruits of men's labor. For the sake of the common good, it requires respect for the universal destination of goods and respect for the right to private property. Christian life strives to order this world's goods to God and to fraternal charity.

2402–2403. In the beginning *God entrusted the earth and its resources to the common stewardship of mankind to take care of them, master them by labor, and enjoy their fruits.* The goods of creation are destined for the whole human race. However, the earth is divided up among men to assure the security of their lives, endangered by poverty and threatened by violence. The appropriation of property is legitimate for guaranteeing the freedom and dignity of persons and for helping each of them to meet his basic needs and the needs of those in his charge. It should allow for a natural solidarity to develop between men. *The right to private property,* acquired by work or received from others by inheritance or gift, *does not do away with the original gift of the earth to the whole of mankind. The universal destination of goods remains primordial,* even if the promotion of the common good requires respect for the right to private property and its exercise.

2404–2406. In his use of things *man should regard the external goods he legitimately owns not merely as exclusive to himself but common to others also, in the sense that they can benefit others as well as himself. The ownership of any property makes its holder a steward of Providence, with the task of making it fruitful and communicating its benefits to others,* first of all his family. Goods of production—material or immaterial—such as land, factories, practical or artistic skills, *oblige their possessors to employ them in ways that will benefit the greatest number. Those who hold goods for use and consumption should use them with moderation, reserving the better part for guests, for the sick and the poor.* Political authority has the right and duty to regulate the legitimate exercise of the right to ownership for the sake of the common good.

2439–2440a. *Rich nations have a grave moral responsibility toward those which are unable to ensure the means of their development by themselves or have been prevented from doing so by tragic historical events. It is a duty in solidarity and charity;* it is also an obligation in justice if the prosperity of the rich nations has come from resources that have not been paid for fairly. *Direct aid is an appropriate response to immediate, extraordinary needs* caused by natural catastrophes, epidemics, and the like.

2441. An increased sense of God and increased self-awareness are fundamental to any full development of human society. This development multiplies material goods and puts them at the service of the person and his freedom. It reduces dire poverty and economic exploitation. It makes for growth in respect for cultural identities and openness to the transcendent.

2442–2444. It is not the role of the Pastors of the Church to intervene directly in the political structuring and organization of social life. This task is part of *the vocation of the lay faithful,* acting on their own initiative with their fellow citizens. *God blesses those who come to the aid of the poor and rebukes those who turn away from them:* "Give to him who begs from you, do not refuse him who would borrow from you"; "you received without pay, give without pay." It is by what they have done for the poor that Jesus Christ will recognize his chosen ones. When "the poor have the good news preached to them," it is the sign of Christ's presence. "The Church's love for the poor . . . is a part of her constant tradition." This love is inspired by the Gospel of the Beatitudes, of the poverty of Jesus, and of his concern for the poor. Love for the poor is even one of the motives for the duty of working so as to "be able to give to those in need." It extends not only to material poverty but also to the many forms of cultural and religious poverty.

2445. *Love for the poor is incompatible with immoderate love of riches or their selfish use:* "Come now, you rich, weep and howl for the miseries that are coming upon you. Your riches have rotted and your garments are moth-eaten. Your gold and silver have rusted, and their rust will be evidence against you and will eat your flesh like fire. You have laid up treasure for the last days. Behold, the wages of the laborers who mowed your fields, which you kept back by fraud, cry out; and the cries of the harvesters have reached the ears of the Lord of hosts. You have lived on the earth in luxury and in pleasure; you have fattened your hearts in a day of slaughter. You have condemned, you have killed the righteous man; he does not resist you."

2447. The works of mercy are charitable actions by which we come to the aid of our neighbor in his spiritual and bodily necessities.... *The corporal works of mercy consist especially in feeding the hungry, sheltering the homeless, clothing the naked, visiting the sick and imprisoned, and burying the dead. Among all these, giving alms to the poor is one of the chief witnesses to fraternal charity: it is also a work of justice pleasing to God:* "He who has two coats, let him share with him who has none and he who has food must do likewise." "But give for alms those things which are within; and behold, everything is clean for you." "If a brother or sister is ill-clad and in lack of daily food, and one of you says to them, 'Go in peace, be warmed and filled,' without giving them the things needed for the body, what does it profit?"

2448. In its various forms—material deprivation, unjust oppression, physical and psychological illness and death—human misery is the obvious sign of the inherited condition of frailty and need for salvation in which man finds himself as a consequence of original sin. This misery elicited the compassion of Christ the Savior, who willingly took it upon himself and identified himself with the least of his brethren. Hence, *those who are oppressed by poverty are the object of a preferential love on the part of the Church which, since her origin and in spite of the failings of many of her members, has not ceased to work for their relief, defense, and liberation through numerous works of charity which remain indispensable always and everywhere.*

2459. Man is himself the author, center, and goal of all economic and social life. The decisive point of the social question is that *goods created by God for everyone should in fact reach everyone in accordance with justice and with the help of charity.*

2544. Jesus enjoins his disciples to prefer him to everything and everyone, and bids them "renounce all that [they have]" for his sake and that of the Gospel. Shortly before his passion he gave them the example of the poor widow of Jerusalem who, out of her poverty, gave all she had to live on. The precept of *detachment from riches is obligatory for entrance into the Kingdom of heaven.*

2545–2546. All Christ's faithful are to "direct their affections rightly, lest they be hindered in their pursuit of perfect charity by the use of worldly things and by an adherence to riches which is contrary to the spirit of evangelical poverty." "Blessed are the poor in spirit." The Beatitudes reveal an order of happiness and grace, of beauty and peace. Jesus celebrates the joy of the poor, to whom the Kingdom already belongs. The Word speaks of voluntary humility as "poverty in spirit"; the Apostle gives an example of God's poverty when he says: "For your sakes he became poor."

2547. The Lord grieves over the rich, because they find their consolation in the abundance of goods. "Let the proud seek and love earthly kingdoms, but blessed are the poor in spirit for theirs is the Kingdom of heaven." Abandonment to the providence of the Father in heaven frees us from anxiety about tomorrow. Trust in God is a preparation for the blessedness of the poor. They shall see God.

Finally, in 1986, the U.S. Catholic Bishops issued a pastoral letter applying Catholic Social Teachings to the U.S. economy. Like the *Catechism* quoted above, the instructions in this pastoral letter on the subjects of wealth, charity, justice, solidarity, and sharing are abundant and complex. For present purposes, we here cite only one selection from the letter specifically addressing the need for "sacrificial giving or tithing" by individuals and households in order to sustain the Church:

351. We bishops commit ourselves to the principle that those who serve the Church—laity, clergy, and religious—should receive a sufficient livelihood and the social benefits provided by responsible employers in our nation. *These obligations, however, cannot be met without the increased contributions of all the members of the Church.* We call on all to recognize their responsibility to contribute monetarily to the support of those who carry out the public mission of the Church. *Sacrificial giving or tithing by all the People of God would provide the funds necessary* to pay these adequate salaries for religious and lay people; the lack of funds is the usual underlying cause for the lack of adequate salaries. *The obligation to sustain the Church's institutions*—education and health care, social service agencies, religious education programs, care of the elderly, youth ministry, and the like—*falls on all the members of the community* because of their baptism; the obligation is not just on the users or on those who staff them. *Increased resources are also needed for the support of elderly members of religious communities.* These dedicated women and men have not always asked for or received the stipends and pensions that would have assured their future. It would be a breach of our obligations to them to let them or their communities face retirement without adequate funds.

Christian and Missionary Alliance

The CMA teaches tithing and proportionate giving directed by heart-felt love for God. Its work of stewardship is headed by a "Great Commission Fund" section of the denomination, whose stated mission is: "Providing stewardship resources to Alliance churches helping Alliance people fulfill their biblical roles as stewards of God's possessions. Our Vision: C&MA churches excelling in the 'grace of giving' through lifestyle stewardship." Its teaching on "The Biblical Background of Tithing" states that, *"Tithing has been found as a key principle in history.* . . . In the Old Testament there were three kinds of tithes. . . . In the New Testament, tithing is specifically mentioned four times. The passages in Matthew 23:23, Luke 11:42, Luke 18:12, and Hebrews 7:4–9 do not constitute a major teaching. As a matter of fact, Jesus does not teach about tithing; but He does not repeal the tithing either. He affirms its importance to discipleship and faithfulness to God." In a 2001 CMA denominational position paper, "Stewardship and the Kingdom of God," the authors write, "The heart is the key issue, and if we are merely stewards of what is ultimately owned by God, then the driving question we must put to ourselves is not, 'How much do I give?' but 'How much dare I keep?'"

Christian Reformed Church (CRC)

The CRC Web site teaches this about Christian stewardship:

> Christian stewardship is the joyous management of all of life and life's resources so that God's mission on earth is accomplished. Every believer, responding in love to God's abundant outpouring of material blessings, shares the responsibility of Christian stewardship. Everything that we "own" is actually "on loan" from God. For as the apostle Paul wrote, "We brought nothing into the world, and we can take nothing out of it" (1 Tim. 6:7). Of course, these material blessings include our money. Some have more; some have less. Regardless of the size of our bank account, we *have the responsibility to give sacrificially for God's mission through His church.* God is pleased with the sacrifices of His people. . . . The Christian Reformed Church believes that Christian stewardship is essential for the health and mission of the church. The gospel is spread on the wings of those who give *generously and sacrificially.* Thank you for your participation as joyous stewards.

The denominational Web site also explains that individual tithing is important in financing the church's various ministries:

> To sustain the work and ministry of this denomination at home and abroad, the Christian Reformed Church relies on the *regular giving* of its churches, members, and friends.... Ministries require more money than...agencies receive through ministry shares [denominational quotas]. Direct gifts to the individual agencies provide the balance. Many Christians *decide what they can give to the church and its work by "tithing," using the biblical principle of offering one-tenth of their income to the Lord.*

Church of the Brethren

An undated *Handbook of Basic Beliefs within the Church of the Brethren* teaches the following, "not to become creeds, but to give guidance, and to point to the great truths of the Christian faith": "The ideals of temperance (1 Corinthians 9:25), purity (1 Corinthians 6:9–11), and simple living (Matthew 6:28–33), are to be taught and observed. *Christians are stewards of their possessions, and should contribute of their means cheerfully, regularly, systematically, proportionately, and liberally* for the advancement of Christ's cause on earth." Furthermore, in 1985, the Annual Conference of the Church of the Brethren issued a statement on "Christian Stewardship: Responsible Freedom" that in its section IV on "Stewardship of Financial Resources" declared the following:

> For the wise and faithful steward, material possessions and money become instruments of service to others, to further the human community God intends. Jesus said, "For where your treasure is, there will your heart be also" (Matt. 6:21).... Sharing material possessions and money to any degree nearing sacrificial giving is difficult for most people. So often security, sense of self-worth, and comparative value as an individual are based on what we have rather than on who we are as children of God and members of the household. The ultimate test of Christian stewardship, however, is how we relate to God and the covenant community, and how we live out that understanding in service and sharing. There are several reasons we share our material possessions and money. We share as a response of gratitude for the love and blessings received from God. How else could we respond? God's love and caring for us is boundless. The natural response to such good news is to share joyfully and unselfishly. We share our wealth also as a ministry of love in helping to supply the material

needs of others. As children of God, we are loved and valued equally. Every being contributes to God's plan and should have the opportunity to develop full potential. As stewards of God, we work together to feed the hungry and oppressed, to befriend the friendless, to work for peace and justice, to work for the equitable distribution of the earth's bounty. Sharing possessions is also a personal journey of discipline and maturity in faith. Jesus' teachings and life of total commitment and sharing are examples to us and challenge us to love our neighbors and serve their needs. Through tithing and proportionate giving we are freed to grow and reach beyond ourselves, to simplify standards of living and keep materialism in perspective. As stewards of God we come together in the faith community to live for the sake of the world.... We unite our unique abilities, our labors, and the fruit of our labor, which is our money, and bring them to God who blesses them and distributes them in the name and service of Christ. As the people of God, we look beyond our own salvation and security and deal with God's yearning that all the peoples of the earth know and accept divine love. It is the call to mission beyond ourselves. Clearly, we are called to share. How then do we know how and how much of our material possessions to share? There are several models for financial stewardship in scripture. When Jesus called his first disciples, "they left everything and followed him" (Luke 5:11). Jesus told the rich ruler, "Sell all that you have and distribute to the poor, and you will have treasure in heaven, and come, follow me" (Luke 18:22). Another New Testament model is that of the early Christians living in community in Jerusalem with shared possessions and goods (Acts 2:43–47; 4:32–35). In I Corinthians 16:2, Paul calls for regular and proportionate giving: "On the first day of every week, each of you is to put something aside and store it up, as he may prosper, so that contributions need not be made when I come." Yet another model is the collection which Paul took up among the Gentile churches to assist believers in Jerusalem, a model emphasizing the responsibility of the well-off for the economically distressed (2 Cor. 8–9). The Old Testament models for financial stewardship include tithing or the giving of the tenth (Lev. 27:30–32), offering of the first fruits (Prov. 3:9), and the time of jubilee or restoration (Lev. 25). Thus stewards were to share *the tenth part* of certain possessions as an offering, to give from the best, and to observe a time when all were restored to the condition God gave them. This was a *part of Jewish law and culture*. The obvious difference between the New Testament and Old

Testament models is that *Christian stewardship requires more.* Jesus was concerned with all of a person's life and possessions. Sharing is to be as one "may prosper" and in response to the need of others. Sharing is to be joyful, celebrative, and out of a response of gratitude. Stewardship is total. That is not to say that the Old Testament model of tithing is irrelevant for today. As a part of Jewish law and culture, the biblical material on tithing remains valuable as an illustration of how the people of God in an earlier period took stewardship seriously. Tithing has illustrative value for us as it provides a model of defining measurable standards of performance for our giving. *Tithing is an appropriate first-step discipline in deciding how much is enough to share.* As Christian stewards, we do not have the ease of a law or formula to determine whether or not we are "faithful and wise." There is no percentage of our income and accumulated wealth that, if shared with the church, automatically discharges our obligation to God, other persons, and the faith community. We must be aware of the use of all of our resources, even those we use to maintain ourselves. We have freedom to choose the portion we share with the church, but it is freedom with responsibility. We are ultimately accountable to God. Our stewardship of wealth must begin somewhere. *Through a discipline such as tithing we take the first step in responsible freedom as God's stewards.* As followers of Christ, and believers of the Word, with knowledge of the inequities and injustices in the world today, *we can do no less.*

Church of the Nazarene

The Nazarene's polity book, *Covenant of Church Conduct,* teaches the following in its section on "Christian Stewardship":

> The Scriptures teach that God is the Owner of all persons and all things. We, therefore, are his stewards of both life and possessions.... We shall be held personally accountable to God for the exercise of our stewardship. God, as a God of system and order in all of His ways, has established a system of giving that acknowledges His ownership and human stewardship. To this end *all His children should faithfully tithe and present offerings for the support of the gospel....* All who are part of the Church of the Nazarene are urged to *contribute faithfully one-tenth of all their increase as a minimum financial obligation to the Lord and freewill offerings in addition as God has prospered them for the support of the whole*

church, *local, district, regional, and general*.... It is [also] essential in the exercise of Christian stewardship that careful thought be given as to what shall be done with the residue of one's income and possessions over which the Lord makes the Christian a steward during this life. Civil laws often do not provide for the distribution of an estate in such a way as to glorify God. Each Christian should give attention to the preparation of a last will and testament in a careful and legal manner, and the Church of the Nazarene through its various ministries of mission, evangelism, education, and benevolence...is recommended for consideration.

Churches of Christ

The Churches of Christ view themselves as an "un-denomination" lacking any central headquarters or president. According to their Web site, their belief "is stated fully and completely in the Bible. There is no other manual or discipline to which the members of the church of Christ give their allegiance." The Internet Ministries of the Churches of Christ provide answers to basic questions, under the section "Who are the churches of Christ and what do they believe in?" written by Batsell Barrett Baxter. The answer to the question, "By what means does the church secure financial support?" is this:

> Each first day of the week the members of the church "lay by in store as they have been prospered" (1 Corinthians 16:2). The amount of any individual gift is generally known only to the one who gave it and to the Lord. This free-will offering is the only call which the church makes. NO assessments or other levies are made. No money-making activities, such as bazaars or suppers, are engaged in.

Church of God (Cleveland, TN)

This denomination teaches tithing as normative financial giving for members. According to the denomination's Web site, which appeals to multiple corroborating scripture references, "the following Doctrinal Commitments [that] represent the core beliefs of the denomination as outlined in Scripture [include]...*tithing* and giving." The denomination's Department of Stewardship provides numerous resources to teach and encourage tithing. Among them is an independent study Internet course, *"Tithing: The Divine Principle,"* described as "An introductory, seminary-level study of biblical tithing in the context of contemporary, Spirit-filled Christian faith and ministry. Primary attention will be given to Scriptural references to tithing, different approaches to the study, interpretation, and application of biblical tithing, the Holy Spirit's role in the matter of tithing, and discernment of appropriate responses, both individual and corporate." Also offered are books, including titles such as *Proving God: Triumphant Living through Tithing.*

Disciples of Christ, Christian Churches

The "Covenant" of the Disciples of Christ affirms the need of members to "share mutually and more fully the stewardship of God's gifts of our life in Christ." Stewardship, as defined on the denomination's Web site, is:

> grateful and responsible use of God's gifts in the light of God's purpose as revealed in Jesus Christ. Christian stewards, empowered by the Holy Spirit, commit themselves to *conscious, purposeful* decisions. Stewardship is lived out in...wisely employing God-given human resources, abilities, and relationships; sharing the material resources we hold and giving them in service, justice, and compassion; providing for future generations.

The denomination's charter, called "The Design of the Christian Church," states, "We commit ourselves to one another and to God...[to] furnish means by which all expressions of the church may fulfill their ministries with faithful Christian stewardship." The Design also states that "congregations demonstrate their mutual concern for the mission and witness of the whole church...[by being] faithful in Christian stewardship, striving to share proportionately in providing the resources for the total life, work, and witness of the Christian Church (Disciples of Christ)," also noting that, "all financial support of the general and regional programs of the Christian Church (Disciples of Christ) by congregations and individuals is voluntary."

The Episcopal Church in the U.S.A.

Common official church teachings for the U.S. Episcopal Church are set by its General Conventions. Most recently, in its 73rd General Convention in 2000, the following resolution, emphasizing tithing as a minimum expression of extravagant giving, was passed:

We believe: We are the children of God, and we need to give. In every aspect of our lives, we are entrusted to be stewards of God's creation. God invites us to give freely and to exercise joyfully our gifts through mission and ministry. We commit ourselves: To boldly claim God's abundant provision in our lives; to offer *extravagantly* our time, talent, and money to do God's work; and to *practice tithing as a minimum standard of giving.* We challenge members of the Episcopal Church: To confront our fears of scarcity; to embrace a new vision of stewardship through a joyful response to God's extravagant gifts; and to empower the mission of Christ through generous giving. We invite: Leadership groups in dioceses and congregations to develop their own stewardship statements in order to promote response to the gospel; and be it further Resolved, That we, the Deputies and Bishops of this convention, give thanks to God for those who *embrace tithing as a faithful individual response to the grace of God.*

This resolution built upon the following prior statement, "Stewardship is the Main Work of the Church," that also recommended tithing, which was adopted by the General Convention of the Episcopal Church meeting in 1988:

Stewardship is the main work of the Church.... Stewardship is more than a duty: it is a thankful response to God's graciousness to us.... Stewardship is an adventure, an expedition into the kingdom where we find our lives through losing them for the sake of the gospel. It is an invitation to offer our gifts for the purpose for which we were created—the only purpose that will fulfill us. It is a challenge to *refocus our lives by designing our budgets around tithing.* It offers us a way to begin breaking the bonds of consumption that involve us, often unwittingly, in perpetuating injustice and oppression.

Evangelical Lutheran Church in America

In its central document on Christian discipleship, "Living Faith: ECLA-wide Call to Discipleship," the ECLA member is enjoined to give financially, as follows:

The growing disciple finds ways to unpack and use...[their] gifts for the sake of Jesus, the church, and the world. Knowing God has entrusted us with abilities and goods, we ask, "How can we use these resources to love God?" Thus we do not waste time striving to be rich in things, but to be rich in love. *The maturing disciple is also maturing in financial stewardship, understands the biblical concept of the tithe and is growing in sacrificial and joyful giving toward and beyond a ten percent* response in all areas of life. *Part of the disciple's job description is to give freely.*

In August, 1999, in its sixth Churchwide Assembly, the ELCA adopted by a more than two-thirds majority vote (872–124) a denominational social statement, "Sufficient Sustainable Livelihood for All." This elaborate statement— one of eight major denominational social statements—analyzes many aspects of poverty, consumerism, economic globalization, and other economic issues that it declares often conflict with Christian moral teachings on economics, wealth, and stewardship. In response, the statement sets the shared goal of *"sufficient, sustainable livelihood for all"* as a benchmark for pursuing faith-informed changes in economic life. Toward that end, the statement commits the church and its members to numerous obligations, a selection of which follows. "We commit ourselves as a church," the statement reads, "and urge members" to:

- *give more* to relieve conditions of poverty, and invest more in initiatives to reduce poverty
- provide counsel, food, clothing, shelter, and *money* for people in need, in ways that respect their dignity
- *generously support* organizations and community-based efforts that enable low-income people to obtain more sufficient, sustainable livelihoods
- examine how we are in bondage to our possessions and can be freed to be faithful stewards of them
- serious and ongoing consideration in our families and congregations of how to resist the allure of consumerism and live lives less oriented toward the accumulation of goods and financial assets
- educate one another, beginning with the young, on how to deal responsibly with money, credit, and spending within one's means
- *give generously of our wealth (for example, through tithing and planned giving), especially for purposes that serve the needs of others*
- learn about, participate in, and *provide financial support for* community economic development and organizing strategies that enhance the current and future well-being of communities and the environment

Greek Orthodox Archdiocese of America

The Greek Orthodox Church in the United States comprises a Department of Stewardship Ministry, which promotes generous financial giving, described as follows:

> Christian Stewardship is a life-style, which acknowledges accountability and responsibility before God. Becoming a Steward begins when we say we believe in God, to whom we give our love, loyalty and trust. We affirm that every aspect of our lives comes as a gift from Him. Stewards are motivated as recipients of God's abundant love, to respond by participating and supporting His plan of salvation and the ministries of the Church, which make salvation possible for them and for others. In the Bible, the Steward is depicted as a person who is given the responsibility of managing something that belongs to the Owner, God. The Steward as the manager is thus accountable to the Owner for all that he possesses and is responsible to return to the Lord his or her fair share in gratitude and thanksgiving. *As God has been generous to us, He expects us to be generous toward the work of Christ and His Church.* Our Stewardship Commitment is the tool of ministry, salvation and healing for us and for others. Christian Stewardship is the privilege and honor of directly supporting God's work on earth through the Church. A flourishing parish Christian Stewardship Program can be compared to a river, which overflows into many tributaries and reaches out in many directions to share with others our rich and profound spiritual inheritance. Success on the local level emanates to greater support and outreach on all levels of ministry: local, national and international....

The Greek Orthodox Church Department of Stewardship Ministry has instituted a "Total Commitment Program," using the biblical passage of 1 Corinthians 16:2 to collect parish funds for use in Archdiocese programs. Believers are taught to *"give on a regular basis, {rather} than to wait until we have enough to meet our spiritual and financial obligation."* The resources and literature that the Archdiocese makes available to members through its Web site teach *proportionate giving and tithing* as normal practices of Christian giving.

International Church of the Foursquare Gospel

This denomination's "Declaration of Faith" states clearly: "We believe that the method ordained of God to sustain His ministry and spread the gospel after His command is *'Tithing'* and is generally accepted throughout all Four-square churches.... In the matter of 'giving' and 'free will offerings,' they are ordered of the Lord.... We know that giving unto His kingdom...is an enjoyable thing, it being more blessed to give than to receive."

International Pentecostal Holiness Church

The core beliefs of this denomination are spelled out in its "Covenant of Commitment," which describes the call to stewardship as follows:

> Our commitment to Jesus Christ includes stewardship. According to the Bible everything belongs to God. We are stewards of His resources. *Our stewardship of possessions begins with the tithe. All our members are expected to return a tenth of all their income to the Lord.* This tithe is to be paid into the "storehouse." This storehouse is the treasury of the local church or conference to which this member belongs. *In addition to the tithe,* all our members are expected to give offerings out of the ninety percent of God's wealth which He allows them to use. Stewardship also includes our time, talent, and spiritual gifts, as well as our money.

Lutheran Church–Missouri Synod

At its 1995 Convention (Resolution 4–07a) the LCMS asked its Department of Stewardship to "articulate the biblical principles of financial stewardship (Bylaw 9.01) which should guide all of our stewardship and appeal efforts, and disseminate these to all synodical entities, agencies and auxiliaries prior to the 1998 convention." The "Biblical Stewardship Principles" that were developed in response and later approved—that are "designed to be used by entities, agencies, auxiliaries and congregations of The Lutheran Church–Missouri Synod in all stewardship education and fund-raising activities"—is clear that Christian stewardship is not simply about money or merely meeting an organization's budget or financial goals. However, the Principles also include the following teaching commitments:

> As children of God through faith in Jesus Christ, and with the Holy Spirit's help, we will: Encourage proper management of all of life and life's resources for God's purposes; Promote materials and approaches to stewards that are firmly grounded in the Owner/manager understanding of stewardship; Encourage cheerful, *first-fruit, proportionate (including*

but not limited to tithing) living and giving in all areas of life by Christian stewards; and, Receive and use God's gifts with thanksgiving.... Recognize the personal and sensitive nature of the steward's response; and yet emphasize the truth that Christian stewards are members of the Body of Christ and are in kingdom work together with fellow Christians; and, Remind Christian stewards that God showers blessings upon those who manage them wisely and well for the common good. As children of God through faith in Jesus Christ, and with the Holy Spirit's help, we will *not:* Minimize the *bringing of regular offerings* as a part of worship and a loving response to God's love for us.

Mennonite Church U.S.A.

The 1995 Confession of Faith in a Mennonite Perspective teaches the following:

We acknowledge that God as Creator is owner of all things. In the Old Testament, the Sabbath year and the Jubilee year were practical expressions of the belief that the land is God's and the people of Israel belong to God. Jesus, at the beginning of his ministry, announced the year of the Lord's favor, often identified with Jubilee. Through Jesus the poor heard good news, captives were released, the blind saw, and the oppressed went free. The first church in Jerusalem put Jubilee into practice by preaching the gospel, healing the sick, and sharing possessions. Other early churches shared financially with those in need.... As stewards of money and possessions, we are to *live simply,* practice mutual aid within the church, uphold economic justice, and *give generously and cheerfully.* As persons dependent on God's providence, we are not to be anxious about the necessities of life, but to seek first the kingdom of God. We cannot be true servants of God and let our lives be ruled by desire for wealth.... Our tradition of simple living is rooted not in frugality for its own sake, but in dependence on God, the owner of everything, for our material needs. We depend on God's gracious gifts for food and clothing, for our salvation, and for life itself. We do not need to hold on tightly to money and possessions, but can *share what God has given us.* The practice of mutual aid is a part of sharing God's gifts so that no one in the family of faith will be without the necessities of life. Whether through community of goods or other forms of financial sharing, mutual aid continues the practice of Israel in giving special care to widows, orphans, aliens, and others in economic need (Deut. 24:17–22).

Tithes and firstfruit offerings were also a part of this economic sharing (Deut. 26; compare Matt. 23:23).... We are to seek first the reign of God and to cease from consumerism, unchecked competition, over-burdened productivity, greed, and possessiveness.

Also, the Mennonite Church encourages its members to give money through a denomination developed "Firstfruits Funding System," the stated program of which is based on the belief that

Households, congregations and institutions are only temporary caretakers of financial resources. They should be an example of generosity, even as they care for their own well-being. The history of God's people shows us a money management pattern of providing a place to gather for worship, scripture study and caring for the poor, being generous to those set apart to lead the congregation, and in being generous—especially to the suffering church. Economic resources are managed with these purposes in mind.

Tithing as a minimum baseline is one of the principles on which financial giving in this "first fruits" system is based, as the program explains:

[Tithing is] a starting point for proportionally giving one's first and best. For those observing the law of Moses, a tithe referred to a ten-percent portion of the harvest, or the income produced if a harvest was sold. Presentation of the tithe took place at the temple as an act of worship. As Western society shifted from an agricultural to a monetary economy, many Christian traditions carried forward the expectation of the tithe as ten percent of gross household income, again as a gift to be presented in worship, usually through the local congregation. However, many remain unaware the Hebrews presented a tithe twice and sometimes three times in a year. The instruction of Jesus is that tithing must be done in conjunction with a deep concern for justice, mercy and faithfulness (Matthew 23:23) or it becomes meaningless. Thus, the concept of firstfruits living, as defined above, is more solidly aligned with Jesus' instruction than the tithe alone. *For those seeking to enforce the tithe, or seeking to abandon it, ten percent of income is the limit of stewardship responsibility. A firstfruits lifestyle, however, finds it is only the beginning.*

Missionary Baptist

The "Church Covenant" of Missionary Baptist churches states that, in response to God's love and salvation, "We engage therefore, by the aid of the

Holy Spirit, to walk together in Christian love; to strive for the advancement of this church in knowledge, holiness, and comfort; to promote its prosperity and spirituality to sustain its worship, ordinances, discipline, and doctrine; *to contribute cheerfully and regularly to the support of the ministry, the expenses of the church, the relief of the poor, and the spread of the gospel through all nations.*"

The Moravian Church in North America

Moravians have stood for certain basic religious principles for more than 500 years, during which it has often put into written form the precepts of its faith and practice. Today that written document is known as the "The Moravian Covenant for Christian Living." In its sections on "Stewardship" and "Love for All," the Moravian Covenant declares:

> We deem it a *sacred responsibility and genuine opportunity* to be faithful stewards of all God has entrusted to us: our time, our talents, our financial resources.... *We will support, according to our ability, the financial needs* of the local congregation, the District, the Province, and the Unity. We will consider the *support of benevolent causes* of the Moravian Church, both at home and abroad, as *a privilege, and opportunity, and a responsibility.* We will *also recognize the support of worthy causes outside of the Church as part of our stewardship....* Together with the universal Christian Church, we have a concern for this world, *opening our heart and hand to our neighbors with the message of the love of God, and being ever ready to minister of our substance to their necessities.*

Documents offered on the Moravian Church Web site recommend—and in some cases call for requiring—proportionate giving and tithing of members. For one example, a record of "Legislation Passed by Our Eastern District Synod of 2004" states as a resolution that "The Synod will encourage *member requirements* to be developed by each congregation to include... *financially supporting the ministry of the church toward the goal of tithing.*"

National Association of Free Will Baptists

The "Church Covenant" of this Baptist Association includes the statement, "We will not forsake the assembling of ourselves together for church conferences, public worship, and the observance of the ordinances of the Gospel;

nor fail to pay according to our ability for the support of the church, of its poor, and all its benevolent work."

National Baptist Convention of America, Inc.

The NBCA's "Doctrinal Statement" includes the following teaching about "Stewardship" as a means for "Carrying Out the Mandate of the Master" under its "Baptist Belief and Proclamation": "Mankind is the steward of another's possessions. Any true sense of stewardship begins with the irrefutable fact that all things belong to God. The Eternal holds mankind responsible for time, talent, and treasure, both in the possession and the use of them.... The truth is that all things belong to God means that all should be used for His glory. Baptists believe that *a proper sense of stewardship begins with the 'tithe'; a presentation of that which belongs to Him. 'The tithe is the Lord's.' We have not given as a result of presenting the tithe. Our giving begins with the offering {after we have tithed}."* The "Mission Statement" of the NBCA states, "The National Baptist Convention of America shall serve to promote and support Christian education, Christian missions and church extension through the combined efforts of Baptist churches and organizations and shall seek to cause the gospel, as understood and practiced by our Baptist faith, to be spread throughout this nation and to the foreign nations. The National Baptist Convention shall seek to positively impact and influence the spiritual, educational, social, and economic conditions of all humankind." The NBCA organizes its financial giving through a denomination-wide "Covenant Action Plan" or CAP, which is a systematic method of financing the objectives of the NBCA, including its outreach ministries. The CAP represents a financial commitment between NBCA and its member churches to pledge and honor that pledge systematically by one of two methods. The CAP plan calls for each member church, association, state convention, or any other affiliate group or person to make monthly contributions or contribute at the three annual meetings based upon their committed ability to give.

Orthodox Presbyterian Church

This Reformed denomination that holds to the Westminster Confession of Faith teaches this in its *Book of Church Order*:

> The bringing of offerings into God's house is a solemn act of thanksgiving to almighty God. In order that the receiving of the offering may stand out as a specific act of worship it is well that the minister

either precede or immediately follow it with a brief prayer, invoking the blessing of God upon the offering and devoting it to his service. It is the duty of the minister to cultivate *the grace of liberal giving in the members of the church* by reminding them of the scriptural admonition that *every one should give as the Lord has prospered him,* of the assurance of Scripture that God loves a cheerful giver, and of the blessed example of the Lord Jesus Christ who, though he was rich, became poor in order that poor sinners through his poverty might become rich. The session shall take care that the offerings of the congregation are used only for the maintenance of public worship, the preaching of the gospel throughout the world, and other Christian objects.

Moreover, the Westminster Larger Catechism embraced by the OPC teaches in answer to the question (Number 147), "What are the duties required in the tenth commandment?" that "The duties required in the tenth commandment are, such a full contentment with our own condition, and *such a charitable frame of the whole soul toward our neighbor,* as that all our inward motions and affections touching him, tend unto, and further all that good which is his."

Pentecostal Church of God

The Doctrinal Statement (Article Three, 2004 Pentecostal Church of God Constitution and Bylaws) of this denomination states: "We recognize the *scriptural duty of all our people, as well as ministers, to pay tithes as unto the Lord.* Tithes should be used for the support of the active ministry and for the propagation of the Gospel and the work of the Lord in general."

Presbyterian Church in America

This Reformed, evangelical denomination defines stewardship in terms of tithing on its denominational Web site:

> As we think about stewardship it is imperative that we acknowledge the sovereignty of God and that we are called to be servants and stewards of all that he gives to our charge. Psalms 24:1 "The earth is the Lord's and everything in it, the world, and all who live in it." As those who are redeemed and adopted into His family we should rejoice in our relationship and also our stewardship. As our days are numbered according to Psalm 139:16, so we are encouraged to "number our days aright, that we may gain a heart of wisdom" Psalm 90:12. This underscores

stewardship of our time. As the Holy Spirit has gifted each believer in the body of Christ (I Cor. 12:7 ff.) so "Each one should use whatever gift he has received to serve others ..." (I Pet. 4:10). This underscores stewardship of our gifts. Finally, *the stewardship of our finances begins with the tithe* in Deuteronomy 14:22 to the Lord's approval in Matthew 23:23, and Luke 11:42, *but it goes beyond* as so much of the Lord's teaching and that of Paul's emphasizes the dangers of money and riches. To the rich, Paul tells Timothy, to command them to do good, to be rich in good deeds, and to be generous and willing to share (II Timothy 6:18).

Presbyterian Church in the U.S.A.

The 213th General Assembly (2001) of the PCUSA approved a new statement of stewardship theology, a first new statement for the denomination in nearly twenty years, reflecting the most recent available understandings it has of biblical and theological stewardship. The denomination describes it as "a foundational piece." Included in the statement are the following teachings, which stress tithing and practices of sacrifice and obedience in the proper management of the possessions that God has entrusted to his people:

> Tangible biblical concepts and images abound that teach us *the life of the steward*. Among those concepts are *tithing* and jubilee. References to tithing occur throughout the Old Testament (from Genesis 14:20 to Malachi 3:10). While Scripture affirms that *the tithe belongs to God,* we diminish the concept of tithing if we confine our discussions only to matters of obligation, calculation, or method. We can fall into *the error of thinking that everything is ours. Nothing could be further from the truth.* The tithe is not given to us as a formula. Rather, *disciplined and proportionate giving* is a regular reminder and a very concrete symbol that the whole belongs to God.... Jubilee does not devalue the material, but teaches that our possessions and relations must be restored to their proper places.... Jubilee frees us from the myth that we are defined by what we own. It tells us that we belong to God—in life and in death.... Christian practices shape that participation and help us learn to live the Christian life the same way we learn other skills—by practicing it. As we participate in various disciplines, space opens up in our lives for the Holy Spirit to transform our ways of thinking and behaving.... We need to become living sacrifices in response to and for the sake of

the gospel. The *discipline of obedience* enables us to understand that neither we nor our resources belong to ourselves. We are not just managing surpluses for the good of humanity. We understand that all resources are God's and that they are to be *used for God's purposes*. And with this discipline, we come full circle for in obedience we gain discernment.

Reformed Church of America (RCA)

The RCA Commission on Theology met in Chicago on February 2–5, 2005 and issued a statement that included a reflection on stewardship that included this passage:

> How can we individually and communally—in our homes, churches, camps, workplaces—resist the rushing current that is our materialistic culture and its siren song of success while cultivating and putting into practice a more faith-filled way of life? Here are...simple strategies: 1. Say no. Don't buy the latest, fastest, biggest. Live simply. 2. Tithe. Give a percentage of your income away—to your church, to Bread for the World, to Church World Service, to missionaries, to the local soup kitchen or homeless shelter.

Seventh-Day Adventist Church

Seventh-day Adventists "accept the Bible as their only creed" and hold certain fundamental beliefs to be the teaching of the Holy Scriptures. These beliefs, as set forth in a document, "Fundamental Beliefs," constitute the church's understanding and expression of the teaching of Scripture. In Section 21 on "Stewardship," the church teaches the following:

> We are God's stewards, entrusted by Him with time and opportunities, abilities and possessions, and the blessings of the earth and its resources. We are responsible to Him for their proper use. We acknowledge God's ownership by faithful service to Him and our fellow men, and *by returning tithes and giving offerings* for the proclamation of His gospel and the support and growth of His church. Stewardship is a privilege given to us by God for nurture in love and the victory over selfishness and covetousness. The steward rejoices in the blessings that come to others as a result of his faithfulness.

Tithing is even more explicitly advanced as the church's normative expectation in the Adventist's *Church Manual*:

> The Tithe. In recognition of the Bible plan and the solemn privilege and responsibility that rest upon church members as children of God and members of His body, the church, *all are encouraged to return a faithful tithe (one tenth of their increase or personal income) into the denomination's treasury....* Thus the local conference/mission/field, the union, and the General Conference are provided with funds with which to support the workers employed and to meet the expense of conducting the work of God in their respective spheres of responsibility and activity. *In addition* to remitting to the union ten percent of their tithe income, local conferences/missions/fields also remit through the union to the General Conference, or its divisions, an additional percentage of their tithe as determined by the General Conference Executive Committee or division committee for the financing of the church's program. These policies have been developed for the gathering and disbursing of funds in all the world and for the conducting of the business affairs of the cause. *The financial and business aspects of the work are of great importance. They cannot be separated from the proclamation of the message of salvation; they are indeed an integral part of it....* The tithe is holy unto the Lord, and *is God's provision for the support of His ministry. Freewill offerings are also part of God's plan for the support of His work throughout the world.*

Southern Baptist Convention

The common teachings of this largest of Protestant denominations in the United States are found in "The Baptist Faith and Message," most recently revised and adopted on June 14, 2000. This summary of faith teaches regular, systematic, proportionate, and liberal financial giving in its Section XIII on "Stewardship:"

> God is the source of all blessings, temporal and spiritual; all that we have and are we owe to Him. Christians have a spiritual debtorship to the whole world, a holy trusteeship in the gospel, and a binding stewardship in their possessions. They are therefore under obligation to serve Him with their time, talents, and material possessions; and should recognize *all these as entrusted to them to use for the glory of God and for helping others.* According to the Scriptures, *Christians should contribute of their means cheerfully, regularly, systematically, proportionately, and liberally for the advancement of the Redeemer's cause on earth.*

United Church of Christ (UCC)

The UCC maintains a strong emphasis on generous financial giving, with tithing as the goal. One denominationally designed bulletin insert with the title, "How Much Should I Give?" answers its own question by saying, "The United Church of Christ *stresses giving in a deliberately chosen percentage of income to support God's mission among people everywhere. Our church urges us to set at least 10% of income as our giving goal* and suggests that we move toward that goal by giving an additional 1% of our income each year." Also, a key denominational resource on "Financing" for new church startups states this on "Teaching Tithing":

> To speak of tithing, giving back to God at least ten percent of one's riches, is an effective way to set a high expectation of spiritual generosity for a new congregation. A tithing church is a generous church, and a generous church will thrive and grow. *When we tithe we place God as our first priority. We trust in God's abundance instead of worrying about not having enough. Tithing churches live out of a vision of abundance rather than a mentality of scarcity.*

The UCC has instituted a number of denominational programs to encourage generous giving. For example, "Covenant Keeper" churches represent about 17 percent of all UCC congregations that support the denomination's "Our Church's Wider Mission" (OCWM) by giving more than 10% of their operating budget to OCWM Basic Support. In addition, the UCC has organized a "StillspeakingMoney®" program of automated giving designed to make it easy for members to give. StillspeakingMoney® automatically deducts givers' gifts from their checking, savings, debit or credit card account on one or more dates each month. In these and many other ways, the UCC clearly communicates the importance of financial giving.

United Methodist Church

This second largest Protestant denomination in the United States explicitly teaches tithing, the giving of 10 percent of income, as a minimum as its most recent official church position. The 2004 *Book of Discipline of the United Methodist Church,* for instance, states that each annual conference, as part of its responsibilities in the area of stewardship, is to "educate the local church that *tithing* is the minimum goal of giving in The United Methodist Church." Furthermore, the 2004 *Book of Resolutions of the United Methodist Church,* in a statement on tithing, says, "the 2000 General Conference adopts as a *high priority* for the next eight years a program for teaching and preaching for spiritual growth in giving, with an emphasis of setting *tithing as a goal for every person* in The United Methodist Church."

Wesleyan Church

Teachings of the Wesleyans on financial giving are published in the denomination's document, "Who Are the Wesleyans?" which teaches the following under the section Our Beliefs: "Those admitted to Covenant Membership in our churches *commit themselves to demonstrate their life in Christ in such ways as* . . . exercis[ing] *faithful stewardship through the wise use of their time and material resources,* practicing careful self-discipline in order to further the mission of Christ's church (*remembering the principle of tithing which is basic to the New Testament standard of stewardship*) *and to demonstrate compassion to those in need."* The same section also speaks of this commitment "toward others," "To do good as much as is possible to all people as God gives opportunity, especially to those in the body of Christ; by giving food to the hungry, by clothing the destitute, by visiting or helping those who are sick or in prison; by instructing, correcting or encouraging them in love." In another section on "Christian Stewardship," the reader finds this instruction:

> The Scriptures teach that God is the owner of all persons and all things, that people are His stewards of both life and possessions, that God's ownership and one's stewardship ought to be acknowledged, and that every person shall be held personally accountable to God for the exercise of their stewardship. *God, as a God of system and order in all of His ways, has established a system of giving which acknowledges His ownership and mankind's stewardship. To this end all His children should faithfully tithe and present offerings for the support of the gospel. Storehouse tithing is a scriptural and practical performance of faithfully and regularly placing the tithe into that church to which the member belongs. Therefore, the financing of the church shall be based on the plan of storehouse tithing,* and The Wesleyan Church shall be regarded by all its people as the storehouse. *All who are a part of The Wesleyan Church are urged to contribute faithfully one-tenth of all their increase as a minimum financial obligation to the Lord and freewill offerings in addition as God has prospered them.*

In a separate "Christian Stewardship" section under "Contemporary Issues," the denomination's basic beliefs document teaches this on "Sharing Our Wealth":

> In a broad sense each man's wealth consists of time, health, and such resources as food, energy, income, and accumulated possessions. It fol-

lows from the basic premise of stewardship that the Christian should use earth's wealth "for the glory of God." The Christian must love God, not the world, and *should share his possessions rather than to hold them selfishly. Sharing possessions is important in fulfilling obligations to God, to family, to government, and to societal needs. Christian sharing should be voluntary, motivated by compassion, and administered with justice.*

Wisconsin Evangelical Lutheran Synod (WELS)

The WELS's Web site page on "Financial Stewardship" states that "Stewardship is part of a Christian's life of sanctification, which includes everything he or she does in grateful response to God's grace and mercy in Christ. It fits in with such activities as worship, prayer, charity and evangelism. It is obvious that God has blessed us richly! Therefore let us generously return a portion of our blessings to Him." Denominational resolutions call for faithful stewardship in financial giving, including one in 2005 stating that "We encourage every individual and congregation of the WELS to excel in the grace of Christian giving." The WELS's 2005–06 Stewardship Program, "Every Soul's a Treasure," teaches members the following:

> **Practice first fruits giving.** Giving first to the Lord before spending on other things expresses my honor to God…by giving him the "best" rather than the leftovers…. When we give our first fruits to the Lord, everything else in life follows suit. **Practice proportionately generous (%) giving** based on your own income and blessings (rather than a comparison with an amount someone else gave). Generosity in giving ought to be the gauge rather than some imposed law or rule. A percentage of the way the Lord has blessed you becomes a guide. (Realize the basis for Old Testament giving started with the tithe = 10%. What should that say to us today?).… **Live not as owners but as stewards (managers) of God's possessions.** Our giving recognizes that God, the Creator, is also the owner of everything and we are the stewards or caretakers of those gifts for his glory. Stewardship plays a large role in refining our character and releasing us from selfishness and greed and serves as a witness to the world that all life and wealth comes from God to be invested for his eternal purposes. **Follow planned, regular giving.** Faithfully save up "on the first day of every week" for a well thought-out gift rather than sporadic, haphazard offerings. Regular consistent offerings acknowledge the regular

consistent ministry activity that accomplishes our mission.... **Test the Lord's Promises with Bold Faith**. This is about stepping out in faith in the Lord who can do the impossible. He creates in us both the willingness and the ability to carry out his will. If our lives test his promises with trusting generosity, he will open unexpected floodgates of blessings in unexpected ways. [Bold highlights in the original.]

The WELS Web site elsewhere teaches the following:

Tithing (giving 10%) was the starting point for giving in the Old Testament, not an upper limit or even a recommendation. For the Old Testament people the tithe was a minimum command. No such law is given to us in the New Testament. It would be a good custom to use a tithe also as a starting point for us today. It would be a sad reflection on us if we, who have so many more blessings than most of the Old Testament people both spiritually and materially, are satisfied with giving less than their minimum. Our freedom from laws of giving is an encouragement to do more, not an incentive to do less.... The Old Testament tithe is [not] useless to us. God's basic message with the tithe was not "give me!" but "trust me!" God was asking his people to believe that he who had blessed them with their money and goods would not fail to continue to bless them. It was a step of faith to take a generous portion of their first and best and give that to God. Giving the tithe was first and foremost not a financial transaction, but a statement of confidence in the continuing goodness of God. Even though the command of the tithe is gone, the lesson to learn remains the same. By taking a percentage, a proportion, of the first and best he gives to us, God is asking us to trust in his continued merciful goodness to us.

Worldwide Church of God

This denomination's published "Statement of Financial Stewardship" maintains, "The church teaches that *Christians have a spiritual duty to financially support their church and encourages each member to give as he or she is able and has been blessed by God.* Thus, most but not all of our revenue is raised from our church members and is solicited, if at all, from verbal or written appeals in accordance with our doctrines. *The practice of tithing, while not mandated, is encouraged as a good standard of Christian financial stewardship.*"

| Data Sources Used in Analysis

D ATA FROM THE following sources are used in this book.

General Social Survey (GSS), 1998 and 1996

The GSS has been conducted by the National Opinion Research Center almost annually since 1972 and biennially beginning in 1994. The GSS is designed as part of a program of social indicator research, replicating questionnaire items and wording in order to facilitate time-trend studies. Items in the 1998 GSS include special modules on religion, with items measuring giving, volunteering, religious self-identification, and congregational affiliation. The 1998 GSS sampled 2,832 cases. The 1996 GSS sampled 2,904 cases. The 1998 and 1996 GSS use a national probability sample that follows the biennial, double sample design adopted in 1994. This biennial, split-sample design was instituted, consisting of two parallel subsamples of approximately 1,500 cases each, with identical cores and different topical ISSP modules. Full probability sampling was employed in 1998 and 1996 for all noninstitutionalized English-speaking persons 18 years of age or older, living in the United States. These national samples used a variation of the stratified "probability proportional to size" (PPS) method. GSS Principal Investigators are James Allan Davis and Tom W. Smith.

The Center on Philanthropy Panel Study, 2001 (COPPS)

COPPS is the Center on Philanthropy at Indiana University's signature research project, designed to follow the same families' philanthropic behaviors throughout their lives. This study provides a unique perspective of families' giving and volunteering behaviors over time. The COPPS is conducted in conjunction with the University of Michigan Institute for Social Research's Panel Study of Income Dynamics (PSID), which has surveyed the same 5,000 households since 1966. As children of these respondents have matured, they have been added to the sample, which now exceeds 7,400 households. In 2001, researchers added the philanthropy component, designed and sponsored by the Center on Philanthropy, which hopes to repeat the survey every two years thereafter, pending funding. The COPPS is the only study that surveys giving and volunteering by the same households over time as families mature, face differing economic circumstances, and encounter changes in their family size, health, and other factors. It also is the only data available that asks families extensively about their wealth and philanthropy as well as income and other relevant factors. Because the PSID employs genealogical sampling (those who are born or marry into sample families are included thereafter), the panel allows researchers to study the transmission of philanthropic behaviors across generations and to study the relationship between helping family members and helping anonymous others. Finally, the panel data helps distinguish types of donors who respond differently to economic, demographic, and environmental factors. The COPPS Principal Investigators are Mark Wilhelm, Eleanor Brown, Patrick Rooney, and Rich Steinberg.

Giving and Volunteering in the United States, 2001 (GVUS 2001)

Sponsored by the Independent Sector—a leadership forum for charities, foundations, and corporate giving programs—this survey provides a broad picture of the giving and volunteering habits of Americans. Fielded as a random-digit-dial telephone survey of 4,216 adult Americans 21 years of age or older, it was conducted in the months of May through July of 2001 by Westat, Inc. The interviews asked about individual volunteering habits in the 12 months prior to the survey and about household giving during the year 2000. A change in the weighting procedures was implemented with the 2001 survey. Analyses must rely on two different weighting schemas, one for households and one for individuals. Respondents were asked two different sets of questions, one set related to household giving and the other to personal volunteering. For this reason, all giving data were weighted to represent the number of households, 105 million, and all volunteering data were weighted to represent the noninstitutionalized adult population, 195 million. Sampling respondents age 21 and older instead of age 18 and older had the effect of removing from the analysis people at the lower end of the giving scale. Changes in methodology in 2001 compared to the same survey in 1994 (see below) mean that comparisons to prior Giving and Volunteering studies cannot easily be made. The latter year asks about religion organization membership and religious service attendance but does not ask religious affiliation or identity.

Giving and Volunteering in the United States, 1994 (GVUS 1994)

Sponsored by the Independent Sector—a leadership forum for charities, foundations, and corporate giving programs—the *Giving and Volunteering in the United States, 1994* survey provides a broad picture of the giving and volunteering habits of Americans. The 1994 representative sample size was 1,509 U.S. adults. Data were gathered through in-home personal interviews conducted by the Gallup Organization from April to May 1994. Sampling employed a replicated multistate area probability sample down to the block level in urban areas and to segments of townships in rural areas. Weights are employed in analyses to adjust toward national representation. See Virginia Hodgkinson and Murray Weitzman, 1994, *Giving and Volunteering in the United States: Findings from a National Survey, 1994 Edition,* Washington, D.C., Independent Sector.

Economic Values Survey, 1993 (EVS)

This is a survey of adult participants in the U.S. labor force, sampled to be representative of the active labor force age 18 and over living in the continental United States. The survey contains 2,013 cases and 489 variables. Data were collected in February and March 1992 through in-person interviews, conducted by the Gallup Organization. The sampling design is that of a replicated probability sample down to the block level in the case of urban areas and to segments of townships in the case of rural areas. The sample design includes stratification by seven size-of-community strata, using 1990 census data. Each of these strata is further stratified into four geographic regions: East, Midwest, South, and West. Within each city-sized regional stratum, the population is arrayed in geographic order and zoned into equal-sized groups of sampling units. Pairs of localities are selected in each zone, with probability of selection and each locality proportional to its population size in the most current U.S. census, producing two replicated samples of localities. Within each subdivision so selected for which block statistics are available, a sample of blocks or block clusters is drawn with probability of selection proportional to the number of dwelling units. In all other subdivisions or areas, blocks or segments are drawn at random or with equal probability. In each cluster of blocks and each segment so selected, a randomly selected starting point is designated on the interviewer's map of the area. Starting at this point, interviewers are required to follow a given direction in the selection of households until their assignment is completed. See Robert Wuthnow, 1994, *God and Mammon in America,* Free Press: New York, pp. 269–311 for details on methodology and the survey instrument. The EVS Principal Investigator was Robert Wuthnow.

Consumer Expenditure Survey (CES), 2000

The CES consists of two surveys collected for the U.S. Bureau of Labor Statistics by the Census Bureau—the quarterly Interview survey and the Diary survey—that provide information on the buying habits of American consumers, including data on their expenditures, income, and consumer unit (families and single consumers) characteristics. The surveys have targeted the total noninstitutionalized population, both urban and rural, of the United States in 1980, 1984, and thereafter. The data are collected in independent quarterly Interview and weekly Diary surveys of approximately 7,500 sample households. Each survey has its own independent sample, and each collects data on household income and socioeconomic characteristics. Included questions ask about expenditures as cash donations to religious organizations as well as educational, charitable, and political organizations. In the Interview Survey, each consumer unit is interviewed every three months over five calendar quarters. In the initial interview, information is collected on demographic and family characteristics and on the consumer unit's inventory of major durable goods. Expenditure information also is collected in this interview but is used only to prevent duplicate reporting in subsequent interviews. Expenditure information is collected in the second through the fifth interviews using uniform questionnaires. Income and employment information is collected in the second and fifth interviews. In the fifth interview, a supplemental section is administered in order to account for changes in assets and liabilities over a one-year period. The Interview survey includes monthly out-of-pocket expenditures such as housing, apparel, transportation, health care, insurance, and entertainment. In the Diary Survey, respondents are asked to keep track of all their purchases made each day for two consecutive one-week periods. Diary survey includes weekly expenditures of frequently purchased items such as food and beverages, tobacco, personal care products, and nonprescription drugs and supplies. Participants receive each weekly diary during a separate visit by a Census Bureau interviewer.

The State of Church Giving through 2003 (SCG)

This detailed hard copy report, written by John L. Ronsvalle and Sylvia Ronsvalle and published by empty tomb, inc. of Champaign, IL, contains extensive information based on the analysis of multiple other data sources. The Ronsvalles and empty tomb, inc. are among the most active analysts of religious financial giving in the United States. This most recent of their reports reviews data for a composite set of denominations from 1968 to 2003 that includes 29 million full or confirmed members, representing about one in three religious congregations in the United States.

Yearbook of American and Canadian Churches (YACC), 2005

The YACC reports annually on data gathered from national religious bodies that reflect the religious affiliations and financial giving patterns of hundreds of millions of Americans. Publication of these data has proceeded almost annually since the 1917 publication of *Federal Council Year Book,* providing excellent longitudinal data. Published data generally represent information gathered two calendar years prior to the date of publication. The *Yearbook* is prepared in the Office of Research, Evaluation and Planning of the National Council of the Churches of Christ in the U.S.A. and is published by Abingdon Press of Nashville, TN.

Other Data Sources

In addition to these data sources, this book also drew on more limited statistics found in the following sources. First we cited some statistics from David Barrett, George Kurian, and Todd Johnson (eds.), 2001, *World Christian*

Encyclopedia, vol. 1 (2nd ed.), Oxford: Oxford University Press. We also quoted some statistics from David Barrett and Todd Johnson (eds.), 2001, *World Christian Trends, AD 30–2200,* Pasadena, Calif.: William Carey Library. We also bring data in from the 2004 General Social Survey (GSS), the 2004 Federal Reserve Board's Survey of Consumer Finances, the 1998 National Congregations Survey (NCS), the 1993 American Congregational Giving Study Survey, the 1996 Religious Identity and Influence Survey (RIIS), the 1996 God and Society in North America Survey, as well as other smaller denominational surveys and the findings of specific surveys reported in books and research reports. Finally, we conducted our own Tithing Experiment Survey, which we describe in detail in chapter 5.

APPENDIX C | Multivariate Regressions
on Charitable Giving

TABLE C.1 Bivariate and multivariate regression on percent of income in total charitable giving, U.S. Christian households.

Variable	Bivariate	Model 1	Model 2	Model 3	Model 4	Model 5	Model 6
Household income (N=1095)							
$0–12,499	(ref)	(ref)	(ref)	(ref)	(ref)	(ref)	(ref)
$12,500–29,999	−0.28	−0.55	−0.58	−0.57	−0.58	−0.66	−0.57
$30,000–39,999	−0.75	−1.01	−1.13	−1.14	−2.04	−0.97	−1.21
$40,000–59,999	−0.4	−1.04	−1.17	−1.09	−1.74	−1.23	−1.25
$60,000–89,999	−0.59	−1.05	−1.23	−1.07	−1.89	−1.51	−1.08
$90,000+	1.87	1.09	1.16	1.29	2.51	2.6	1.43
Church attendance (N=1081)							
2–3 Times/Month+	5.12**	5.11**	5.05**	4.97**	5.55**	5.85**	5.08**
Region (N=1095)							
Northeast	(ref)		(ref)	(ref)	(ref)	(ref)	(ref)
Midwest	0.65		0.56	0.31	0.25	0.95	0.4
Southeast	2.71**		2.64**	2.20*	2.26	2.83*	2.33*
Southcentral	1.47		1.14	0.68	1.08	1.29	0.62
West	0.54		0.6	0.4	0.35	0.43	0.64
Religious preference (N=1094)							
Protestant	(ref)			(ref)			
Catholic	−2.24**			−1.60**			
Protestant identity (N=509)							
Fundamentalist	(ref)				(ref)		
Evangelical	2.08				0.83		
Mainline	−1.58				−2.06		

	N=880 R-Sq=.10	N=880 R-Sq=.11	N=880 R-Sq=.12	N=504 R-Sq=.13	N=575 R-Sq=.13	N=845 R-Sq=.12
Liberal	**-3.44***			-2.52		
None / Other	**-3.09***			-1.93		
Denomination (N=582)						
Southern Baptist	(ref)			(ref)		
Other Baptist	**-3.36***			-2.57		
United Methodist	-2.12			-1.29		
Luthern–MO Synod	-1.77			-2.09		
Episcopal	0.59			0.38		
All others	0.37			0.45		
Denominational type (N=1035)						
Moderate	(ref)			(ref)		
Fundamentalist	**2.19****			**1.37***		
Liberal	1.14			0.93		
R-square:	N=880 R-Sq=.10	N=880 R-Sq=.11	N=880 R-Sq=.12	N=504 R-Sq=.13	N=575 R-Sq=.13	N=845 R-Sq=.12

Note: significant coefficients in bold, * p<.05 **p<.01 ***p<.001; (ref)=reference group; the reference group for church attendance is less than 2–3 times per month.

TABLE C.2 Bivariate and multivariate regression on percent of income in total charitable giving, U.S. households.

Variable	Bivariate	Model 1	Model 2	Model 3	Model 4	Model 5	Model 6	Model 7
Household income (N=1095)								
$0–12,499	(ref)	(ref)	(ref)	(ref)	(ref)	(ref)	(ref)	(ref)
$12,500–29,999	-.37	-.37	-.49	-.56	-.51	-.58	-.66	-.52
$30,000–39,999	-.54	-.54	-.76	-.90	-.91	-2.03	-.97	-.92
$40,000–59,999	-.38	-.38	-.81	-.94	-.87	-1.74	-1.23	-.92
$60,000–89,999	-.53	-.53	-.75	-.84	-.74	-1.89	-1.51	-.85
$90,000+	1.80	1.80	1.39	1.44	1.39	2.51	2.6	1.38
Church attendance (N=1081)								
2–3 Times/Month+	5.01***	5.00***	4.91***	4.76***	5.55***	5.85***	4.83***	5.05***
Region (N=1095)								
Northeast	(ref)		(ref)	(ref)	(ref)	(ref)	(ref)	(ref)
Midwest	0.61		0.6	0.38	0.25	0.95	0.58	0.51
Southeast	2.59**		2.39**	1.98**	2.26	2.83*	2.37**	2.23**
Southcentral	1.38		1	0.66	1.08	1.29	1.05	0.63
West	0.37		0.61	0.53	0.35	0.43	0.66	0.68
Religious preference (N=1094)								
Protestant	(ref)			(ref)				
Catholic	-2.24***			-1.65**				
Non-Christian	-.80			.49				
None	-3.33***			1.25				
Other	-2.42			-2.41				

Protestant identity (N=509)

Category	(1)	(2)
Fundamentalist	(ref)	(ref)
Evangelical	2.08	0.83
Mainline	-1.58	-2.06
Liberal	-3.44*	-2.52
None / Other	-3.09*	-1.93

Denomination (N=582)

Category	(1)	(2)
Southern Baptist	(ref)	(ref)
Other Baptist	-3.36*	-2.57
United Methodist	-2.12	-1.29
Luthern–MO Synod	-1.77	0.38
Episcopal	0.59	0.45
All Others	0.37	0.98

Major religious type (N=1094)

Category	(1)	(2)
Non-Christian	(ref)	(ref)
Christians	0.45	-.74
None	-2.12	-1.33

Denominational type (N=1035)

Category	(1)	(2)
Moderate	(ref)	(ref)
Fundamentalist	2.19***	1.40*
Liberal	-.28	0.5

R-square:

N= 1081	N=1081	N=1080	N=504	N=575	N=1080	N=1022
R-Sq=.008	R-Sq=.10	R-Sq=.13	R-Sq=.13	R-Sq=.13	R-Sq=.12	R-Sq=.13

Note: significant coefficients in bold, * p<.05 **p<.01 ***p<.001; (ref)=reference group; the reference group for church attendance is less than 2–3 times per month.

TABLE C.3 Bivariate and multivariate regressions on charitable total giving, U.S. Christian households.

Variable	Bivariate	Model 1	Model 2	Model 3	Model 4	Model 5	Model 6
Household income (N=1103)							
$0–12,499	(ref)	(ref)	(ref)	(ref)	(ref)	(ref)	(ref)
$12,500–29,999	609.57	549.05	526.5	528.85	530.43	611.81	567.93
$30,000–39,999	578.64	523.86	457.82	451.18	358.91	590.33	457.37
$40,000–59,999	1,097.64	887.15	820.11	870.14	918.69	903.64	827.06
$60,000–89,999	1,693.99**	1,556.23*	1,472.18*	1,568.55*	1,785.27	1,682.85	1,624.61*
$90,000+	5,399.67**	5,127.49**	5,161.05**	5,240.63**	7,199.60**	6,897.82**	5,488.82**
Church attendance (N=1184)							
2–3 Times/Month+	2,162.74**	2,104.57**	2,070.98**	2,030.27**	2,425.41**	2,365.92**	2,079.54**
Region (N=1201)							
Northeast	(ref)		(ref)	(ref)	(ref)	(ref)	(ref)
Midwest	420.93		411.29	265.91	−21.29	518.65	294.99
Southeast	1,317.00*		1,306.40*	1,056.30	994.13	1,309.89	1,081.00
Southcentral	597.59		637.49	375.99	467.79	738.39	295.99
West	809.26		355.54	244.67	169.8	330.78	367.43
Religious preference (N=1998)							
Protestant	(ref)			(ref)			
Catholic	−1,075.01**			−914.37*			

	(1)	(2)	(3)	(4)	(5)	(6)
Protestant identity (N=534)						
Fundamentalist	(ref)			(ref)		
Evangelical	651.89			341.31		
Mainline	−544.21			−1,100.68		
Liberal	−1,550.83			−925.92		
None / Other	−1,473.25			−719.81		
Denomination (N=624)						
Southern Baptist		(ref)			(ref)	
Other Baptist		−1,118.36			−669.76	
United Methodist		37.78			−103.97	
Luthern–MO Synod		1,987.21			1,715.51	
Episcopal		1,339.88			940.52	
All Others		811.14			653.76	
Denominational type (N=1387)						
Moderate			(ref)			(ref)
Fundamentalist			971.34**			907.83*
Liberal			784.54			562.63
R-square:	N=887 R-Sq=.113	N=877 R-Sq=.119	N=877 R-Sq=.128	N-509 R-Sq=.167	N=581 R-Sq=.15	N=853 R-Sq=.13

Note: significant coefficients in bold, * p<.05 **p<.01 ***p<.001; (ref)=reference group; the reference group for church attendance is less than 2–3 times per month.

TABLE C.4 Bivariate and multivariate regressions on charitable total Giving, U.S. households.

Variable	Bivariate	Model 1	Model 2	Model 3	Model 4	Model 5	Model 6	Model 7
Household income (N=1103)								
$0–12,499	(ref)	(ref)	(ref)	(ref)	(ref)	(ref)	(ref)	(ref)
$12,500–29,999	495.44	486.00	417.73	466.84	530.43	611.81	449.49	476.16
$30,000–39,999	552.24	501.78	423.32	430.15	358.91	590.33	366.22	367.33
$40,000–59,999	964.03	815.56	740.65	805.28	918.69	903.64	730.95	738.44
$60,000–89,999	2024.09**	1962.69**	1948.95**	1996.91**	1785.27	1682.85	1891.97**	1531.29**
$90,000+	4912.42***	4777.19***	4791.10***	4778.94***	7199.60***	6897.82***	4661.73***	4973.36***
Church attendance (N=1184)								
2–3 Times/Month+	2275.85***	2315.44***	2269***	2177.99***	2425.41***	2365.92***	2288.43***	2163.77***
Region (N=1201)								
Northeast	(ref)		(ref)	(ref)	(ref)	(ref)	(ref)	(ref)
Midwest	681.82		819.81	625.66	−21.29	518.65	816.51	489.6

Southeast	1258.62**	1253.27*	983.08	994.13	1309.89	1288.93*	1149.85*
Southcentral	550.23	606.47	397.17	467.79	738.39	685.79	399.83
West	555.61	434.5	289.18	169.8	330.78	453.62	474.87
Religious preference (N=1998)							
Protestant	(ref)		(ref)				
Catholic	−1075.01**		−912.02*				
Non-Christian	629.06		355.32				
None	−1469.26***		−593.68				
Other	741.86		481.07				
Protestant identity (N=534)							
Fundamentalist	(ref)			(ref)			
Evangelical	651.89			341.31			
Mainline	−544.21			1100.68			
Liberal	−1550.82			925.92			
None / Other	−1473.25			71981			

(continued)

TABLE C.4 (Continued)

Variable	Bivariate	Model 1	Model 2	Model 3	Model 4	Model 5	Model 6	Model 7
Denomi-nation (N=624)								
Southern Baptist	(ref)					(ref)		
Other Baptist	−1118.36					−669.76		
United Methodist	−37.78					−103.97		
Luthern– MO Synod	1987.21					1715.51		
Episcopal	1339.89					940.52		
All Others	811.14					653.76		
Major religious type (N=1998)								
Non-Christian	(ref)						(ref)	
Christians	−1909.67*						−2041.61*	
None	−3005.08**						−2235.38*	

Denominational type (N=1387)							
Moderate	(ref)						(ref)
Fundamentalist	**971.34****						**858.55***
Liberal	100.17						326.28
R-square:	N= 1089 R-Sq=.11	N=1089 R-Sq=.12	N=1088 R-Sq=.12	N= 509 R-Sq=.17	N= 581 R-Sq=.15	N= 1088 R-Sq=.12	N= 1029 R-Sq=.14

Note: significant coefficients in bold, * p<.05 **p<.01 ***p<.001; (ref)=reference group; the reference group for church attendance is less than 2–3 times per month.

Introduction

1. For examples of works on religious giving, see Robert Wuthnow, 1997, *The Crisis in the Churches: Spiritual Malaise, Fiscal Woe,* New York: Oxford University Press; Charles Zech, 2000, *Why Catholics Don't Give ... And What Can Be Done about It,* Huntington, IN: Our Sunday Visitor Publishing; Andrew Greeley and William McManus, 1987, *Catholic Contributions: Sociology and Policy,* Chicago: Thomas More Press; John and Sylvia Ronsvalle, 2005, *The State of Church Giving through 2003,* Champaign, IL: empty tomb, inc.; Dean Hoge, Charles Zech, Patrick McNamara, and Michael Donahue, 1996, *Money Matters: Personal Giving in American Churches,* Louisville, KY: Westminster John Knox Press; Mark Chaves and Sharon Miller (eds.), 1999, *Financing American Religion,* Walnut Creek, CA: Alta Mira; Loren Mead, 1998, *Financial Meltdown in the Mainline?* Herndon, VA: Alban Institute Press; Ronald Vallet and Charles Zech (eds.), 1995, *The Mainline Church's Funding Crisis,* Grand Rapids, MI: William B. Eerdmans Publishing; Michael Durall, 2003, *Beyond the Collection Plate: Overcoming Obstacles to Faithful Giving,* Nashville: Abingdon; David Barrett and Todd Johnson (eds.), 2001, *World Christian Trends, AD 30–AD 2002,* Pasadena: William Carey Library; John and Sylvia Ronsvalle, 1996, *Behind the Stained Glass Window: Money Dynamics in the Church,* Grand Rapids, MI: Baker Books; David Neff (ed.), 1990, *The Midas Trap,* Wheaton, IL: Victor Books; Ronald Vallet, 1998, *Congregations at the Crossroads,* Grand Rapids, MI: William B. Eerdmans Publishing; Eugene Grimm, 1992, *Generous People: How to Encourage Vital Stewardship,* Nashville: Abingdon; Patrick McNamara, 2003, *Called to Be Stewards: Bringing New Life to Catholic Parishes,* Collegeville, MN: Liturgical Press; Michael Durall, 1999, *Creating Congregations of Generous People,* Herndon, VA: Alban Institute Press; Kennon Callahan, 1992, *Giving and Stewardship in an Effective Church,* San Francisco: Jossey-Bass; George Barna,

1997, *How to Increase Giving in Your Church,* Ventura, CA: Regal; Independent Sector, 2002, *Faith and Philanthropy: The Connection between Charitable Behavior and Giving to Religion,* Washington, D.C.: Independent Sector; Robert Fogal, Dwight Burlingame, Charles Hamilton, and Warren Ilchman (eds.), 1995, *Cultures of Giving: How Region and Religion Influence Philanthropy, New Directions for Philanthropic Fundraising* (7) (spring), San Francisco: Jossey-Bass; Dean Hoge, Patrick McNamara, and Charles Zech, 1997, *Plain Talk about Churches and Money,* N.p.: Alban Institute Press.

Selected works from an immense literature on faithful Christian treatment of money, income, wealth, and possessions include Craig Blomberg, 2001, *Neither Poverty nor Riches: A Biblical Theology of Possessions,* Downers Grove, IL: Inter-Varisty Press; Gene Getz, 2004, *Rich in Every Way: Everything God Says about Money and Possessions,* West Monroe, LA: Howard Books; James Reapsome and Martha Reapsome, 2003, *Where Your Treasure Is: What the Bible Says about Money,* Colorado Springs: Shaw; Randy Alcorn, 1998, *Money, Possessions, and Eternity,* Wheaton, IL: Tyndale House; Arthur Simon, 1975, *Bread for the World,* New York: Paulist Press; Ronald Sider, 1977, *Rich Christians in an Age of Hunger: A Biblical Study,* Downers Grove, IL: Inter-Varsity Press; Larry Burkett, 1985, *Using Your Money Wisely,* Chicago: Moody Press; Richard Foster, 1981, *Freedom of Simplicity,* New York: Harper and Row; John White, 1979, *The Golden Cow: Materialism in the Twentieth-Century Church,* Downers Grove, IL: Inter-Varsity Press; Virgil Vogt, 1982, *Treasure in Heaven: The Biblical Teaching about Money, Finances, and Possessions,* Ann Arbor, MI: Servant Books; Vernard Eller, 1973, *The Simple Life: The Christian Stance toward Possessions,* Grand Rapids, MI: William B. Eerdmans; John Taylor, 1975, *Enough Is Enough: A Biblical Call for Moderation in a Consumer-Oriented Society,* Minneapolis: Augsburg; John Francis Kavanaugh, 1981, *Following Christ in a Consumer Society: The Spirituality of Cultural Resistance,* Maryknoll, NY: Orbis Books; Donald Kraybill, 1978, *The Upside-Down Kingdom,* Scottdale, PA: Herald Press; J. A. Walter, 1979, *Sacred Cows: Exploring Contemporary Idolatry,* Grand Rapids, MI: Zondervan Publishing; Tom Sine, 1991, *Wild Hope,* Dallas: Word Publishing; Arthur Gish, 1973, *Beyond the Rat Race,* New Canaan, CT: Keats; Jim Wallis, 1976, *Agenda for Biblical People,* New York: Harper and Row. For some historical perspective, see Mark Noll (ed.), 2001, *God and Mammon: Protestants, Money, and the Market, 1790–1860,* New York: Oxford University Press.

2. Regarding social mechanisms in sociology, see Peter Hedström and Richard Swedberg, 1998, *Social Mechanisms,* Cambridge: Cambridge University Press; Jon Elster, 1989, *Nuts and Bolts for the Social Sciences,* Cambridge: Cambridge University Press; Charles Tilly, 1998, *Durable Inequality,* Berkeley: California, particularly chapter 1.

3. If anything, to the extent that we are normative, our general approach reflects less a theological framework than a Kantian categorical-imperative concern with the consequences of everybody (or nobody) acting along certain moral lines.

4. For related works, see, for example, Michael McCullough, "Other-Regarding Virtues," Research Topic White Paper #4, Institute on Research on Unlimited Love, Altruism, Compassion, and Service, Southern Methodist University; Linda Gold-Greenberg, 2005, "The Psychology of 'Giving,'" paper presented at the CCAE Senior Development Forum, October 8; Catherine Eckel and Philip Grossman, 2004, "Giving to Secular Causes by the Religious and Nonreligious," *Nonprofit and Voluntary Sector Quarterly* 33(2) (June): 271–289; Jane Allyn Piliavin and Hong-Wen Charng, 1990, "Altruism: A Review of Recent Theory and Research," *Annual Review of Sociology* 16: 27–65.

5. See, for example, Alexander Karp, Gary Tobin, Aryeh Weinberg, 2004, "An Exceptional Nation: American Philanthropy Is Different Because America Is Different," November/December, The Philanthropy Roundtable, http://www.philanthropyroundtable.org/article.asp?article=796&paper=0&cat=147; Arnaud Marts, 1966, *The Generosity of Americans: Its Source, Its Achievement,* Englewood Cliffs, NJ: Prentice-Hall.

6. Kieran Healy, 2006, *Last Best Gifts: Altruism and the Market for Human Blood and Organs,* Chicago: University of Chicago Press.

7. In this book, we use the words "United States" and "American" interchangeably for the sake of convenience and readability, even though we are aware that "American" broadly comprises much more than what pertains to the United States, including most of Latin America.

8. Dean Hoge, Charles Zech, Patrick McNamara, and Michael Donahue, 1996, *Money Matters: Personal Giving in American Churches,* Louisville, KY: Westminster John Knox Press, p. 12.

9. The sample design for the Knowledge Networks Panel Sample in which our Tithing Experiment Survey module questions were included began as an equal probability design that is self-weighting with several known deviations to make the sample more flexible and efficient. Adjustments are calculated and applied to base sampling weights to account for these known deviations. There are also other sources of survey error that are an inherent part of any survey process such as non-response, non-coverage, and response error. We addressed these sources of sampling and non-sampling survey error using multiple adjustments to the weights, described below. To reduce the effects of potential non-response and non-coverage bias in panel estimates, a cell post-stratification adjustment is applied to panel weights after accounting for sample design factors using demographic distributions from the most recent data from the Current Population Survey. The post-stratification variables include age, race, gender, and Hispanic ethnicity and were applied prior to selection of our Tithing Experiment Survey sample from the Knowledge Networks Panel sample. The sample universe for our Tithing Experiment Survey is all people 18+ who live in the United States who are Baptist, Protestant, Catholic, Pentecostal, Eastern Orthodox, or other Christian. The sample was selected from Knowledge Networks Panel members using information they had previously provided on their religious affiliation.

Panel members numbering 1,439 were assigned to the survey; 1,030 of those completed our survey questions, for a survey response rate of 72 percent. Once the Tithing Experiment Survey data were returned from the field, we subjected them to a post-stratification process to adjust for variable non-response and non-coverage. Demographic and geographic distributions from the Knowledge Networks Panel were used in the post-stratification. The primary purpose of a post-stratification adjustment to Knowledge Networks Panel data is to reduce the sampling variance for characteristics highly correlated with known demographic and geographic totals—population benchmarks. The Knowledge Networks Panel comprises a much larger sample of the U.S. population than the sample fielded for our 2006 Tithing Experiment Survey. This post-stratification adjustment also helps reduce bias due to variable non-response. The following benchmark distributions were utilized for the post-stratification adjustment of the Tithing Experiment Survey data: Gender (Male, Female); Age (18–29, 30–44, 45–59, 60+); Race/Hispanic ethnicity (White/Non-Hispanic, Black/Non-Hispanic, Other/Non-Hispanic, 2+ Races/Non-Hispanic, Hispanic); Education (Less than high school, High school, Some college, Bachelor and beyond); Census Region (Northeast, Midwest, South, West); Metropolitan Area (Yes, No); Internet Access (Yes, No); Religious affiliation (Baptist, Protestant, Catholic, Pentecostal, Eastern Orthodox, other Christian). Comparable distributions were calculated using all completed cases from the survey. Since the sample sizes are typically too small to accommodate a complete cross-tabulation of all the survey variables with the benchmark variables, we apply an approach called iterative proportional fitting for the post-stratification weighting adjustment. Iterative proportional fitting adjusts the sample data back to all of the benchmarks by iteratively fitting the weighted sample data to the marginal distributions of the benchmark data until the sample distributions converge to the benchmark distributions. After the post-stratification adjustment, we examined the distribution of the weights calculated above for all survey respondents to identify and truncate outliers to the upper and lower tails of the weight distribution for the sample. Finally, the post-stratified and truncated weights of all were scaled so that the weights sum to the qualified sample size. The final weighted data set should as a result represent the population we intended to sample: adult Christians who live in the United States.

10. Our sample of interview subjects is in no way nationally representative. We used a convenience, quota sample method to identify our interview respondents. Our goal is not to use interviews to represent different groups at a national level—since that is what survey findings do—but rather more modestly to converse with ordinary clergy and believers to gain insights and to illustrate some of the larger points of the book. Our interview respondents consisted of 26 pastors and 51 parishioners, 6 of whom were interviewed as couples.

11. See, for example, Judith Dean, Julie Schaffner, and Stephen Smith, 2006, "Global Poverty: Academics and Practitioners Respond," *The Review of Faith and International Affairs,* 4(1) (spring): 13–20.

12. Independent Sector, 2002, *Giving and Volunteering in the United States,* Washington, D.C.: Independent Sector; Independent Sector, 2002, *Faith and Philanthropy: The Connection between Charitable Behavior and Giving to Religion,* Washington, D.C.: Independent Sector; Arthur Brooks, 2003, "Religious Faith and Charitable Giving," *Policy Review* (121); Grace Terzian, 2006, "Hudson Institute Launches First *Index of Global Philanthropy: American Private Giving Abroad Vastly Exceeds U.S. Government Aid,*" News Release, New York: Hudson Institute.

13. The Gospel of Luke 21: 3–4.

14. Some existing works on religious and racial minority giving include Steven M. Cohen, 2004, *Philanthropic Giving among American Jews,* New York: United Jewish Communities; Gary Tobin, 2001, *The Transition of Communal Values and Behavior in Jewish Philanthropy,* San Francisco: Institute for Jewish and Community Research; Barry Kosmin and Paul Ritterband (eds.), 1991, *Contemporary Jewish Philanthropy in America,* Savage, MD: Rowman and Littlefield; Jack Wertheimer, 1997, "Current Trends in American Jewish Philanthropy," *American Jewish Yearbook 1997,* New York: American Jewish Committee, pp. 3–92; Gordon Dahl and Michael Ransom, 1999, "Does Where You Stand Depend on Where You Sit: Tithing Donations and Self-Serving Beliefs" [on Mormon giving], *American Economic Review,* 89(4) (September): 703–727; Walter Collier et al., 1998, *A Study on Financing African-American Churches, National Survey on Church Giving, A Research Report,* Atlanta: Institute of Church Administration and Management; African American Philanthropy Study Design Group, 2004, *African American Philanthropy in Metro Atlanta,* Atlanta: Community Foundation of Greater Atlanta; also see Warren Ilchman, Stanley Katz, and Edward Queen II, 1998, *Philanthropy in the World's Traditions,* Bloomington: Indiana University Press, chapters 4, 5, 9, 11, 12, 13.

Chapter 1

1. The religion statistics above are based on analyses of the 2002 National Election Survey, the 2002 Explaining Religious America Survey, the 2002 Religion and Public Life Survey, with some extrapolations based on 2002 and 2005 U.S. Census data. Income figures are calculated using 1998 GSS data adjusted for inflation to 2005 dollars.

2. We calculated this figure in a few different ways using different data points, in order to confirm through triangulation the likely validity of our final estimates. First, we began with the average salary of committed Christians in 1998 ($41,967.78) and adjusted that down for an after-tax income, to $29,377.45. We then calculated 10 percent of that after-tax household income to be $2,937.75. That is $697.88 more per household than the amount reported as actually contributed by committed Christian households. This, adjusted to 2005 dollars using the consumer price index of the U.S. Department of Commerce Bureau of Economic Analysis, is $836.17. We then multiplied that number by the

estimated number of committed Christian households in 2005 (54,398,851), providing a grand total figure of $45,486,687,240 of additional money that committed Christians in the United States would give if they contributed exactly but no more than 10 percent of their after-tax income. Our second calculation began with the estimated $187.92 billion that all Americans gave to charity in 2004 and then reckoned the share of that total that committed Christians gave. Survey data analyses suggest that, although what we are counting as committed Christians represent 46.15 percent of all Americans, they are more likely than their American counterparts to donate money to charity—giving an estimated 72.4 percent of the total charitable dollars given. We thus estimated $136.1 billion as the share of all charitable giving in 2004 that was contributed by committed Christians. We calculated from 1998 General Social Survey data that this group gives, on average—including the number of very big givers at the high end— 5.38 percent of its pre-tax income, which translates into 7.69 percent of after-tax income (at a 30 percent tax rate). Based on this information, we calculated that they would have to give an extra $40,869,300,000 to increase their giving to 10 percent of their after-tax incomes. Adjusted to 2005 dollars raises that number to $48,967,997,000. Our third estimate began again with the average 1998 household pre-tax income of committed Christians, $41,967.78. Again, we calculated from 1998 General Social Survey data that this group gives, on average—including the number of very big givers at the high end—7.69 percent of its after-tax income. This left a 2.31 percent gap in post-tax giving, which, as a share of average household income, means an average additional $678.62 per year to close the gap and bring this group to the level of tithing on post-tax income. This figure we adjusted up, using the consumer price index, for the real difference in dollar value from 1998 to 2005, which brought it to $813.10. We then multiplied that number by the estimated number of U.S. households representing this religious group in 2005 (54,398,851, or 46.15 percent of U.S. households) to estimate the number of *new* dollars, in addition to current giving, that committed U.S. Christians would give if they all gave a full (but no more than) 10 percent of their after-tax income. That number came to $44,231,705,748. These three final figures are modestly different from each other. But, given the different sources of data used in these calculations, the estimations involved, and the influence of small percentage fractions in affecting the magnitude of the amounts in question, these estimates provide assuring confirmation that the figure we are seeking to calculate is approximately $46 billion.

3. We do not here attempt to provide detailed documentation of and justification for the costs of all of the following proposals, since that is not the point of what follows. Suffice it to say that, in estimating these numbers, we referenced reliable information from such organizations as World Vision, the World Health Organization, Habitat for Humanity, The Heifer Project, Christian Aid,

Mennonite Central Committee, Feed the Children, and so on. Specific publications consulted for present purposes included the following, for example: Gareth Jones, Richard Stekett, Robert Black, Zulfiqar Bhutta, Saul Morris, and the Bellagio Child Survival Study Group, 2003, "How Many Child Deaths Can We Prevent This Year?" *Lancet* 326 (July 5): 65–71; Carol Bellamy, 2005, *The State of the World's Children*, 2005, New York: United Nations Children's Fund; Bellagio Study Group on Child Survival, 2003, "Knowledge into Action for Child Survival," *Lancet* 362 (July 26): 323–327.

4. Consistent with the fourth fact described in chapter 1, the average 1998 income of the group of committed Christians who gave more than 10 percent of their means was $42,929.58, a mere $961.80 (or 2.3 percent of income) greater than the average income of all committed Christians. Their generous giving beyond 10 percent of income is clearly not the result of an extra abundance of wealth. Again, see David Johnston, 2005, "Study Shows the Superrich Are Not the Most Generous," *New York Times,* December 19; New Tithing Group, 2004, "The Generosity of Rich and Poor: How the Newly Discovered 'Middle Rich' Stack Up—An Analysis of New IRS Income Categories Sheds Light on the Wealth and Charity of the Middle Rich," research report, New Tithing Group.

5. With mathematical adjustments removing the "freewill bounty giving" dollars above 10 percent, as described here, the mean percentage of pre-tax income given by committed Christians in 1998 was 3.57 percent (or $1,476; contributions of the median giver were 1.89 percent of income, or $600). The average after-tax income (70 percent of total income) of this group was $29,338.46, such that 10 percent giving on after-tax income would have been $2,934 per year for each household. The average gap between 10 percent giving and actual giving, therefore, calculates to $1,458. Adjusted into 2005 dollars using the consumer price index of the U.S. Department of Commerce Bureau of Economic Analysis, that amount rises to $1,746.92. Multiplying this amount by the number of U.S. households representing committed Christians in 2005 (54,398,851) gives us an estimated total of $95,030,446,029. Subtracting the lost contributions of the 10 percent of committed Christians who, for the sake of realism, we are assuming (for reasons of unemployment, illness, family disruption, and the like) are legitimately unable to give any money to any cause reduces that figure to $85,527,401,427. Finally, since we are calculating the *net* gain in giving, over and above the scenario calculated in the previous section, we subtract $46 billion, leaving for this estimation an extra potential, contributable amount of $39,527,401,427.

6. Calculations of 1998 GSS data show that the dollars given by committed Christians above and beyond 10 percent of income represent 35.99 percent of all the dollars given by committed Christians up to and including 10 percent of income, which calculates to $34,623,560,000 in 2005 dollars.

7. According to GSS data, the mean 1998 income for these "less commit-ted" Christians—those Americans who self-identify as Christian but who attend church less than twice a month and do not consider themselves strong Christians—was $39,754.54, which translates to $27,828.18 in after-tax income. Five percent of that after-tax income is $1,391.41—which is $943.50 more than the $477.91 actual mean annual dollar amount given by this group. Adjusted to 2005 dollars, that difference is $1,130.47. One-third of the 30 per-cent of America's less committed Christians represents 11,787,400 households in 2005. Multiplying this number of households by the additional $1,130.47 per household needed to bring giving for this group up to five percent of income produces an increased dollar amount of $13,325,240,784.

Chapter 2

1. We use 1998 GSS, not more recent, data here because that year's survey included special questions on financial giving.
2. Note, however, that the results for Mormons, Jehovah's Witnesses, and other non-Christians should be treated with caution, because of their small numbers (N=25, 21, and 46, respectively). We include these cases here, nevertheless, because these findings are illuminating and consistent with those of other studies.
3. The 1996 GSS giving questions did not ask dollar amounts given, only whether respondents had given money to different causes or not (yes/no). Note that the giving reported here does not include possible "informal" giving of money to needy relatives, neighbors, or homeless people—which, for some respon-dents, might include informally loaning money. Even on that informal giving measure, 19 percent of all Christians, 18 percent of Protestants, 22 percent of Catholics, 20 percent of fundamentalist Protestants, 14 percent of evan-gelical Protestants, 17 percent of mainline Protestants, 24 percent of theologi-cally liberal Protestants, 19 percent of "other/none" self-identified Protestants, 13 percent of Southern Baptists, 25 percent of United Methodists, 30 percent of Missouri Synod Lutherans, 18 percent of Presbyterians, 26 percent of Episcopalians, and 18 percent of nondenominational Christians did not give any money informally to needy relatives, neighbors, or homeless people. Those informal giving numbers decline only modestly for frequently church attend-ing believers in these groups: 17 percent of regularly attending Christians, 16 percent of regularly attending Protestants, and 19 percent of regularly attending Catholics reported in 1996 not giving any money to needy relatives, neighbors, or homeless people. Even when *all* possible kinds of giving were combined (formal and informal), still 11 percent of U.S. Christians, 11 percent of Protestants, and 12 percent of Catholics did not give, or even possibly loan, money, however little the amount, to anyone by any means. Amazingly, seven percent of U.S. Christians who attend church two times a month or more—that is, more than every 15th person sitting in the pews—gave no money, however little or informal, to anyone by any means.

4. Readers are reminded that these survey-based numbers are sampled estimates; taken individually they may include some error, but taken collectively they portray a reliable general picture. Differences in figures presented between different years of GSS surveys may reflect question wording differences.

5. The following statistics come from these sources: Giving USA Foundation, 2005, "Charitable Giving Rises 5 Percent to Nearly $250 Billion in 2004," 2005 Press Release, New York: AAFRC Trust for Philanthropy; Mark Wilhelm, 2004, "The Quality and Comparability of Survey Data on Charitable Giving," working paper of the Indiana University Center for Philanthopy, October; Ann Kaplan (ed.), 1996, *Giving USA,* New York: AAFRC Trust for Philanthropy, p. 55; Independent Sector, 2002, *Giving and Volunteering in the United States, 2001,* Washington, D.C.: Independent Sector, p. 87; Independent Sector, 1994, *Giving and Volunteering in the United States,* Washington, D.C.: Independent Sector, pp. 16, 39; Dean Hoge, Charles Zech, Patrick McNamara, and Michael Donahue, 1996, *Money Matters: Personal Giving in American Churches,* Louisville, KY: Westminster John Knox Press, p. 14; Stephen Hart, 1990, "Religious Giving: Patterns and Variations," Paper presented at the annual meeting of the Religious Research Association and the Society for the Scientific Study of Religion, November 9, 1990.

6. The exact numbers for percent of all giving contributed to religion are as follows: Presbyterian (53.9%), Episcopalians (55.2%), Lutherans (61.8%), Methodists (61.5%), other Protestants (53.3%), Catholic (50.7%), Baptist (77.9%), Pentecostal (86.3%), Jewish (39.8%), Mormon (89.9%), Jehovah's Witness (71.7%), other non-Christian (28.1%), nonreligious (31.6%).

7. As a simple example—illuminating the key difference between mean and median averages through exaggeration—if, in a group of ten people, four gave $1, four gave $10, one gave $100, and one gave $5,000, the median (middle positioned on a list from least to most) amount given would be $10, while the mean [($5,000+$100+$40+$4) divided by 10] amount given would be $511.40. The $501.40 jump in the mean representation of central tendency is explained, of course, by the single giver's $5,000 donation grossly inflating the average, which is then, misleadingly, typically said to represent all 10 givers. If we want to portray how generous the ten givers are, the median figure will provide more insight than the mean.

8. According to National Congregation Survey data, the mean contribution per adult church participant in the typical U.S. Christian church in 1998 was $1,074.63 and the median contribution was $900.

9. The following statistics come from these sources: New Strategist Publications, 2003, *Household Spending: Who Spends How Much on What,* Ithaca, NY: New Strategist Publications, p. 272; Urban Institute, n.d., "Profiles of Individual Charitable Contributions by State," 2003, Washington, D.C.: Urban Institute Center on Nonprofits and Philanthropy; Independent Sector, 1994, *Giving and Volunteering in the United States,* Washington, D.C.: Independent Sector, p. 39;

John and Sylvia Ronsvalle, 2005, *The State of Church Giving through 2003*, Champaign, IL: empty tomb, inc., pp. 7, 89; Stephen Hart, 1990, "Religious Giving: Patterns and Variations," Paper presented at the annual meeting of the Religious Research Association and the Society for the Scientific Study of Religion, November 9, 1990; Barna Research Group, Ltd., 2003, "Tithing Down 62% in the Past Year," *Barna Update*, Ventura, CA, May 19, 2003.

10. New Strategist Publications, 2003, *Household Spending: Who Spends How Much on What*, Ithaca, NY: New Strategist Publications, p. 272.

11. See René Bekkers and Mark Wilhelm, 2006, "Helping Behavior, Dispositional Empathetic Concern, and Principles of Care," working paper, Utrecht University and Indiana University—Purdue University at Indianapolis, pp. 19–20, 23–24, for research along these lines comparing cooperative and uncooperative survey respondents. Bekkers and Wilhelm's research shows that very cooperative survey respondents were 11.4 percentage points more likely to have given to charity than uncooperative respondents. Also compare tables 1 and 3 in Mark Wilhelm, 2006, "The Quality and Comparability of Survey Data on Charitable Giving," *Nonprofit and Voluntary Sector Quarterly*, forthcoming. Existing research, however, comprises scant analyses of survey respondents compared to true non-respondents as correlated with charitable giving, although the consensus of all of the expert researchers in this area who we inquired with on this point was that survey non-respondents are very likely to contribute less in charitable financial giving.

12. For recent reports on U.S. Jewish private philanthropy, see Steven M. Cohen, 2004, *Philanthropic Giving among American Jews*, New York: United Jewish Communities; and Gary Tobin, 2001, *The Transition of Communal Values and Behavior in Jewish Philanthropy*, San Francisco: Institute for Jewish and Community Research. According to Dean Hoge et al.'s analysis of 1987–89 General Social Survey data, U.S. Latter Day Saints (Mormons) give more than seven percent of their income, much more than the average two to three percent of income that the majority of Christians collectively give (Dean Hoge, Charles Zech, Patrick McNamara, and Michael Donahue, 1996, *Money Matters: Personal Giving in American Churches*, Louisville, KY: Westminster John Knox Press, pp. 11–13). IRS tax return data show the highest charitable contribution as a percent of income by state is Utah, the state with the highest concentration of Mormons (Urban Institute, n.d., "Profiles of Individual Charitable Contributions by State, 2003," Washington, D.C.: Urban Institute Center on Nonprofits and Philanthropy).

13. Independent Sector, 2002, *Giving and Volunteering in the United States*, Washington, D.C.: Independent Sector, pp. 24–25. Among *contributing* households, Independent Sector reports that American givers contribute an average of 3.1 percent of household income; respondents who attend religious services at least once a month give a mean of 4.3 percent of household income; respondents who attend services less than once a month but more than never give a

mean of 1.8 percent of household income; and respondents who never attend religious services give a mean of 1.5 percent of household income (Independent Sector, 2002, *Giving and Volunteering in the United States,* Washington, D.C.: Independent Sector, pp. 28–29, 85–87).

14. Because the number of cases on which figures 2.3 and 2.4 report could not be evenly divided into perfect five percentile groups, we assigned extra cases to the lower percentiles, actually slightly distributing giving toward the lower end.

15. We recognize that the actual entire "income" of the lowest category reported here may include non-cash goods—such as Medicaid, food stamps, and housing subsidies—that are not counted in the annual incomes reported in the survey, which would revise our findings slightly.

16. Independent Sector, 2002, *Giving and Volunteering in the United States,* Washington, D.C.: Independent Sector, pp. 32, 119. Also see New Tithing Group, 2004, "The Generosity of Rich and Poor: How the Newly Discovered 'Middle Rich' Stack Up—An Analysis of New IRS Income Categories Sheds Light on the Wealth and Charity of the Middle Rich," research report, New Tithing Group; David Johnston, 2005, "Study Shows the Superrich Are Not the Most Generous," *New York Times,* December 19. To be clear, larger proportions of wealthier households give at least something to charity—77 percent of households earning less than $25,000, compared to 97 percent of households earning more than $100,000, for instance—and give a larger total number of dollars; but as a percent of income, wealthier households give lower proportionately (Independent Sector, 2002, *Giving and Volunteering in the United States,* Washington, D.C.: Independent Sector, pp. 2–3, 17, 110–111).

17. On a related view, estimates actually suggest that members of numerous Christian denominations located in much poorer nations than the U.S. give of their financial means as a proportion of income not that much less generously and sometimes more generously than do much wealthier U.S. Christians. Global Christianity researchers David Barrett and Todd Johnson, for example, write that "[c]ontrary to popular stereotype, many denominations in the Third World, even in areas of abject poverty and neglect, generate vast annual income[s].... The largest Third-World denomination, the Assemblies of God in Brazil, has 19 million members [with a collective] personal income of $57 billion, and church income averages $1 billion a year [i.e., an estimated 1.8 percent of personal income].... China's 89 million Christians have [a collective] personal income of $49 billion of which $2 billion is donated to and used by their churches [i.e., an estimated 4.1 percent of personal income].... The Kimbanguist Church of Zaire ... has ... 9.5 million members handling $2 billion in personal annual income, of which they donate over $20 million to their denomination annually [i.e., 1 percent of income]. In South Africa, Zion Christian Church's 7.2 million members have [a collective] personal income of $21 billion, from which the ZCC gets a church income of $200 million [i.e., an estimated 1 percent of

income]." See David Barrett and Todd Johnson (eds.), 2001, *World Christian Trends, AD 30–AD 2002*, Pasadena: William Carey Library, p. 656.

18. We are indebted to John and Sylvia Ronsvalle, of empty tomb, inc., for this historical analysis, published in their report, *The State of Church Giving through 2003* (Champaign, IL: empty tomb, inc., 2005), and for their permission to use their published figure (p. 36) here as our figure 2.12.

19. Andrew Greeley and William McManus, 1987, *Catholic Contributions: Sociology and Policy,* Chicago: Thomas More Press; Stephen Hart, 1990, "Religious Giving: Patterns and Variations," Paper presented at the annual meeting of the Religious Research Association and the Society for the Scientific Study of Religion, November 9, 1990.

20. Also see Charles Zech, 2000, *Why Catholics Don't Give ... And What Can Be Done About It,* Huntington, IN: Our Sunday Visitor Publishing.

21. John and Sylvia Ronsvalle, 2005, *The State of Church Giving through 2003,* Champaign, IL: empty tomb, inc.

22. Mark Wilhelm, Patrick Rooney, and Eugene Tempel, 2005, "Changes in Religious Giving Reflect Changes in Involvement: Life-Cycle and Cross-Cohort Evidence on Religious Giving, Secular Giving, and Attendance," Center on Philanthropy at Indiana University Working Paper, pp. 4, 20; also see Mark Wilhelm, Patrick Rooney, and Eugene Tempel, 2003, "Religious Giving over the Life Cycle and across Cohorts," Center on Philanthropy at Indiana University Working Paper.

23. David Barrett and Todd Johnson (eds.), 2001, *World Christian Trends, AD 30–AD 2002*, Pasadena: William Carey Library, pp. 656, 660–61; statistics cited are based on lines 53, 55, 56, 78, and 84 in table 20–3 found on p. 661.

24. Susan Wiener, Arthur Kirsch, Michael McCormack, with Michelle Weber, Pamela Zappardino, and Charles Collyer, 2002, *Balancing the Scales: Measuring the Roles and Contributions of Nonprofit Organizations and Religious Congregations,* Washington, D.C.: Independent Sector; Susan Saxon-Harrold, Susan Wiener, Michael McCormack, and Michelle Weber, 2001, *America's Religious Congregations: Measuring Their Contribution to Society,* Washington, D.C.: Independent Sector.

25. Virginia Hodgkinson, Murray Weitzman, and Arthur Kirsch, 1988, *From Belief to Commitment: The Activities and Finances of Religious Congregations in the United States—Findings from a National Survey,* Washington, D.C.: Independent Sector, p. 48.

26. See table 3 in Mark Chaves, 1993, "Denominations as Dual Structures: An Organizational Analysis," *Sociology of Religion* 54(2): 147–169.

27. John and Sylvia Ronsvalle, 2005, *The State of Church Giving through 2003,* Champaign, IL: empty tomb, inc., pp. 51–62.

28. Walter Collier et al., 1998, *A Study on Financing African-American Churches, National Survey on Church Giving, A Research Report,* Atlanta: Institute of Church Administration and Management, pp. 51–52.

1. For example, Dean Hoge, Charles Zech, Patrick McNamara, and Michael Donahue, 1996, *Money Matters: Personal Giving in American Churches,* Louisville, KY: Westminster John Knox Press, pp. 56–79, 91–92; Dean Hoge and Fengang Yang, 1994, "Determinants of Religious Giving in American Denominations," *Review of Religious Research* 36(2): 123–148; Peter Zaleski and Charles Zech, 1994, "Economic and Attitudinal Factors in Catholic and Protestant Religious Giving," *Review of Religious Research* 36(2): 158–167; James Davidson and Ralph Pyle, 1994, "Passing the Plate in Affluent Churches: Why Some Members Give More than Others," *Review of Religious Research* 36(2): 181–196; Dean Hoge and Boguslaw Augustyn, 1997, "Financial Contributions to Catholic Parishes," *Review of Religious Research* 39(1): 46–60; Dean Hoge, 1994, "The Problem of Understanding Church Giving," *Review of Religious Research* 36(2): 101–110; Roger Nemeth and Donald Luidens, 1994, "Congregational vs. Denominational Giving," *Review of Religious Research* 36(2): 111–122; Donald Luidens and Roger Nemeth, 1994, "Social Sources of Family Contributions," *Review of Religious Research* 36(2): 207–217; Michael Donahue, 1994, "Correlates of Religious Giving in Six Denominations," *Review of Religious Research* 36(2): 149–157; Jeff Rexhausen and Michael Cieslak, 1994, "Relationship of Parish Characteristics to Sunday Giving among Catholics in the Archdiocese of Cincinnati," *Review of Religious Research* 36(2): 218–229. Also see John Havens, Mary O'Herlihy, and Paul Schervish, 2006, "Charitable Giving: How Much, by Whom, to What, and How?" pp. 542–567 in Richard Steinberg and Walter Powell (eds.), *The Non-Profit Sector* (2nd ed.), New Haven: Yale University Press; Paul Schervish and John Havens, 1997, "Social Participation and Charitable Giving: A Multivariate Analysis," *Voluntas* 8(3): 235–260; Lise Vesterlund, 2006, "Why Do People Give?" pp. 568–587 in Richard Steinberg and Walter Powell (eds.), *The Non-Profit Sector* (2nd ed.), New Haven: Yale University Press; Eleanor Brown, 1999, "Patterns and Purposes of Philanthropic Giving," pp. 212–230 in Charles Clotfelter and Thomas Ehrlich (eds.), *Philanthropy and the Nonprofit Sector in a Changing America,* Bloomington: Indiana University Press; Eleanor Brown, 2005, "College, Social Capital, and Charitable Giving," pp. 185–204 in Arthur Brooks (ed.), *Gifts of Time and Money in America's Communities,* Lanham, MD: Rowman and Littlefield; James Andreoni, 2006, "Philanthropy," pp. 1201–1269 in *Handbook of the Economics of Giving, Altruism, and Reciprocity,* vol. 2, Serge-Christophe Kolm and Jean Mercier Ythiere (eds.), Amsterdam: Elsevier; Gregory Krohn, 1995, "The Receipts and Benevolences of Presbyterian Congregations, 1973–1988," *Journal for the Scientific Study of Religion* 34(1): 17–34; Warren Hrung, 2004, "After-Life Consumption and Charitable Giving," *American Journal of Economics and Sociology* 63(3): 731–745; Catherine Eckel and Philip Grossman, 2004, "Giving to Secular Causes by the Religious and Nonreligious," *Nonprofit and Voluntary Sector Quarterly* 33(2): 271–289; Kevin

Forbes and Ernest Zampelli, 1997, "Religious Giving by Individuals: A Cross-Denominational Study," *American Journal of Economics and Sociology* 56(1): 17–30; Dennis Sullivan, 1985, "Simultaneous Determination of Church Contribution and Church Attendance," *Economic Inquiry* 23(2): 309–320.

2. Note that this approach is derived not from the currently dominant mentality and methods of sociology (rooted in positivism, the Humean theory of causation as constant [or, modified, regular] conjunction, and statistical methods focused on significant correlations between variables) but in the philosophy of social science known as critical realism. The dominant framework of sociology for many decades has been explaining observed variance in factors by correlating them with variance on other factors. That is exactly what popular statistical methods, such as multivariate regression analyses, do best. Critical realism, however, also seeks to understand social facts that may reflect little variance but that are still the important effects of real social causes. In our case here, the social fact reflecting little variance but nevertheless requiring explanation is the extremely low giving of the vast majority of U.S. Christians. For background on critical realism, see Berth Danermark, Mats Ekström, Liselotte Jakobsen, and Jan Ch. Karlsson, 2002, *Explaining Society: Critical Realism in the Social Sciences,* New York: Routledge; Andrew Collier, 1994, *Critical Realism,* New York: Verso; Andrew Sayer, 2000, *Realism and Social Science,* Thousand Oaks, CA: Sage; Andrew Sayer, 1992, *Method in Social Science: A Realist Approach,* New York: Routledge; Margaret Archer, Roy Bhaskar, Andrew Collier, Tony Lawson, and Alan Norrie (eds.), 1998, *Critical Realism: Essential Readings,* New York: Routledge; Margaret Archer, 1995, *Realist Social Theory,* Cambridge: Cambridge University Press; Jose Lopez and Garry Potter, 2001, *After Postmodernism: An Introduction to Critical Realism,* New York: Athlone; Andrew Collier, 1994, *Critical Realism,* New York: Verso; Roy Bhaskar, 1998, *The Possibility of Naturalism,* New York: Routledge.

3. John DeGraaf, David Wann, Thomas Naylor, 2005, *Affluenza: The All-Consuming Epidemic,* 2nd ed., San Francisco: Berrett-Koehler Publishers; Robert Frank, 1999, *Luxury Fever,* New York: Free Press; Juliet Schor, 1998, *The Overspent American: Upscaling, Downshifting, and the New Consumer,* New York: Basic Books. On the effects on savings rates, see Christopher Thornberg and Jon Havevan, 2006, "Savings and Asset Accumulation among Americans 25–34," American Institute of Certified Public Accountants, Los Angeles: Beacon Economics.

4. Elizabeth Warren and Amelia Warren Tyagi, 2003, *The Two-Income Trap: Why Middle Class Mothers and Fathers Are Going Broke,* New York: Basic Books; Teresa Sullivan, Elizabeth Warren, and Jay Lawrence Westbrook, 2000, *The Fragile Middle Class: Americans in Debt,* New Haven: Yale University Press; Elizabeth Warren, 2006, "The Middle Class on the Precipice," *Harvard Magazine,* January-February, pp. 28–31, 89. Also see Barbara Ehrenreich, 1989, *Fear of Falling: The Inner Life of the Middle Class,* New York: Harper; Katherine Newman, 1988, *Falling from Grace: The Experience of Downward Mobility in the American Middle Class,* New York: Free Press; Tamara Draut, 2005, *Strapped: Why America's*

20- and 30-Somethings Can't Get Ahead, New York: Anchor Books; Anya Kamenetz, 2006, *Generation Debt,* New York: Riverhead Trade.

5. Independent Sector, 2002, *Giving and Volunteering in the United States, 2001,* Washington, D.C.: Independent Sector, p. 66.

6. Data from the ELCA Annual Congregational Report Forms on a denomination-sponsored U.S. Congregations study in 2001, prepared by the ELCA Department for Research and Evaluation, available at http://www.elca.org/research/USCongs/giving_1.pdf.

7. Independent Sector, 2002, *Giving and Volunteering in the United States, 2001,* Washington, D.C.: Independent Sector, pp. 64, 65, 115.

8. Neil Tseng, 2003, "Expenditures on Entertainment," in *Consumer Expenditure Survey Anthology, 2003,* Washington, D.C.: U.S. Department of Labor, Bureau of Labor Statistics, Report Number 967: 73–75; Peter Kuhback and Bradlee Herauf, 2006, "U.S. Travel and Tourism Satellite Accounts for 2002–2005," *Survey of Current Business,* June, Washington, D.C.: U.S. Department of Labor, Bureau of Labor Statistics: 14–30; U.S. Census Bureau, "Historic Census of Housing Tables, Vacation Homes," *Housing and Household Economic Statistics Division,* Washington, D.C.: U.S. Census Bureau; American Beverage Association, n.d., "Fact Sheet: Industry Basics," Washington, D.C.: American Beverage Association; National Confectioners Association, 2006, *NCA's 2006 Year in Review: Issues, Trends, Performance,* Vienna, VA: National Confectioners Association; NMMA, 2005, "Facts and Figures: Retail Boating Market," Chicago: National Marine Manufacturers Association; Unity Marketing, 2006, *Jewelry Report, 2006 Update: The Who, What, Where, Why and How Much of Jewelry Shopping,* Stevens, PA: Unity Marketing; U.S. Census Bureau, 2005, "Median and Average Square Feet of Floor Area in New One-Family Houses Sold by Location" and "Square Feet of Floor Area in New One-Family Houses Completed," U.S. Census Bureau Tables, Washington, D.C.: U.S. Census Bureau; Geoffrey Paulin, 2003, "Consumer Expenditures for Alcohol in 2000," in *Consumer Expenditure Survey Anthology, 2003,* Washington, D.C.: U.S. Department of Labor, Bureau of Labor Statistics, Report Number 967: 39–48; Mark Vendemia, 2005, "Tobacco Expenditures by Education, Occupation, and Age," in *Consumer Expenditure Survey Anthology, 2005,* Washington, D.C.: U.S. Department of Labor, Bureau of Labor Statistics, Report Number 981: 51–55; Alicia Hansen, 2004, "Background Paper: Lotteries and State Fiscal Policy," Washington, D.C.: Tax Foundation; Iowa Public Television, 2003, "The Super-Sizing of America," *Market to Market,* December 5, 2003, Johnston, IA: Iowa Public Television; Scott Hettrick, 2005, "Spending on DVDs up 10%," *Variety,* December 30, 2005; Larry Moran and Clinton McCully, 2001, "Trends in Consumer Spending, 1959–2000," *Survey of Current Business,* March, Washington, D.C.: U.S. Department of Labor, Bureau of Labor Statistics: 15–21.

9. Pamela Danziger, 2004, *Why People Buy Things They Don't Need: Understanding and Predicting Consumer Behavior,* Chicago: Kaplan Business; Pamela Danziger,

2004, *Let Them Eat Cake: Marketing Luxury to the Masses—As well as the Classes,* Chicago: Kaplan Business; Michael Silverstein, Neil Fiske, and John Butman, 2004, *Trading Up: Why Consumers Want New Luxury Goods ... And How Companies Create Them,* New York: Penguin Books; Paul Nunes and Brian Johnson, 2004, *Mass Affluence: Seven New Rules of Marketing to Today's Consumer,* Cambridge, MA: Harvard Business School Press; James B. Twitchell, 2003, *Living It Up: America's Love Affair with Luxury,* New York: Simon and Schuster.

10. See Katharine Bradbury and Jane Katz, 2002, "Issues in Economics: Are Lifetime Incomes Growing More Unequal?" *Regional Review,* Quarter 4, Boston: Federal Reserve Bank of Boston, pp. 2–5.

11. Brian Bucks, Arthur Kennickell, and Kevin Moore, 2006, "Recent Changes in U.S. Family Finances: Evidence from the 2001 and 2004 Survey of Consumer Finances," Washington, D.C.: U.S. Federal Reserve Board.

12. Juliet Schor, 1998, *The Overspent American: Upscaling, Downshifting, and the New Consumer,* New York: Basic Books.

13. Liz Pulliam Weston, 2006, "The Truth about Credit Cards," Internet article on moneycentral.msn.com, http://moneycentral.msn.com/content/Banking/credit-cardsmarts/P74808.asp.

14. In early 2006, for example, home purchase choices drove the cost of U.S. housing to 94.5 percent of the maximum prices American home buyers could afford, as a comparison of the median-priced home to the median family income; this pushing of home purchases to maximum levels of affordability helps to explain the fact that 4.56 percent of all housing loans in the United States in the first half of 2006 were delinquent in payment or being foreclosed, as one out of twenty home buyers appears to have overreached their abilities to pay for the homes they purchased; see U.S. Department of Housing and Urban Development, 2006, "U.S. Housing Market Conditions, 2nd Quarter, 2006," Washington, D.C.: HUD, pp. 6, 11. According to U.S. Census Bureau data drawn from the 2005 American Community Survey, 34.5 percent of mortgage owners in the United States spend 30 percent or more on household ownership costs (mortgage, real estate taxes, homeowner's insurance, utilities, and fuels); 47.7 percent of residents of California paid more than 30 percent of their household incomes on housing costs; see U.S. Census Bureau, R2513, "Percent of Mortgaged Owners Spending 30 Percent or More of Household Income on Selected Housing Owner Costs, 2005," Washington, D.C.: U.S. Census Bureau. Of course, housing prices are dynamically set by buyer demand, such that the higher proportions of income that buyers spend on housing, the higher the price of housing rises.

15. One related question that arises about objective resource constraints and financial giving is the effect of household size. Are families with more children less able to give money away because of their greater financial obligations for caring for children? The answer is no. The statistical evidence shows that, while family income is curvilinear to household size (average household income increases

with more children up to two children, but then decreases starting with three children, according to 1998 GSS data), family size and financial generosity are unrelated. That is, giving as a percent of income does not statistically significantly increase or decrease as household size increases. Multivariate regression analyses of 1998 GSS data, for instance, controlling for standard demographic variables, including income, show that number of children entered as categorical dummy variables is statistically insignificant at all levels for a whole variety of models. However, when calculated in bivariate analyses as percent of income given per household child (calculated as [total giving] / [income/number of children], which indirectly controls for income), those families with more children are actually more generous than those with fewer, giving away higher average percents of income per child. So the idea that increased child-rearing expenses increase objective resource constraints which decreases voluntary financial charitable giving is not supported by available data.

16. See table 5.4 in chapter 5.

17. These findings are based on multiple regression analyses using twelve control variables (age, sex, marital status, education, race, household size, urban residence, regional location, Internet access, religious affiliation, church attendance, and perceptions of church expectations of financial giving), the results of which are reported in tables 5.6 and 5.8 in chapter 5.

18. Iain Walker and Heather Smith, 2001, *Relative Deprivation: Specification, Development, and Integration,* Cambridge: Cambridge University Press, 2001; James M. Olson, C. Peter Herman, Mark Zanna (eds.), 1986, *Relative Deprivation and Social Comparison,* Mahwah, NJ: Lawrence Erlbaum Associates; John Masters and William Smith (eds.), 1987, *Social Comparison, Social Justice, and Relative Deprivation,* Mahwah, NJ: Lawrence Erlbaum Associates; Ted Robert Gurr, 1970, *Why Men Rebel,* Princeton, NJ: Princeton University Press.

19. Dean Hoge, Charles Zech, Patrick McNamara, and Michael Donahue, 1996, *Money Matters: Personal Giving in American Churches,* Louisville, KY: Westminster John Knox Press, 42.

20. Christian Smith et al., 1998, *American Evangelicalism: Embattled and Thriving,* Chicago: University of Chicago Press, p. 38.

21. Independent Sector, 2002, *Giving and Volunteering in the United States, 2001,* Washington, D.C.: Independent Sector, p. 52.

22. John Dovidio, Jane Piliavin, David Schroeder, Louis Penner, 2006, *The Social Psychology of Prosocial Behavior,* Florence, KY: Lawrence Erlbaum, pp. 67–85. Social Contact Theory explaining changes in racial attitudes and relations provides a parallel to the motivational social psychology of understood abstractions versus concrete experiences; see Thomas Pettigrew and Linda Tropp, 2006, "A Meta-Analytic Test of Intergroup Contact Theory," *Journal of Personality and Social Psychology* 90(5): 751–783; Linda Tropp and Thomas Pettigrew, 2005, "Relationships between Intergroup Contact and Prejudice among Minority and Majority Status Groups," *Psychological Science* 16(12) (Dec.): 951–957;

E. A. Plant, 2004, "Responses to Interracial Interactions over Time," *Personality and Social Psychology* 76: 790–801. For an analysis of the importance of concrete experience on political mobilization, see Christian Smith, 1996, *Resisting Reagan: The U.S. Central America Peace Movement*, Chicago: University of Chicago Press, pp. 151–157, 165–168.

23. For details on survey methodology, see endnote 7 in chapter 1. The exact wording for this question was: "About what *percent of after-tax income* do you think *your own local church expects its members to donate* in religious and charitable giving (based on what is taught and generally expected in your church)?:

    1. 0 percent
    2. 1–2 percent
    3. 3–4 percent
    4. 5–6 percent
    5. 7–9 percent
    6. 10 percent
    7. 11–12 percent
    8. more than 12 percent."

24. Robert Wuthnow, 1997, *The Crisis in the Churches: Spiritual Malaise, Financial Woe*, New York: Oxford University Press, 139–157; Loren Mead, 1998, *Financial Meltdown in the Mainline?* Herndon, VA: Alban Institute; Daniel Conway, 1999, "Clergy As Reluctant Stewards of Congregational Resources," in Mark Chaves and Sharon Miller (eds.), *Financing American Religion*, Walnut Creek, CA: AltaMira; Dean Hoge, Charles Zech, Patrick McNamara, and Michael Donahue, 1996, *Money Matters: Personal Giving in American Churches,* Louisville, KY: Westminster John Knox Press, 116–117; Dean Hoge, Patrick McNamara, and Charles Zech, 1997, *Plain Talk about Churches and Money,* Herndon, VA: Alban Institute. On the other hand, one nonrandom national study of African American churches found that 60 percent of the churches teach tithing, 29 percent teach tithing plus the giving of additional offerings, seven percent teach proportionate giving, and only four percent teach that tithing is not obligatory (Walter Collier et al., 1998, *A Study on Financing African-American Churches, National Survey on Church Giving, A Research Report,* Atlanta: Institute of Church Administration and Management, p. 46).

25. Daniel Conway, 1999, "Clergy As Reluctant Stewards of Congregational Resources," in Mark Chaves and Sharon Miller (eds.), *Financing American Religion,* Walnut Creek, CA: AltaMira.

26. Loren Mead, 1998, *Financial Meltdown in the Mainline?* Herndon, VA: Alban Institute, p. 117.

27. We acknowledge, however, that the word "rules" here could be depressing this statistic.

28. Other demographic variables explain little variance in defining stewardship in distinctly financial terms. Working Americans sampled in the 1992 Economic

Values Survey differ on this question by race, geographic region, education, and income by only a few percentage points. Age appears to be slightly associated, with respondents 55 years old or older being twice as likely (at 16 percent) as 18–24 year olds (at 8 percent) to view stewardship in financial terms.

29. Yet another indirect way to try to assess this hypothesis is to see if there is a correlation between views of biblical authority and financial giving. The Bible, both Old and New Testaments, is packed full of teachings about generosity, self-sacrifice, tithing, stewardship, care for the poor, honoring God with one's money, and so on. If hypothesis 4 were true, then we might expect to see an association between the life directing authority that readers attribute to the Bible and levels of financial giving. This approach emphasizes more the teaching authority of the Bible than relative ignorance about those teachings. Still, it provides another angle on the question worth viewing. The GSS regularly asks its survey respondents a question about their view of the Bible. Answer categories are: (1) The Bible is the actual word of God and is to be taken literally, word for word; (2) The Bible is the inspired word of God but not everything in it should be taken literally, word for word; and (3) The Bible is an ancient book of fables, legends, history, and moral precepts recorded by men. Analyses of 1998 GSS data show that those who believe in a literal view of the Bible ("literalists") give away more money than both those who view the Bible as God's inspired word not to be read literally ("non-literalists") and as an ancient book of fables ("skeptics"), even though they earn lower incomes. Among all U.S. Christians, literalists gave a mean of 5 percent of their income, non-literalists gave a mean of 2.7 percent of their income, while skeptics gave a mean of 1.8 percent of their income; the median percent of income given (calculated by dividing median giving by median income for each group) was 1.1, 1.1, and .3 percent, respectively. The same patterns hold for only Christians who attend church regularly and for only those Christians who give any money. Thus, U.S. Christians who profess to believe that the Bible's teachings can be read literally tend to give away more money, suggesting the possibility that a more pointed understanding of teachings on money might encourage more generous giving. However, we cannot tell from these data whether it is the view of the Bible per se that increases giving or whether it is other factors, such as denominational cultures, congregational organizational processes, or the larger underlying personal faith commitments of the survey respondents.

30. Note, however, that the 2001 Independent Sector survey shows that contributing Americans who give money "to fulfill religious obligations or beliefs" give an average of 4.3 percent of their household income, compared to 1.9 percent of income given by those who do not give for this reason (Independent Sector 2002, 60).

31. Robert Wuthnow, 1997, *The Crisis in the Churches: Spiritual Malaise, Financial Woe*, New York: Oxford University Press, p. 148.

32. Independent Sector, 2002, *Giving and Volunteering in the United States, 2001*, Washington, D.C.: Independent Sector, pp. 52, 53.

33. Dean Hoge, Charles Zech, Patrick McNamara, and Michael Donahue, 1996, *Money Matters: Personal Giving in American Churches,* Louisville, KY: Westminster John Knox Press, pp. 43, 45, 48.

34. Robert Wuthnow, 1997, *The Crisis in the Churches: Spiritual Malaise, Financial Woe,* New York: Oxford University Press; Loren Mead, 1998, *Financial Meltdown in the Mainline?* Herndon, VA: Alban Institute; Daniel Conway, 1999, "Clergy As Reluctant Stewards of Congregational Resources," in Mark Chaves and Sharon Miller (eds.), *Financing American Religion,* Walnut Creek, CA: AltaMira; Dean Hoge, Charles Zech, Patrick McNamara, and Michael Donahue, 1996, *Money Matters: Personal Giving in American Churches,* Louisville, KY: Westminster John Knox Press, pp. 116–117; Dean Hoge, Patrick McNamara, and Charles Zech, 1997, *Plain Talk about Churches and Money,* Herndon, VA: Alban Institute, pp. 139–157.

35. See Dean Hoge, Charles Zech, Patrick McNamara, and Michael Donahue, 1996, *Money Matters: Personal Giving in American Churches,* Louisville, KY: Westminster John Knox Press, p. 37.

36. Robert Wuthnow, 1997, *The Crisis in the Churches: Spiritual Malaise, Financial Woe,* New York: Oxford University Press, p. 147.

37. Daniel Ludow, 1992, "Tithing Settlement," *Encyclopedia of Mormonism,* New York: Macmillan, p. 1481. A popular Mormon children's verse conveys their teaching emphasis on tithing: "I want to give the Lord my tenth, for ev'ry time I do, it makes me think of all the gifts, He gives to me and you. He gives us life, this lovely world. And though my tenth seems small, it shows my faith and gratitude, to him, the Lord of all." See Patrick Allitt, 2006, "The Art of Tithing," *In Character* 2(3): 48–59. Also see: http://www.lds.org/pa/e-learn/mp/tithingsettlement/index.htm.

38. Quoted in Julia Duin, 2001, "Giving in Different Denominations: Religious Giving Has Reached All-Time Lows," *Philanthropy* (May): no page number given; also see Charles Zech, 2000, *Why Catholics Don't Give … and What Can Be Done about It,* Huntington, IN: Our Sunday Visitor, pp. 74–75. Also see Christopher Scheitle and Roger Finke, n.d., "Maximizing Organizational Resources: Selection versus Production," unpublished paper, Pennsylvania State University; Roger Finke, Matt Bahr, and Christopher Scheitle, n.d., "Toward Explaining Congregational Giving," unpublished paper, Pennsylvania State University.

39. Dean Hoge, Charles Zech, Patrick McNamara, and Michael Donahue, 1996, *Money Matters: Personal Giving in American Churches,* Louisville, KY: Westminster John Knox Press, pp. 49, 75–76, 82.

40. Reported in Dean Hoge, Charles Zech, Patrick McNamara, and Michael Donahue, 1996, *Money Matters: Personal Giving in American Churches,* Louisville, KY: Westminster John Knox Press, pp. 76, 82, 182–183.

41. The remaining 10 percent of sampled Christians either claimed they approached charitable giving by some other method (6 percent) or refused to answer or did not know the answer (4 percent).

42. Non-Christians, non-givers, and those who refused or reported "Don't know" to the religious giving question were excluded from the analysis. For details on this survey, see Robert Wuthnow, 1994, *God and Mammon in America,* New York: Free Press.

43. Dean Hoge, Charles, Zech, Patrick McNamara, and Michael Donahue, 1996, *Money Matters: Personal Giving in American Churches,* Louisville, KY: Westminster John Knox Press: 49;

44. Dean Hoge, Charles Zech, Patrick McNamara, and Michael Donahue, 1996, *Money Matters: Personal Giving in American Churches,* Louisville, KY: Westminster John Knox Press, p. 75.

45. We actually had a tenth hypothesis but absolutely no data with which to test it. Hypothesis 10 would be the Paradox of Choice hypothesis: American Christians have too many options to which they might give, and the proliferation of choices is somewhat paralyzing. The logic of this hypothesis runs counter to that of rational choice free-market explanations, which predict greater participation with more options. But Barry Schwartz has gathered an impressive body of social psychology evidence suggesting that people can actually choose more decisively and reasonably when they have *fewer* options from which to choose (Barry Schwartz, 2005, *The Paradox of Choice: Why More Is Less,* New York: Harper). For our purposes, this might mean that if American Christians had only a handful of giving targets to consider, they might be more decisive and committed in their giving. Available evidence to evaluate that hypothesis is, however, scant. The only anecdotal evidence, relying on a simple correlation without controls for other variables, that we can think of is the fact that U.S. Latter Day Saints are generally taught to think about financial giving as a one-target consideration—the Church—and they give at relatively very high rates on the whole, compared to American Christians who "enjoy" innumerable giving options and tend to give money at lower levels. More research is needed to better assess this hypothesis. Thanks to Steve Vaisey for suggesting it to us.

Chapter 4

1. See Mark Wilhelm, Eleanor Brown, Patrick Rooney, and Richard Steinberg, 2006, "The Intergenerational Transmission of Generosity," unpublished paper, IUPUI Center on Philanthropy at Indiana University.

2. Formally, we cannot make a strong claim about congregational culture insofar as we did not conduct ethnographic fieldwork in congregations; our interview data suggest, however, that these discourses do form distinct cultures in congregations.

3. Some of the pastors whom we interviewed were clearly 100 percent Live-the-Vision while others seemed a mixture of Live-the-Vision and Pay-the-Bills (see the next subsection below on Mixed Cultures); here we quote both types.

4. See Sharon Louise Miller, 1999, "The Symbolic Meaning of Religious Giving," Ph.D. dissertation, University of Notre Dame.

Chapter 5

1. Thanks to Steve Vaisey for pointing out the decoupling mechanism here.

Conclusion

1. Vincent Miller, 2004, *Consuming Religion: Christian Faith and Practice in a Consumer Culture*, New York: Continuum; R. Laurence Moore, 1995, *Selling God: American Religion in the Marketplace of Culture*, New York: Oxford University Press; Wade Clark Roof, 1999, *Spiritual Marketplace: Baby Boomers and the Remaking of American Religion*, Princeton: Princeton University Press; Leigh Eric Schmidt, 1997, *Consumer Rites: The Buying and Selling of American Holidays*, Princeton: Princeton University Press; J. Carrette, 2004, *Selling Spirituality*, New York: Routledge; Paul Stiles, 2005, *Is the American Dream Killing You?: How "The Market" Rules Our Lives*, New York: Collins, pp. 207–237.

2. Many Americans would of course see biblical basis for at least some of these beliefs, for instance, private property, making the sorting through of conflicts between them more complicated.

3. See: http://ecfa.org/, http://www.ministrywatch.com/mw2.1/H_Home.asp, and http://www.thegoodsteward.com/.

4. See Sharon Louise Miller, 1999, "The Symbolic Meaning of Religious Giving," Ph.D. dissertation, University of Notre Dame.

5. Emile Durkheim, 1995 [1912], *The Elementary Forms of the Religious Life*, New York: Free Press.

6. See Peter Berger and Thomas Luckman, 1967, *The Social Construction of Reality*, New York: Anchor; Anthony Giddens, 1984, *The Constitution of Society*, Berkeley: University of California Press; Margaret Archer, 2003, *Realist Social Theory*, Cambridge: Cambridge University Press.